Books on Asia

from the Near East

to the Far East

Books on Asia
from the Near East
to the Far East

A guide for the general reader

Selected and annotated by

Eleazar Birnbaum

University of Toronto Press

© University of Toronto Press/1971
Toronto and Buffalo

Printed in Canada

ISBN 0-8020-1683-9
Microfiche ISBN 0-8020-0031-2

LC 75-151361

Contents

Preface

The word Asia is no longer an uncommon one to the average man. For some decades now he has come across it more and more frequently in his newspaper and on the radio. Since the 1950s an ever increasing number of homes have television, so that innumerable people have witnessed, in their own living-rooms, scenes of life and death from a continent which to most of them had been merely a place on the map. Today, more often than not, when Asia appears on television it is in news and current affairs broadcasts, and the subjects concern conflict and destruction; nevertheless the viewer could hardly fail to become aware of that continent's rich historical and cultural background, as well as its current problems.

What is Asia? In European classical antiquity, it meant a portion of the western coastline of Anatolia (in present-day Turkey) together with its immediate hinterland. Over the centuries, the word came to designate an ever widening territorial expanse, until it now covers the whole immense land mass east of the Bosphorus and the Ural mountains, the home of the vast majority of the world's population and the seat of its oldest civilizations. It has frequently been referred to by the parallel and often synonymous terms "the Orient" and "the East," descriptions implying a world in which Europe is at the centre, and tending to lump all of Asia together. In the past, however, that continent was never more than a geographical unity. It is only recently that this situation has been changing somewhat. Many of the peoples of Asia are now coming to consider the fact of their *not* being Europeans as a positive common link. Despite the enormous differences between their various traditions, they are looking upon themselves as consciously "Asian." Political developments have, of course, been largely responsible for this change in feeling.

Until comparatively recent times, very few of the heirs to European civilization (whom we may, for convenience, call Westerners) took a real interest in any civilization other than that in which they grew up. To them "literature" meant western literature, "history" meant European (or, more recently, also North American) history. To this day the English term "modern languages" refers exclusively to European languages. There were, of course, rare individuals who were genuinely concerned with different civilizations, and not merely in terms of export markets for goods or as lands of benighted heathens requiring conversion. But such people were a small minority, and were often regarded as eccentrics. The degree of interest considered normal for an average educated man was possibly a dilettante's taste for "travel books" and for such minor literary by-products of the East as the *Arabian Nights.* (Perhaps this offered to repressed monogamous Europeans the vicarious pleasure of contemplating forbidden delights like harems and Turkish baths filled with languid odalisques without the attendant problems of maintaining such establishments!) If serious attention to the brilliant cultures of Asia was slight in Europe, it was still slighter in North America, and, for historical reasons, interest developed there even later. In the past twenty years, however, there has been a rapid and growing demand for more information. Numerous books have been published to meet the need, but, as one might expect, their quality has been very uneven. Many of the "popular" ones are mere pot-boilers, teeming with errors and misconceptions, thrown together hastily by people ill acquainted at first hand with their subject. At the other extreme are reliable, learned tomes, which are too erudite and detailed for the non-specialist, and more liable to dampen his interest in an unfamiliar subject than to encourage him. It is clear that the general reader would find it very useful to have a guide that could lead him to such books as are likely to meet his needs. In barren areas of study, where there are few works worthy of wholehearted recommendation, he requires also a helpful warning of the major shortcomings in the books that are available.

A number of general bibliographies of Asia have been published in the western world during the past few years. Several of these interpret Asia as exclusive of the Near or Middle East. Some are quite comprehensive and cover popular as well as specialized books, including those that are available as well as those that are out of print. Others are limited to paperbacks, many of them poor in quality, and yet others are very short and elementary. Most of those printed in English confine themselves to books in that language, and, unfortunately, the majority of these bibliographies are now out of date. One selective reading guide which was very helpful to the general reader in its time was the *Book List on Asia* compiled by Professor G. M. Wickens, published in 1961 and long out of print.* Of the nearly 500 books listed there (including 21 in French), many have been superseded or are no longer available. In the past ten years a host of new books addressed to non-specialists have also appeared. The present work seeks to bring the best of these and of the older works still in print to the attention of the anonymous but ubiquitous "intelligent general reader." It may also be found useful by teachers and students, as well as librarians, journalists, discussion-group leaders, and booksellers. Good works on Asia, its heritage and present condition, have been printed in many languages, but as English and French are the most internationally known, the books included have been confined to these two. Thousands of volumes were examined in preparing the guide but only about 2,000 were selected for inclusion. The range of subjects covered is very wide, yet the general reader will sometimes fail to find a recommended book on a matter in which he has a special interest. Ten years ago Professor Wickens noted, in the preface to his work, that "in some cases the fact has to be faced that there is no really good book at all in French or English (if indeed in any other Western language) on a given topic." Coverage has improved greatly in the past decade, but the statement is still essentially true.

*G. M. Wickens (comp.), *Book list on Asia, including parts of Africa, for Canadians/Liste de livres sur l'Asie et certaines parties de l'Afrique à l'intention des Canadiens* (Ottawa, Canadian National Commission for Unesco/Commission nationale canadienne pour l'Unesco, 1961).

The brief notes accompanying the book titles are intended to assist the general reader in his choice. Brevity entails the risks inherent in generalization and oversimplification, yet they have been gladly taken, since the aim is to provide orientation for the novice rather than education for the specialist.

I have seen most of the works listed in one edition or another. For annotations to those in fields outside my own (Islamic studies) I have availed myself of information contained in book reviews, standard works, and printed subject bibliographies, as well as of suggestions and comments kindly offered by colleagues. To all of them I am indebted. In the preparation of this book for printing, Miss L. Ourom of the University of Toronto Press has been very helpful. My special gratitude is due to my wife, who bore my long absences in the library and at my desk with considerable fortitude.

Department of Islamic Studies   E.B.
University of Toronto

Introduction

For the purposes of this work, Asia may conveniently be divided into three great culture or civilization areas, which often transcend geographical, national, political, or linguistic boundaries, whether ancient or modern: (1) the Islamic World, (2) India, South and Southeast Asia, (3) the Far East. In each of these civilization groups, the basic moulding factor has been not economics, geography, language, or race, although each of these has played a part, but religion (defined more or less broadly). It has been religion which created in all three areas the fundamental cultural entity called a civilization, out of a heterogeneous collection of peoples of different languages and origins.

Our reading guide consists of four main divisions, whose scope may be defined as follows:

I. *Asia as a Whole* contains works dealing with areas of Asia (i.e. the Near East to the Far East) wider than any single one of the three divisions below.

II. *The Islamic World* extends from Morocco* in the west to Pakistan and Muslim India in the east, and from Soviet Central Asia in the north to the Yemen in the south. (Material on Muslim peoples in Asia outside this area, such as Malaysia and Indonesia, appears in part III.) It was somewhat arbitrarily decided to omit works on the pre-Islamic Near East (the Ancient Near East, and biblical and early Jewish and Christian studies) since Islam is the main living civilization of the area. Another reason for doing so was the need to avoid extending the size of the work unduly; other bibliographies are available to meet specific needs on the pre-Islamic Near East. Works on the non-Muslim elements in post-Islamic times are, however, included.

III. *India, South and Southeast Asia* includes the Indian subcontinent (with the exception of Pakistan since its independence, and of material specifically devoted to the Muslims of India, both covered in part II) and the peninsulas and islands extending to the east and southeast.

IV. *The Far East* takes in China, Japan, and Korea, which, in spite of major differences, contain enough common elements to constitute a distinct group vis-à-vis their neighbours.

The main divisions within each of these four parts are similar, but the subdivisions vary considerably from part to part, according to the nature of the material and the number of books available.

---

*The Muslim lands along the southern shores of the Mediterranean (Morocco, Algeria, Tunisia, Libya, and Egypt) are, of course, geographically part of Africa and not Asia, yet it would have been artificial and pedantic to exclude them from this reading guide. They have been an integral part of the Islamic heartlands since the first century of Islam. (Muslim Spain is included for similar reasons.) Other parts of Africa which are more distant and later additions to the Islamic world are, however, excluded.

CHOICE OF TITLES

Books on Asia does not set out to be a guide to Asian current events. Controversial or ephemeral works are excluded on principle, as are many excellent books which were felt to be too detailed or specific for the general reader. The aim in selecting entries has been to provide a long-term historical perspective, which will sometimes do much to explain current affairs implicitly if not always explicitly. The historical and social studies sections within each part are therefore relatively large. Since, axiomatically, to understand other people one must try to see them through their own eyes, considerable attention has been given to translations of the religious, philosophical, and literary texts which have moulded the Asian peoples and embody their ideas, their ideals, and their self-images.*

Some works originally written in English have been cited only in their French translations. This indicates that the French translation is useful for those who do not read English easily, but that those who are fluent in English will find that another work in English on the same topic, cited in the same section, is likely to be more satisfactory.

As a convenience for the general reader who may be interested in purchasing some of the volumes, inexpensive ones have been given preference. Most of those listed can be bought for less than 10 dollars, and the paperbacks for much less, of course. Really expensive works, even when good, have rarely been included. The comparatively small number of items cited costing more than 10 dollars consists mainly of art books, and most of these are priced below 20 dollars.

Every effort has been made to list only books in print and available at the time of compilation, so that prospective purchasers do not waste their own time or that of booksellers. Unfortunately this has meant the exclusion of a considerable number of old favourites (of which some may be reprinted) and their replacement by available works which I consider less good. It should be noted too that books are constantly going out of print, and it cannot, of course, be guaranteed that every book listed will continue to be available.

The general reader should remember that there are additional sources of information on Asia in the reference section of his public library. Asian subjects are covered in general encyclopaedias, as well as in specialized ones,† and the articles are often quite intelligible to the layman. Reference librarians can also

---

*The National Commissions for Unesco in various countries of Asia have sponsored the translation into English or French of well-known works. Issued by various publishers, they bear one of two series titles: "Unesco Collection of Representative Works" (mostly "classics") or "Unesco Collection of Contemporary Works." Those in each series which are most suitable for the general reader have been included in the relevant section below. A complete listing can be found in the *Catalogue [du] programme Unesco de traduction d'oeuvres littéraires/Catalogue [of the] Unesco literature translations programme* ([Paris], Unesco [2nd ed., in press, 1970]).

†E.g., James Hastings, *Encyclopaedia of religion and ethics*; and the *Encyclopaedia of the social sciences.*

help those interested in following up a subject by directing them to relevant articles in reliable periodicals.*

Oriental languages are a fascinating study but they are not learned casually by general readers, whose interests and capacities vary greatly. For this reason it was decided to exclude language textbooks, grammars, and dictionaries. To cover adequately the broad and complex linguistic spectrum of Asian languages would require a cooperative bibliography annotated by people experienced in teaching a wide variety of languages to western students, a task which is beyond the scope of this book. Suffice it to say that the average layman needs a teacher. A book title may claim that you can "teach yourself," or the publisher's blurb may assure you that "you will find it easy to learn the language in a few weeks, in the comfort of your own home," but naive acceptance of such statements is likely to lead to disappointment.†

Guide-books to Asian countries have also been excluded. Although some contain good general introductions to the history and culture of the lands described, the majority are too specific and detailed for armchair travellers. A useful classified and briefly annotated listing of guide-books is now available for consultation in many libraries.‡

CLASSIFICATION

The classification has been devised for general convenience, and a complete listing of the subsections is included at the beginning of each part. It must be remembered, however, that many books could justifiably be classified in more than one category: e.g. the borderline between "History" and "Modern Period" is often blurred; a collection of translations from literature with copious introductory material might fall equally well into either "History of Literature" and "Literature in Translation." If a particular author or a specific title is being sought, use of the indexes is recommended.

*For the Islamic world the essential key to periodicals is *Index Islamicus,* compiled by J. D. Pearson (Cambridge, Heffer, 1958; with supplements every five years). Books and articles on Asia east of Afghanistan are indexed in the annual *Bibliography of Asian studies,* published since 1941 as a separate section of the *Journal of Asian studies.* Like *Index Islamicus* it is classified by subject and, like it again, unfortunately it has no evaluative notes.

†General information on individual Asian languages may be found in the usual encyclopaedias. Those with access to a good library and a knowledge of French will find a reliable description of each language with a select bibliography in: *Les langues du monde,* par une groupe de linguistes, sous la direction de A. Meillet et Marcel Cohen. [2ᵉ éd.] Paris, Centre Nationale de la Recherche Scientifique, 1952.

‡J. A. Neal, *Reference guide for travelers* (New York, Bowker, 1969). Experienced travellers will know the general reliability of many of the traditional guide-book series, such as Blue Guides, Nagel, Hachette, and Murray's. The introductory sections of these are often readable and informative, although the body of the text (the itineraries) may tend to be somewhat turgid. Guides in the Fodor series often make lighter and easier reading, but contain less detailed information. In addition there are many guides to individual countries which do not belong to series.

FORM OF ENTRIES

The "entry word" and the rest of the entry conform as far as possible to the current rules of the American and British Library Associations and the Library of Congress, which are followed by most libraries in English-speaking countries. This should be helpful to library users and librarians alike.

Entries have been arranged alphabetically within each subdivision, under the author's or editor's surname (or equivalent). Other elements of the name are given after a comma. Where an author has no surname (or equivalent), the elements are not inverted. When a writer normally uses a pseudonym ("pen name") this is employed instead of his real name. Sacred books and epics with no known individual author have been entered under the title (e.g. Mahābhārata), but using the common Anglicized form if there is one (e.g. Koran). If a work has been translated from English into French or vice-versa, and editions in both languages are listed, the work in its original language is cited first. If translated from some other language, then the English translation is given before the French. If various persons have contributed to a book, such as an anthology, it is entered under the name of the editor, translator, or compiler (abbreviated ed., tr., and comp., following the name); if two people have collaborated on it, it is entered under the name which appears first on the title-page.

SUBTITLES Subtitles which appear on the original title-pages have been reproduced in full, since they often explain the scope of a book or the author's approach. (Many bibliographies omit subtitles and are much the poorer for it.)

PLACE OF PUBLICATION, PUBLISHER, AND DATE The original place of publication and publisher are given first. American, Canadian, British, and French publishers or distributors are cited if known, particularly if they are noted on the books themselves: e.g. "London, Macmillan; New York, St. Martin's; Toronto, Saunders, 1968" (in this example, 1968 applies to all three places of publication). The date of the latest known edition is given.

PAPERBACKS Many very valuable works are available quite inexpensively in paperback editions, and much effort has been expended to give details of them. Such editions are marked by the letter "P" following the date: "1965 P" means published in paperback in 1965. An entry such as "1963, 1965 P" means that the 1963 edition was hardcover and the 1965 paperback. If the original hardcover edition was out of print at the time of compilation and only the paperback was available, the hardcover edition has not been mentioned. If a publisher simultaneously issued hardcover and paperback editions of a book, a notation "C&P" (C = clothbound/hardcover) is inserted following the date. Many hardcover books come out in paperback a year or two after original publication, but some paperbacks are original. Where no paperback edition of a British, American, or Canadian book in English is listed here, and the reader wishes to ascertain whether such an edition has become available, he is advised to consult the current monthly issue of *Paperbound books in print* (New York, Bowker) for North American publications and of *Paperbacks in print* (London, Whittaker) for British publications. A useful source of information on North American paperback and hardbound books in preparation, which includes estimated publication dates, is the latest quarterly issue of *Forthcoming books, now including new books in print* (New York, Bowker).

EDITION This is noted in as brief a form as possible, publishers' advertising verbiage being reduced to essentials (e.g. "New revised and enlarged edition" becomes "[2nd ed.]").

REPRINTS OR IMPRESSIONS Details are not given for unchanged reprints or impressions. For example, if the title-page or its verso reads "3rd ed. 1965, 5th impression, 1970," the entry is reduced to "3rd ed. 1965 (and repr.)." If the original work was published very long ago by a different publisher, this is indicated thus: "1967 (repr. of 1914 ed.)"; if the publisher is still the same, thus: "1914 repr. 1967."

SERIES Publication series are indicated in parentheses after the date of publication. These often act as useful guides in showing the level of a work. For example, "Collection 'Que sais-je?'" is enough to tell one that the work will probably be quite a sound outline or a survey of a subject in about 128 small pages, and "Pelican Books" indicates a slightly more detailed, reliable introduction to a subject.

An ASTERISK preceding an entry indicates a particularly useful work of its type, suitable for purchase by the general reader who wishes to own a basic book.

ANNOTATIONS The annotations aim to define the scope of the work, where this is not clear from the title and the subtitle, and often attempt a brief evaluation for the benefit of the non-specialist. Brevity here of necessity entails oversimplification. A work described as "popular" tends to be on the borderline with good journalese, and is sometimes characterized by the presence of many debatable general statements and an absence of documentation. "Good nontechnical" indicates a more reliable work by an expert, of the kind described in French as "haute vulgarisation." Conversely, "partly technical" or "detailed" means that the layman will probably wish to omit large portions of the book.

INDEXES The Index of Names contains entries not only for the main authors and editors, but also for most "second joint authors," for the subjects of biographies, and for some editors and translators whose names appear on the books but have not been chosen as "entry words."

ABBREVIATIONS

C	clothbound; hardcover edition
comp.	compiler; compiled by
ed.	edited by; editor; edition
jt.	joint
P	paperback edition
rev.	revised (by), revision; revu(e)
tr.	translated by; translator; translation; traduction
*	particularly useful work of its type

I Asia as a whole

A REFERENCE WORKS

*AMERICAN UNIVERSITIES FIELD STAFF. *Select bibliography: Asia, Africa, Eastern Europe, Latin America.* Ed. Phillips Talbot. New York, American Universities Field Staff, 1959
  – *Supplements*, 1961, 1963, 1965, 1967. New York, American Universities Field Staff, 1961-68
    A competent selective general bibliography, with supplements of new publications issued every two years. Most entries are annotated, generally quite well, but some are decidedly inadequate, apparently uncritically based on the publisher's blurb or the claims of the title-pages.

ASIA SOCIETY, New York. *A guide to Asian collections in American museums.* New York, Asia Society, 1964 P
    Details of collections of Asian art (i.e. Afghanistan to Japan) in forty-one American and three Canadian institutions, with indication of particular areas of strength.

*ASIA SOCIETY, New York. *A guide to films, filmstrips, maps, and globes [and] records on Asia,* selected and annotated. New York, Asia Society, 1964 P
*– *Supplement, including a new section on slides,* selected and annotated. New York, Asia Society, 1967 P
    An indispensable key to its subjects, compiled by experts in each field. ("Asia" is defined as "Afghanistan to Japan.") The section on records is particularly well annotated. Details for obtaining the items reviewed are given and whether by purchase, rental, or loan.

*EMBREE, Ainslie T. (ed.) *Asia: a guide to paperbacks.* [2nd ed.] By Ainslie T. Embree, Jackson H. Bailey, Samuel C. Chu, Donn V. Hart, George Alexander Lensen. New York, Asia Society, 1968 P
    The most valuable and comprehensive source of information on paperbacks currently available on the lands from Afghanistan to the Pacific Islands. Well arranged by subject in each geographical-cultural area, with helpful annotations to each title. Since the book aims to list all American paperbacks available, the items cited include works which are unreliable or ephemeral, reprints of out-of-date and superseded books, and material too detailed for the general reader. The annotation "serious work" usually means "too specialized for the layman."

*EMBREE, Ainslie T. (comp.) *Asia: a guide to basic books.* Compilers and annotators: Ainslie T. Embree, John Meskill, Robert Van Niel, Walter F. Vella. New York, Asia Society, 1966 P
    A well-compiled classified listing of 316 "basic books on Asia which are especially useful for teachers, mature students and adults," Asia being de-

fined as "Afghanistan to Japan." The selections are generally good, though too thin in places, and the annotations usually helpful. Some of the books cited are, however, out of print.

KAHIN, George McTurnan (ed.) *Major governments of Asia.* 2nd ed. Ithaca, Cornell University Press, 1963
   A thorough, readable conspectus of the politics and policies of China, India, Indonesia, Japan, and Pakistan by experts on these countries.

MORGAN, Kenneth W. *Asian religions: an introduction to the study of Hinduism, Buddhism, Islam, Confucianism, and Taoism.* Washington, American Historical Association; New York, Macmillan, 1964 P (Service Center for Teachers of History, Publications series)
   A very helpful 30-page bibliographical essay evaluating relevant books suitable for laymen.

*PEARSON, James D. *Oriental and Asian bibliography: an introduction, with some reference to Africa.* London, Crosby Lockwood; Hamden, Conn., Archon, 1966
   A valuable survey which describes and evaluates the bibliographical aids available for various fields of Asian study.

PHILIPS, Cyril Henry (ed.) *Handbook of oriental history.* By members of the Department of Oriental History, School of Oriental and African Studies, University of London. London, Royal Historical Society, 1951 (and repr.)
   A short reference book which is very helpful for certain types of information. Individual experts cover the Near East, India and Pakistan, Southeast Asia, China, and Japan. Each cultural area section is subdivided to cover (1) the romanization of words, (2) forms of personal names and titles, (3) place names, (4) select glossary of semitechnical terms, (5) calendars and dating systems, (6) lists of dynasties and rulers.

QUAN, L. King. *Introduction to Asia: a selective guide to background reading.* Prepared by L. King Quan. Washington, The Library of Congress, Reference Dept., 1955
   Informative annotations on nearly 800 useful works published before the mid-1950s.

*WINT, Guy (ed.) *Asia: a handbook.* London, Blond, 1965; New York, Praeger, 1966 (and repr.); rev. and abridged ed. Harmondsworth, Baltimore, Penguin, 1969 P
   A very handy and quite authoritative reference book of basic information written by a team of experts. Deals with Asia east of Iran in four sections: (1) basic information for each country, including statistics; (2) political and social history, etc.; (3) cultural aspects (art, literature, religion, etc.); (4) treaties. Comprehensive bibliographies are included.

B GENERAL WORKS

BARTOL'D, Vasiliĭ Vladimirovich. *La découverte de l'Asie*. Histoire de l'orientalisme en Europe et en Russie. [Par] W. Barthold. Traduit du russe et annoté par B. Nikitine. Paris, Payot, 1947 P (Collection Bibliothèque Historique)
> An important study of the development of European scholarly interest in Asia. Over-emphasis on Russia's contribution.

DE BARY, William Theodore (ed.) *Approaches to Asian civilizations*. Ed. Wm. Theodore de Bary and Ainslie T. Embree. New York, London, Columbia University Press, 1964
> How can a basic knowledge of Asian civilizations — history, cultures, thought — be introduced to non-specialist western undergraduates? This book consists of illuminating papers on the subject presented by specialists to a conference of college teachers.

FINKELSTEIN, Louis (ed.) *The Jews: their history, culture and religion*. 3rd ed. 2 vols. New York, Harper, 1960
> This wide-ranging work contains studies by experts on the history, culture, languages, and literatures of the Jews in various Asian countries in the mediaeval and modern periods, especially the Arab lands and Persia.

*GROUSSET, René. *La face de l'Asie*. Par René Grousset et George Deniker. Paris, Payot, 1962 P (Collection Petit Bibliothèque Payot)
> A masterly, though brief general view of the contributions, in the past and present, of the Semitic, Turkic, Iranian, Indian, Chinese, and Japanese peoples.

LACH, Donald Frederick. *Asia in the making of Europe*. Vol. 1: *The century of discovery*. Books 1-2. Chicago, University of Chicago Press, 1965
> The first parts of a major work on the impact of Asia on the West. These two volumes go to 1600 and deal mainly with India, Southeast Asia, and the Far East. Several sections have been reprinted separately (noted in the relevant places below) under the titles *China (India, Japan, Southeast Asia) in the eyes of Europe* (Chicago, University of Chicago Press, 1968 P).

LACH, Donald Frederick (ed.) *Asia on the eve of Europe's expansion*. By Donald F. Lach and Carol Flaumenhaft. Englewood Cliffs, N.J., Prentice-Hall, 1965 C&P
> A handy book of travel accounts by Europeans of the 16th and 17th centuries and writings of contemporary Asians.

LATTIMORE, Owen (ed.) *Silks, spices and empire: Asia seen through the eyes of its explorers*. Edited, annotated and introduced by Owen and Eleanor Lattimore. New York, Delacorte, 1968

A very interesting selection of descriptions by travellers, both oriental and western, from ancient times to the 20th century. Covers the area from India to Japan and from Mongolia to Malaya.

*MATTHEW, Helen G. (ed.) *Asia in the modern world.* Toronto, New York, New American Library, 1963 P (Mentor Books)

A good introductory volume, particularly directed at high school and college students, with general sections on Asian religions, arts, and geography, followed by chapters on individual countries of South and Southeast Asia and the Far East. Useful chapter on "Resources for teaching and further study" and classified bibliography of recent books, especially paperbacks.

MICHAUX, Henri. *Un barbare en Asie.* Nouvelle éd. Paris, Gallimard, repr. 1967 (Collection Soleil)

Acute, witty, and ironical observations on Asians and their civilizations, from India to Japan.

MICHAUX, Henri. *A barbarian in Asia.* Tr. Sylvia Beach. New York, New Directions, 1949

See preceding note.

POLO, Marco. *The travels of Marco Polo.* Ed. Milton Rugoff. New York, New American Library, 1961 P (Signet Classics)

A modern popular translation, with brief notes, of the travel book which describes the 25-year journey of the great 13th-14th century traveller who went overland from Europe across Turkey, Iraq, Persia, Afghanistan, and Central Asia to China.

C HISTORY, SOCIAL SCIENCES, AND LAW

BINGHAM, Woodbridge. *A history of Asia.* By Woodbridge Bingham, Hilary
Conroy, and Frank W. Iklé. 2 vols. Boston, Allyn, 1964-65
   A general history, covering a vast field. Tends to dogmatize, but nevertheless a useful introduction. Each chapter is followed by two booklists: (a)
supplemental, (b) advanced.

BUSS, Claude A. *Asia in the modern world: a history of China, Japan, South
and Southeast Asia.* New York, Macmillan; London, Toronto, Collier-Macmillan,
1964
   A useful work, which attaches importance to Asian points of view.

CRESSEY, George Babcock. *Asia's lands and peoples: a geography of one-third
of the earth and two-thirds of its people.* 3rd ed. New York, Toronto, McGraw-
Hill, 1963
   An excellent general geography, physical, social, economic, and cultural.

DEAN, Vera Micheles. *The nature of the non-western world.* [Rev. (2nd) ed.]
New York, Toronto, New American Library; London, New English Library,
1966 P (Mentor Books)
   An elementary, though practical book, based on an undergraduate course;
somewhat naive.

DEAN, Vera Micheles (ed.) *West and non-West: new perspectives.* An anthology, edited by Vera Micheles Dean and Harry D. Harootunian. New York, Holt,
1963 C&P
   Selections from the works of historians, political scientists, economists, so-
ciologists, scientists, and novelists. Useful for college students and laymen.

EDWARDES, Michael. *Asia in the European age.* London, Thames & Hudson,
1961
   An interesting study of the impact of the West on Asia's history from the
beginning of the 16th to the middle of the 20th century. Noteworthy analysis of the motives of European colonialists. Covers India, China, Japan,
Southeast and Central Asia.

GINSBURG, Norton Sydney (ed.) *The pattern of Asia.* Englewood Cliffs, N.J.,
Prentice-Hall, 1958 (and repr.)
   A reliable and standard political and economic general geography covering
the whole of Asia.

GROUSSET, René. *Histoire de l'Asie.* 8ᵉ éd. Paris, Presses Universitaires de France, 1966 P (Collection "Que sais-je?")
>A rapid review by a master of the field.

GROUSSET, René. *A history of Asia.* Tr. Douglas Scott. New York, Walker; Toronto, McLeod, 1963 C&P (Walker Sun Books)
>See preceding note.

HÜRLIMANN, Martin. *Traveller in the Orient.* Tr. Isobel Neilson. London, Thames & Hudson, 1960
>An evocative series of 223 photographs taken by an excellent photographer in the Lebanon, Pakistan, India, China, Japan, and Thailand, with accompanying text.

KIERNAN, Victor Gordon. *The lords of human kind: European attitudes towards the outside world in the Imperial Age.* London, Weidenfeld, 1969
>An entertainingly written survey, based on an immense number of works by 18th and 19th century travellers, literary figures, and officials. The "mysterious East" which they described is a mixture of solid fact, misunderstanding, romantic day-dreaming, contempt, and admiration. To a lesser degree the book also records the impressions gained by the non-Europeans of the strange men from the West.

LENSEN, George Alexander. *The world beyond Europe: an introduction to the history of Africa, India, Southeast Asia and the Far East.* 2nd ed. Boston, Houghton, 1966
>A summary of traditional societies and handy short surveys of European influences on their subsequent histories.

MÉTRAUX, Guy S. (ed.) *The new Asia: readings in the history of mankind.* Edited for the International Commission for a History of the Scientific and Cultural Development of Mankind, by Guy S. Métraux and François Crouzet. New York, Toronto, New American Library; London, New English Library, 1965 P (Mentor Books)
>Thirteen outstanding articles, mostly by Asian scholars, assessing the changes in various Asian societies in the last two centuries.

MONGAIT, Aleksandr Lvovich. *Archaeology in the USSR.* Translated and adapted by M. W. Thompson. Harmondsworth, Baltimore, Penguin, 1961 P (Pelican Books)
>A useful survey including much material about the archaeology of the Asian portions of the USSR, especially in prehistoric times. Pronounced communist slant in the writing at times.

PANIKKAR, Kavalam M. *Asia and western dominance.* 2nd ed. London, Allen & Unwin, 1959 (and repr.)

A critical historical account of the role of the West in Asia since the 15th century, by a leading Indian historian and politician.

PANIKKAR, Kavalam M. *L'Asie et la domination occidentale du XVe siècle à nos jours*. Tr. Paule et Ernest Bolo. Paris, Seuil, 1957
See preceding note.

ROMEIN, Jan. *The Asian century: a history of modern nationalism in Asia*. Tr. R. T. Clark. London, Allen & Unwin; Berkely, University of California Press, 1962 (and repr.)
An examination of the rise of nationalism in Asia since 1900; described by its Dutch author as "frankly anti-colonial and written more or less from the Asian point of view, because only in this way can we hope to explain Asian nationalism." Doctrinaire but interesting.

SPENCER, Joseph Earle. *Asia, east by south: a cultural geography*. New York, Wiley; London, Chapman, 1954 (and repr.)
A well-written geographical survey, from India to Japan, with strong cultural emphasis. Many maps.

*STAMP, Lawrence Dudley. *Asia: a regional and economic geography*. 12th ed. London, Methuen; New York, Dutton, and Barnes & Noble, 1967
A standard work.

*WARD, Robert E. (ed.) *Major political systems*. Vol. 1: *Asia*. Ed. Robert E. Ward and Roy C. Macridis. Englewood Cliffs, N.J., Prentice-Hall, 1963
Good survey essays on governments, political structure, and processes in all the main Asian countries from Israel eastwards. Less detailed than the two volumes edited by G. M. Kahin, *Major governments of Asia* (section A above) and *Government and politics of Southeast Asia* (see section III D1), but more countries are covered.

WARD, Robert E. (ed.) *Political modernization in Japan and Turkey*. Ed. Robert E. Ward and Dankwart A. Rustow. Princeton, Princeton University Press, 1964; 1968 P (Studies in Political Development series)
An excellent item-by-item review of the progress of modernization in two of the most advanced countries of Asia, situated at opposite ends of the continent.

WOODCOCK, George. *Asia, gods and cities: Aden to Tokyo*. London, Faber, 1966
A kaleidoscopic travelogue about a journey in 1963 through Pakistan, Malaya, Thailand, Cambodia, Hong Kong, and Japan.

D HISTORY OF LITERATURE, AND LITERATURE IN TRANSLATION

ANDERSON, George Lincoln (ed.) *The genius of the oriental theater.* New York, Toronto, New American Library, 1966 P (Mentor Books)
 Fair translations of two classical Indian plays and eight Japanese plays, of the Nō, Kabuki, and Jōruri varieties.

ANDERSON, George Lincoln (ed.) *Masterpieces of the Orient.* New York, Norton, 1961 P
 Selected long passages of prose and poetry from four civilizations: Near East (two Arabic works, one Persian), India (three), China (four), Japan (six). Uneven choice is inevitable in the circumstances. One modern writer is included in each section. Helpful introductions and bibliographical notes.

Asian PEN anthology. Ed. F. Sionil Jose. New York, Taplinger, 1967
 A "regional anthology" of short stories and poetry by modern writers from Pakistan to Japan. Its stated purpose is "to introduce Asian writers to Asians," but it is illuminating reading for westerners too. Often mediocre and uneven, yet enough is good or characteristic to make this a useful book.

*CEADEL, Eric B. (ed.) *Literatures of the East: an appreciation.* London, Murray, 1953 (Wisdom of the East series). The same as *Literatures of the East: a survey.* New York, Grove, 1959 P
 Lectures for laymen by experts. Brief but good surveys of the "essentials" of the following literatures: ancient Hebrew, Arabic, Iranian, Persian, ancient Indian, Chinese, Japanese.

DANIEL, Milton L. (ed.) *A treasury of modern Asian stories.* Ed. Milton L. Daniel and William Clifford. New York, New American Library, 1961 P (Mentor Books)
 Short stories and extracts from novels by recognized 20th century leaders of modern Asian writing in many countries from Turkey to Japan. A good selection, adequately translated.

*DE BARY, William Theodore (ed.) *A guide to oriental classics.* Prepared by the staff of the Oriental Studies Programme, Columbia College. Ed. Wm. Theodore de Bary and Ainslie T. Embree. New York, London, Columbia University Press, 1959; 1964 P
 Lists English translations of many major works of oriental literatures (Islamic, Chinese, Japanese, and Indian) and suggests supplementary readings and topics for discussion. Very helpful for non-specialists and general study groups.

DHINGRA, Baldoon (comp.) *Asia through Asian eyes. Parables, poetry, proverbs, stories, and epigrams of the Asian peoples.* London, Thames & Hudson, 1959

> A varied selection of brief quotations from many Asian countries on a wide variety of subjects, arranged topically.

HANRAHAN, Gene Z. (ed.) *Fifty great oriental stories.* New York, Toronto, London, Bantam, 1965 P

> Half the stories are from classical literature, the rest are 20th century. Mainly from China, Japan, India, and Southeast Asia; none from the Near and Middle East. Pleasant reading.

Histoire des littératures. Dir. et préf. par Raymond Queneau. 3 vols. Paris, Gallimard, 1956-58 (Encyclopédie de la Pléiade)

> An excellent composite work, with good summaries of the main features and authors of most of the major oriental literatures, each section written by a specialist. Asian literatures are dealt with in the first two volumes. Tome 1 (1956): *Littératures anciennes, orientales et orales.* Tome 2 (1957): *Littératures occidentales,* includes *Littérature hebraïque moderne* and *Littératures non-slaves d'URSS.*

*JACQUOT, Jean (ed.) *Les théâtres d'Asie.* Paris, Editions du Centre National de la Recherche Scientifique, 1961 (Collection Le Choeur des Muses)

> A series of valuable lectures by 19 different experts on the traditional drama of India, China, Japan, Viet Nam, Indonesia, Tibet, and Persia.

*SHIMER, Dorothy Blair (comp.) *The Mentor book of modern Asian literature: from the Khyber Pass to Fuji.* New York, Toronto, New American Library; London, New English Literature, 1969 P (Mentor Books)

> An attractive selection of literature from the 18th century to the present, selected from existing translations. Includes poetry, drama, essay, novel, and short story genres.

*YOHANNAN, John D. (ed.) *A treasury of Asian literature.* New York, Day; London, Phoenix House, 1956; New York, Toronto, New American Library; London, New English Library, 1958 P (and repr.) (Mentor Books)

> A pleasant introduction to some 24 major works of classical Arabic, Persian, Indian, Chinese, and Japanese literatures. The extracts are taken from existing translations and are divided into (1) story, (2) drama, (3) song (i.e. poetry), (4) scripture.

E RELIGION AND IDEAS

ADAMS, Charles J. (ed.) *A reader's guide to the great religions.* New York, Free Press; Toronto, Collier-Macmillan, 1965
Eight good essays by experts, containing selections from the sacred literature of major religious groups and evaluations of them. Good bibliographical coverage. The following are described: primitive religion, the religions of Japan and China, Hinduism, pre-mediaeval Buddhism, Islam, and Christianity.

ARCHER, John Clark. *Faiths men live by.* Rev. Carl E. Purinton. 2nd ed. New York, Ronald, 1958
A useful popular general outline, devoted mostly to a description of Asian religions.

BALLOU, Robert O. (ed.) *The Bible of the world.* Ed. Robert O. Ballou, in collaboration with Friedrich Spiegelberg. New York, Viking; Toronto, Macmillan, 1939 (and repr.)
Well-chosen longish selections from Hindu, Buddhist, Confucian, Taoist, Zoroastrian, Jewish, Christian, and Muslim scriptures.

BALLOU, Robert O. (ed.) *The portable world Bible. Selections from the sacred scriptures of the eight great basic religions of the world.* New York, [194?] C&P
A serviceable shorter version of the book cited above.

BOUQUET, A. C. (ed.) *Sacred books of the world.* An anthology with full commentary, illustrating the development from the formulas and invocations of primitive magic to the hymns and revelations of the twentieth century. Harmondsworth, Baltimore, Penguin, 1954 P (Pelican Books)
Representative selections from Asian scriptures.

BRADEN, Charles Samuel. *Les livres sacrés de l'humanité.* Tr. H. E. del Medico. Paris, Payot, 1955 P (Collection Bibliothèque Historique)
A fair selection of extracts translated from the main religious literatures of Asia.

FINEGAN, Jack. *The archeology of world religions.* Princeton, Princeton University Press; London, Oxford University Press, 1952; 3 vols., 1965 P
A widely used large college textbook, giving details of the following religions: "Primitivism," Zoroastrianism, Hinduism, Jainism, Buddhism, Confucianism, Taoism, Shintoism, Islam, Sikhism. Their basic tenets and early forms of development, sacred literature, and art are described in detail and illustrated by extracts in translation and numerous photographs. The emphasis is always on the earlier, not the current, forms of the religions.

GLASENAPP, Helmuth von. *Croyances et rites des grandes religions.* Tr. L. Jospin. Paris, Payot, 1966 P (Collection Bibliothèque Historique)

GRIMAL, Pierre (ed.) *Mythologies de la Méditerranée au Ganges.* Paris, Larousse, 1963
    Chapters on the classical Middle Eastern and Indian mythologies. Excellent illustrations.

GRIMAL, Pierre (ed.) *Mythologies des montagnes, des forêts et des îles.* Paris, Larousse, 1963
    Sections include Finno-Ugrian, Chinese, Japanese, and Siberian mythology. Excellent illustrations in this encyclopaedic survey.

GRIMAL, Pierre (ed.) *Larousse world mythology.* [Translated by Patricia Beardsworth from *Mythologies de la Méditerranée au Gange* and *Mythologies des steppes, des îles et des forêts.*] London, Hamlyn; New York, Putnam, 1965
    A richly illustrated survey, including chapters on the mythologies of the classical Near and Middle East, India, China, and Japan.

Histoire de la philosophie. I: Orient, Antiquité, Moyen Âge. Publié sous la direction de Brice Parain. Paris, Gallimard, 1969 (Encyclopédie de la Pléiade)
    The Asian sections of this work take up about one-third of the text and are a valuable summary.

KITAGAWA, Joseph Mitsuo. *Religions orientales: communautés spirituelles de l'Orient.* Tr. George Deniker. Paris, Payot, 1961 P (Collection Bibliothèque Scientifique)
    Covers Chinese religions, Hinduism, Buddhism, and Islam.

*MORGAN, Kenneth W. *Asian religions: an introduction to the study of Hinduism, Buddhism, Islam, Confucianism and Taoism.* Washington, American Historical Association; New York, Macmillan, 1964 (American Historical Society, Publications series)
    A very helpful 30-page pamphlet which evaluates relevant books suitable for the general reader.

*SCHOEPS, Hans-Joachim. *The religions of mankind: their origin and development.* Tr. Richard and Clara Winston. Garden City, N.Y., Doubleday, 1966; 1968 P (British edition entitled: *An intelligent person's guide to the religions of mankind.* London, Gollancz, 1967)
    Good sympathetic accounts of the main religions of Asia take up the major part of this volume.

SMITH, Huston. *The religions of man.* New York, London, Harper, 1958; 1965 P; New York, New American Library, 1959 P (and repr.) (Perennial Library)

The meaning of Hinduism, Buddhism, Confucianism, and Taoism to members of these religions. Not a historical account of their development.

*SMITH, Wilfred Cantwell. *The faith of other men.* New York, Toronto, New American Library; London, New English Library, 1965 P (Mentor Books)
Seven illuminating radio talks on Hindus, Buddhists, Muslims, the Chinese, Christians, and Jews; followed by a paper on "The Christian in a religiously plural world."

STACE, Walter T. (ed.) *The teachings of the mystics: being selections from the great mystics and mystical writings of the world.* With interpretative commentaries. New York, Toronto, New American Library, 1960 P (Mentor Books)
Includes Hindu, Buddhist, Taoist, Islamic, and Jewish mysticism.

*ZAEHNER, Robert Charles (ed.) *The concise encyclopaedia of living faiths.* New York, Hawthorn, 1959; Boston, Beacon; Toronto, Saunders, 1967 P; rev. ed., London, Hutchinson, 1964 (New Horizon series)
A series of excellent general essays on the essentials of the historical development, doctrines, and literature of the great religions. Almost three-quarters of the book deals with Asian religions and there are good bibliographies.

F ARTS AND CRAFTS, ARCHITECTURE, AND SCIENCE

ASIA SOCIETY, New York. *Masterpieces of Asian art in American collections.*
New York, Asia Society, 1960
    A fine illustrated catalogue of an exhibition of East, South, and Southeast
    Asian art.

BOWERS, Faubion. *Theatre in the East: a survey of Asian dance and drama.*
London, Nelson; New York, Grove, 1956; 1960 P
    A useful general introduction.

DIRINGER, David. *Writing.* London, Thames & Hudson; New York, Praeger,
1962 (and repr.) (Ancient Peoples and Places series)
    An illustrated survey which includes accounts of the writing systems used
    for Asian languages. Contains some rash generalizations.

FÉVRIER, James. *Histoire de l'écriture.* [2e éd.] Paris, Payot, 1959 P (Collection Bibliothèque Historique)
    A standard work, dealing largely with Asian writing systems.

GORDON, Beate. *An introduction to the dance of India, China, Korea and Japan.* 2nd ed. By Beate and Joseph Gordon. New York, Asia Society, 1965
    A handy 10-page introductory essay giving some fundamental facts about
    the dance in South and East Asia. The last portion compares Asian and
    western dance.

*GROUSSET, René. *The civilizations of the East.* Tr. Catherine Alison Phillips.
4 vols. New York, Cooper Square, 1968 (repr. of 1931-34 ed.)
    Vol. 1: *The Near and Middle East.* Vol. 2: *India.* Vol. 3: *China.* Vol. 4: *Ja-
    pan.* A readable account of oriental art against the local historical and cul-
    tural background.

HAACK, Hermann. *Oriental rugs: an illustrated guide.* Ed. & tr. George and
Cornelia Wingfield Digby. London, Faber, 1960 (and repr.)
    A serviceable layman's introduction.

HOSKING, R. F. (ed.) *A handbook of Asian scripts.* Ed. R. F. Hosking and G.
M. Meredith-Owens. London, British Museum, 1966 P
    A handy little book describing the world's non-western writing systems,
    their origins and relationships.

LILLYS, William (ed.) *Oriental miniatures: Persian, Indian, Turkish.* Edited
with introductions and notes by William Lillys, Robert Reiff, and Emel Esin.
Rutland, Vt., Tuttle, 1965

Short general introductions and 33 good colour plates, each with notes, make this a pleasant book for the general reader. Mrs. Esin's portion, "Turkish miniatures," is also published separately.

The oriental world. India and Southeast Asia [by] Jeannine Auboyer; China, Korea, and Japan [by] Roger Goepper. New York, Toronto, McGraw-Hill; London, Hamlyn, 1967 (Landmarks of the World's Art series)
An attractively illustrated introduction to the arts of a vast region over a long period.

PURCELL, William L. *An introduction to Asian music.* New York, Asia Society, 1966 P
An 11-page booklet providing excellent basic minimum information on the traditions and conventions of the music of India, China, Japan, and Indonesia. Includes good brief bibliography in two parts: (1) for reading, (2) for listening, the latter listing phonograph records.

ROWLAND, Benjamin. *Art in East and West: an introduction through comparisons.* Cambridge, Mass., Harvard University Press, 1954; Boston, Beacon, 1964 P
An interesting and authoritative comparison of the assumptions and characteristics of oriental and western art.

ROWLAND, Benjamin. *The Harvard outline and reading lists for oriental art.* Rev. ed. Cambridge, Mass., Harvard University Press, 1958
Oriental art (excluding Islamic art west of Persia) divided into artistic-historical periods in each region. The reading lists are helpful for non-specialist needs, but suffer from two disadvantages: they are now rather old and therefore exclude some good relevant material, and they are not annotated.

SPEISER, Werner. *Oriental architecture in colour: Islamic, Indian, Far Eastern.* Translated from the German by Charles W. E. Kessler. London, Thames & Hudson; New York, Viking, 1965 (Architecture of the World series)
A series of 112 fine photographs with explanatory text, plans, and commentary. Text not always accurate or adequate as a historical survey.

WINTER, H. J. J. *Eastern science: an outline of its scope and contribution.* London, Murray; New York, Paragon, 1952 (Wisdom of the East series)
A short introduction for laymen to the ancient and mediaeval science of the Near East, India, and China. More details are to be found in the appropriate sections of important general works on the history of science, such as Charles Singer's *History of technology* – 5 vols., Oxford, Clarendon (O.U.P.), 1954-58 (and repr.) – and George Sarton's *Introduction to the history of science* – 3 vols., Baltimore, Williams & Wilkins (for Carnegie Institution), 1927-48 (and repr.).

II The Islamic world *

*Including non-Muslims in the area, and also former and
partially Islamic lands.
†Including original works in English or French by Asian
and North African writers.

INTRODUCTION

Islam, the youngest of the three monotheistic religions, arose in the full light of history less than 14 centuries ago and quickly developed into a world faith; its adherents now number one-seventh of mankind and cover an immense geographical area. It was also the inspiration for a rich, complex, and multifaceted civilization. Islam's historical relationship with Judaism and Christianity is still obvious in many respects. The Koran describes the Jews and Christians as "the People of the Book (i.e. the Scripture)," and the same term may be applied to Muslims, for it is their holy book, the Koran (Qur'ān), which has moulded them. It is, for them, divine revelation to "the final prophet," Muḥammad. In it are mingled sublime religious poetry, moral exhortation, parables, history, and law. This scripture and its interpretation, and the traditions of the deeds, habits, and words of Islam's prophet, were studied and restudied and became the basis of the Muslim way of life. The ideal was a world governed by the divine law as expounded by the sages of Islam (in the same general pattern found in Judaism). Although in practice the society administered by the Muslim rulers and their ministers may have been very far from this ideal theocratic one of the learned men of religion and the believing masses, the vision itself was yet a reality, acting as a point of reference by which the society could take its bearings.

All the "sciences" of Islamic civilization had originally a religious motivation: ancient Arabic was studied to elucidate the full range of meanings of the words in the Koran, Arabic grammar was analysed to determine the exact sense and usage of the Koran's language, and the Muslims' study of history began in an effort to establish details of the life of Muḥammad and the early Muslims, as reported in the traditions. As the civilization broadened and deepened throughout the centuries it continued to receive constant inspiration from religious sources, even in the most apparently worldly or secular spheres. By sanction of the Koran itself Jews and Christians had their guaranteed place as partly autonomous communities; in the classical days of Islam, they formed an integral part of Islamic society and made notable contributions to its civilization, without necessarily compromising their faithfulness to their own traditions. (For this reason books dealing with the historic Jewish and Christian communities of the Islamic world appear in this section.)

The world of Islam expanded with incredible speed. In its first half-century, it grew from a small portion of Arabia to take in Egypt and the coast of North Africa up to Morocco, then also Spain and Portugal in the West, and Palestine, Syria, Iraq, Persia, and parts of Central Asia and Northwest India in the East. In the subsequent period, millions of people of many "races" and religions, speaking a great many different languages, became converts to Islam, and thus ultimately members of the ruling society. The growth continued, until the domain of Islam had expanded over Anatolia ("Turkey") and parts of Southeast Europe, further tracts of Central Asia up to the borders of China, more of India, and then gradually through the mainland of Southeast Asia and the neighbouring islands of Indonesia. Great Muslim empires rose, flourished, and broke up. The most notable was the Ottoman Empire which endured for over 600 years. For centuries "the Turks" were the terror of Europe, feared and yet admired for many of their achievements, military, social, and artistic. It is remarkable that a disproportionately large number of the Muslim states which have existed were founded by men of Turkish or Turkic speech.

Islam was particularly fruitful in the mediaeval period. In theology and law, in literature and philology, history and architecture, marvellous works were produced. In the sciences, mathematics, medicine, and philosophy, the Greek heritage (which had been long neglected or rejected by mediaeval Europe) was taken up and developed, to be returned to Europe later as a major factor in producing the Renaissance. Arabic became the international literary language of the Muslim world, written and read by scholars in every part of that world, whatever their native tongue might be (and it was frequently Persian or Turkish). In certain areas, however, much important work (especially in the fields of literature and history) was also written in Persian (in Persia, Turkey, and India) and Turkish (the Ottoman Empire, parts of Persia, and much of Central Asia).

The traditional Islamic world had an obvious all-pervading basic unity, in spite of the frequent political changes within it. In recent times, however, this unity has been rather seriously shaken. Like the other great civilizations of the East, and like the West earlier, the Muslim lands have been undergoing violent and linked upheavals: rapid economic and social transformation, nationalism, and secularization. The Muslim world is now riven by language-based nationalisms, Turkish, Arab, Persian, and so on. Yet nationalist and secular concepts are somewhat anomalous to Islam, being in conflict with the unifying outlook of traditional Islamic society. The conflict between twin nationalisms, Arab and Zionist, divides and exhausts much of the Middle East. It remains to be seen whether a modus vivendi may yet develop, an expression in modern terms of the Arab-Jewish cultural symbiosis which characterized the Islamic world of mediaeval times.

A few specific remarks regarding the following list of books should be made. Since a thorough understanding of Israel's complexities requires a detailed knowledge of Jewish history in many parts of the world, for which a much more extensive bibliography than is possible within the scope of this work would be needed, only a very limited number of general books on Zionism and Israel in recent times have been included. Other works on the Jews (and Christians) in Islamic lands do, however, appear in the relevant general subsections.

Many books relating to Indian Muslims in the larger context of Indian history, etc., will be found in part III C (India), and works on Muslims in the countries of Southeast Asia (Malaysia, Indonesia) will be found under their national headings in part III D.

A REFERENCE WORKS

AMERICAN INSTITUTE OF ISLAMIC STUDIES. *Islam in paperback.* Denver, American Institute of Islamic Studies, 1969 P (Bibliographic series)
> A useful listing of all US and British paperback publications known to compilers which relate to the Islamic area (defined culturally, including anthropology, history, politics, literature, religion, etc.) from ancient times to the present. As it does not set out to be selective, a fair proportion of specialized works as well as poor-quality books are included. Annotations aim to describe scope only and are not critical. Books are arranged by subject. The lack of an author and title index is lamentable. An annual revised edition is planned.

*BOSWORTH, Clifford Edmund. *The Islamic dynasties: a chronological and genealogical handbook.* Edinburgh, Edinburgh University Press; Chicago, Aldine, 1967 (Islamic Surveys series)
> A useful book, listing the rulers of 82 Islamic dynasties in all parts of the Muslim world from the beginnings of Islam to the present day. Each dynastic table is preceded by an informative, very brief history of the dynasty.

The Encyclopaedia of Islam. New [2nd] ed. Prepared by a number of leading orientalists. Leiden, Brill; London, Luzac, 1954-   [in progress]
> Vol. 1: A – B; vol. 2: C – G; vol. 3: H – I. The most important reference work in its field, covering many aspects of Islamic history and civilization in detail, and giving some account of the present time. Articles are generally authoritative, sometimes rather technical. Several fascicles appear each year. When completed, this edition will supersede the first edition (4 vols. and supplement, London, Leiden, 1913-38).

Encylopédie de l'Islam. Nouvelle [2e] éd. Établie avec le concours des principaux orientalistes. Leiden, Brill; Paris, G.-P. Maisonneuve, 1954-   [in progress]
> French edition of the preceding work.

ETTINGHAUSEN, Richard. *A selected and annotated bibliography of books and periodicals in western languages dealing with the Near and Middle East, with special emphasis on medieval and modern times.* Completed summer 1951. With supplement, December 1953. Washington, Middle East Institute, 1954.
> This useful general bibliography with helpful annotations is now partly out of date and totally out of print. It is cited here because the Middle East Institute, Washington, plans to publish an expanded and revised edition.

MASSIGNON, Louis (ed.) *Annuaire du monde musulman: statistique, historique, social et economique.* Paris, Presses Universitaires de France, 1955
> A sound general reference work, containing important statistics.

*The Middle East and North Africa: a survey and directory. 17th ed. London, Europa Publications, 1970

> An indispensable standard annual containing a mass of current information on every country in the area, with geographical, historical and political, cultural and economic surveys, and a Who's Who of 200 prominent living personalities of the region.

*PAREJA, Felice Maria. Islamologie. Par F. M. Pareja, en collaboration avec L. Hertling, A. Bausani et Th. Bois. Beyrouth, Imprimerie Catholique, 1957-63 [published 1964]

> A remarkable one-volume survey (in 1072 large pages plus good index) of the whole field of Islamic studies. Bibliographies at the end of each chapter are good for material published before World War II, but rather poor for later publications. In spite of some unevenness, this book is the best available one-volume treatment of its subject. (An English translation is to be published at some indefinite date by Rutgers University Press.)

*PEARSON, James Douglas. Index Islamicus, 1906-1955. A catalogue of articles on Islamic subjects in periodicals and other collective publications. Cambridge, Heffer, 1958; Supplement, 1956-60, Cambridge, Heffer, 1962; Second Supplement, 1961-65, Cambridge, Heffer, 1967

> The indispensable tool for locating serious articles published in periodicals, Festschriften, and collective works in western languages and relating to the Islamic world in all its aspects. The articles are arranged in over 40 main subject groups, each subdivided further. An index to authors and a list of periodicals and Festschriften analysed are also provided.

POUNDS, Norman J. G. An atlas of Middle Eastern affairs. Text by N. J. G. Pounds, maps by Robert C. Kingsbury. 2nd ed. London, Methuen; New York, Praeger, 1964

> A useful little book, consisting of 58 outline maps summarizing the basic geographical, historical, national, cultural, and economic factors. Each map is accompanied by a page of commentary.

RONART, Stephan. The concise encyclopaedia of Arabic civilization. By Stephan and Nandy Ronart. Vols. 1-2. Amsterdam, Djambatan, 1959-66; New York, Praeger, 1960-66

> Vol. 1, The Arab east, covers the Arabian peninsula, Egypt, Iraq, Jordan, Lebanon, and Syria. Vol. 2, The Arab west, covers Morocco, Algeria, Tunisia, Libya, and the Sudan. (Vol. 3: Supplement, in preparation.) A handy if rather uneven short reference work on many aspects of Muslim civilization, both traditional and modern.

*ROOLVINK, Roelof. Historical atlas of the Muslim peoples ... compiled with the collaboration of Saleh el Ali, Hussain Monès, Mohd. Salim, with a foreword by H. A. R. Gibb. Amsterdam, Djambatan; Cambridge, Mass., Harvard University Press; London, Allen & Unwin, 1958 C&P

The best atlas of its kind. An excellent cartographic presentation of Islamic history in 40 pages of well-drawn coloured maps.

*SAUVAGET, Jean. *Introduction to the history of the Muslim East: a bibliographical guide.* Based on the second edition as recast by Claude Cahen. Berkeley, University of California Press; London, Cambridge University Press, 1965

The best book of its kind, indispensable for serious students. Divided into three main parts: (1) Sources of Muslim history; (2) Tools of research and general works; (3) Historical bibliography. Hundreds of important books and articles are briefly evaluated in a narrative text. Bibliographical citation is sometimes inadequate or inaccurate, but it remains by far the most comprehensive book of its type.

B GENERAL WORKS

ARBERRY, Arthur John. *Oriental essays: portraits of seven scholars.* London, Allen & Unwin; New York, Macmillan, 1960
>What makes Orientalists tick? An interesting group of biographical essays on some well-known scholars of the past centuries, containing also extracts from their works.

*ARNOLD, Thomas Walker (ed.) *The legacy of Islam.* Ed. Thomas Arnold and Alfred Guillaume. London, Toronto, New York, Oxford University Press, 1931, repr. 1965
>An excellent introduction to Islamic civilization for laymen. Particular attention is paid to its relationship with European culture. Individual scholars write chapters on such subjects as history, geography and commerce, art and architecture, literature, mysticism, philosophy and theology, law, science, and music.

BAMMATE, Haïdar. *Visages de l'Islam.* 2e éd. Lausanne, Payot, 1958
>An enthusiastic survey of Islamic culture, with little emphasis on political history except in the post-war period. Somewhat apologetic in tone.

*BULLARD, Reader William (ed.) *The Middle East: a political and economic survey.* 3rd ed. London, Toronto, New York, Oxford University Press (for the Royal Institute of International Affairs), 1958
>An excellent cooperative work describing the region in general from many points of view — history, religion, economics, and society — and then each country individually under these main headings: Land and People, History and Politics, Government, Social and Economic Surveys.

GIBB, Hamilton Alexander Roskeen. *Studies on the civilization of Islam.* Ed. Stanford J. Shaw and William R. Polk. Boston, Beacon; London, Routledge; Toronto, Saunders, 1962; 1968 P (Beacon Books on World Affairs series)
>Illuminating surveys by a leading scholar, covering three main fields: (1) mediaeval Islamic history; (2) Islamic institutions, philosophy; and (3) modern intellectual currents in the Muslim world.

HITTI, Philip Khuri. *Islam and the West: a historical cultural survey.* Princeton, Van Nostrand, 1962 P (Anvil Books)
>An elementary outline.

STEWART, Desmond. *Early Islam.* By Desmond Stewart and the editors of Time-Life Books. New York, Toronto, Time Inc., 1967 (Great Ages of Man series)
>An imaginative introduction to Islamic religion and civilization. Rather elementary and simplified, but generally interesting and well written, with

numerous beautiful photographs and colour reproductions from miniatures. History is treated very sketchily.

VON GRUNEBAUM, Gustave E. *Islam: essays in the nature and growth of a cultural tradition.* 2nd ed. New York, Barnes & Noble; London, Routledge, 1961
A series of stimulating chapters on Islam, past and present.

YOUNG, Theodore Cuyler (ed.) *Near Eastern culture and society: a symposium on the meeting of East and West.* Princeton, Princeton University Press, 1951, repr. 1966
An interesting collection of essays, particularly on the growth of western interest in various aspects of Islamic culture.

C HISTORY, SOCIAL SCIENCES, AND LAW†

1 GENERAL WORKS

ANDERSON, James Norman Dalrymple. *Islamic law in the modern world.*
New York, New York University Press; London, Stevens, 1959
Five lectures describing traditional Islamic law and contemporary trends.

*ARBERRY, Arthur John. *Aspects of Islamic civilization as depicted in the original texts.* London, Allen & Unwin; Cranbury, N.J., Barnes Yoseloff, 1965; Ann Arbor, University of Michigan Press, 1967 P
A variety of Islamic texts from the 7th century to the present, which give a good composite picture of the civilization as seen from within. Arranged by subject.

ARNOLD, Thomas W. *The caliphate.* With a concluding chapter by Sylvia G. Haim. London, Routledge, 1965
An important study (first published in 1924 and now rather dated) of the place of the office of caliph in Islamic political theory. The abolition of this institution in 1924 and its consequences are discussed in the additional chapter.

BIROT, Pierre. *La Méditerranée et le Moyen-Orient.* Par P. Birot et J. Dresch. 2 vols. 2ᵉ éd. Paris, Presses Universitaires de France, 1964-
A detailed physical and geographical study, including human geography. Vol. 1 includes North Africa. Vol. 2 (in preparation) will cover the Mediterranean and the Middle East.

*BISHAI, Wilson B. *Islamic history of the Middle East: backgrounds, development, and fall of the Arab Empire.* Boston, Allyn, 1968
A simply written history to the end of the Abbasid caliphate in 1258. This is one of the best college textbooks.

---

† Those who wish to read further about the history of specific areas, periods, and subjects may find it useful to consult the following two helpful articles, which contain "model syllabi" accompanied by detailed bibliographies prepared specially for use in university courses. (1) "Syllabus: History of the medieval Middle East, A.D. 622-1799," edited and written by Robert Geran Landen (in *Middle East Studies Association Bulletin,* vol. 4, no. 3, Oct. 1970, pp. 16-54). The bibliography (pp. 28-54) is subdivided by subject, and special symbols mark material particularly suitable for undergraduate history courses, paperbacks, and translations of Islamic texts. There are no annotations. (2) "Syllabus: History of the modern Middle East," edited and written by James Jankowski (in the same *MESA Bulletin,* vol. 4, no. 2, May 1970, pp. 20-32). This covers the period since the beginning of the 19th century and includes a good bibliography (pp. 26-32) of books recommended for, and keyed to, the courses listed in the syllabus.

*BROCKELMANN, Carl. *History of the Islamic peoples.* Tr. Joel Carmichael and Moshe Perlmann. New York, Putnam, 1947 (and repr.); New York, Capricorn, 1960 P (and repr.); London, Routledge, 1949, repr. 1964
  Packed with solid information, especially political history, but is indigestible for continuous reading. Good for quick reference. Excludes post-mediaeval Muslim India, Indonesia, and Central Asia.

*BROCKELMANN, Carl. *Histoire des peuples islamiques.* Tr. M. Tazerout. Paris, Payot, 1949 P (Collection Bibliothèque Historique)
  See preceding note. The French translation is inadequate.

BULLARD, Reader William. *Britain and the Middle East from the earliest times to 1963.* 3rd ed. London, Toronto, New York, Hutchinson, 1964
  A good short review, by a well-informed British former diplomat.

Cambridge History of Islam. Ed. P. M. Holt, Ann K. S. Lambton, Bernard Lewis. 2 vols. Cambridge, New York, [Cambridge] University Press, 1970
  New large standard work on all aspects of Islamic history and civilization, written by a team of experts.

CHARLES, Raymond. *Le droit musulman.* 3e éd. Paris, Presses Universitaires de France, 1965 (Collection "Que sais-je?")
  The main lines of traditional Muslim law, with a brief survey of its present position in various Muslim countries.

COON, Carleton S. *Caravan: the story of the Middle East.* [2nd ed.] New York, Holt, 1958
  A lively and well-written introduction to the peoples and lands of the region, from an anthropologist's viewpoint.

COULSON, Noel James. *A history of Islamic law.* Edinburgh, Edinburgh University Press; Chicago, Aldine, 1964 (Islamic Surveys series)
  A concise introduction, with an informative section on Islamic law in the modern world and a review of the problems of legal reform in the light of Islamic legal history.

COULSON, Noel James. *Conflicts and tensions in Islamic jurisprudence.* Chicago, London, University of Chicago Press, 1969
  Six good lectures addressed to those who are interested in law and the underlying assumptions; not a technical book for Islamic scholars. It examines the main currents of Islamic legal thought, including the relationship between revelation and reason.

DAVISON, Roderic Hollett. *The Near and Middle East: an introduction to history and bibliography.* Washington, Service Center for Teachers of History; New York, Macmillan, 1957 (Service Center for Teachers of History, American Historical Association, Publications series)

An unpretentious little book, which fulfils its purpose of describing books useful for teachers in secondary schools and colleges. Only books in English are cited. For more advanced reading, J. Sauvaget's *Introduction* (section A above) is essential.

ESIN, Emel. *Mecca the blessed, Madinah the radiant.* Photographs by Haluk Doganbey. London, Elek; New York, Crown, 1963
A popular, brief modern Muslim account of Islamic history, religion, and civilization, with special emphasis on the two Holy Cities of Islam. The text is reverent, but somewhat unhistorical. The illustrations are wonderful — colour photographs and copious reproductions of miniature paintings from Islamic manuscripts.

ESIN, Emel. *La Mecque ville bénie, Médine ville radieuse.* Tr. Cathérine Grégoire. Paris, Albin Michel, 1963
See preceding note.

FISCHEL, Walter J. *Jews in the economic and political life of mediaeval Islam.* London, Luzac, 1937, repr. 1968 (Royal Asiatic Society Monograph series)
The Jews played an important part in many parts of the Islamic world, especially in trade.

*FISHER, Sydney Nettleton. *The Middle East: a history.* 2nd ed. New York, Knopf; Toronto, Random House, 1969
A good textbook in spite of over-simplification. The second half deals with the modern period. Useful annotated bibliographies after each chapter.

*FISHER, William Bayne. *The Middle East: a physical, social and regional geography.* 5th ed. London, Methuen, 1963; New York, Dutton, 1966
Very good.

FURON, Raymond. *Le Proche-Orient: Syrie, Liban, Israël, Jordanie, Iraq, Arabie.* Paris, Payot, 1957 (Collection Bibliothèque Géographique)
Summary of geography and history (the latter not always reliable) with emphasis on oil.

FYZEE, Asaf Ali Asghar. *Outlines of Muhammadan law.* 3rd ed. London, Toronto, New York, Oxford University Press, 1964
Deals with the Hanafi traditional school of Islamic law as applied in India and Pakistan, showing the law in practice, not merely in theory.

*GAUDEFROY-DEMOMBYNES, Maurice. *Les institutions musulmanes.* Paris, Flammarion, 1921, repr. 1953
A comprehensive introduction, particularly to social and political institutions.

*GAUDEFROY-DEMOMBYNES, Maurice. *Muslim institutions.* Tr. John P. MacGregor. London, Allen & Unwin, 1950; New York, Barnes & Noble, 1961
See preceding note.

GAUTIER, Emile Félix. *Moeurs et coutumes des musulmans.* Paris, Payot, 1959 P (Collection Bibliothèque Historique)

GOITEIN, Solomon Dov. *Studies in Islamic history and institutions.* Leiden, Brill, 1966
A series of outstanding studies in three groups: (1) the nature and development of Islam; (2) Islamic religious and political institutions; (3) Islamic social history.

ISSAWI, Charles (ed.) *The economic history of the Middle East, 1800-1914: a book of readings.* Chicago, University of Chicago Press, 1966 C&P
A good broad selection of 19th century and modern writings by scholars, diplomats, and others, about a period when European influence began to transform the area. Country by country. Persia excluded.

KIMCHE, Jon. *The second Arab awakening.* London, Thames & Hudson, 1970
An interesting interpretation of Middle Eastern history since the beginning of the 20th century. Based partly on new evidence concerning Great Power involvements and emerging nationalisms. The last third of the book is devoted to the rise of Zionism, Israel, and the role of the Palestinians.

LAPIDUS, Ira Marvin. *Muslim cities in the later Middle Ages.* Cambridge, Mass., Harvard University Press, 1967
Islamic civilization is essentially urban. This is a good study of traditional urban Islam.

LEVY, Reuben. *The social structure of Islam.* Cambridge, Cambridge University Press, 1957; 1962 P
An examination of some of the basic social institutions of the Islamic world.

LEWIS, A. R. *Naval power and trade in the Mediterranean, A.D. 500-1100.* Princeton, Princeton University Press, 1951 (Princeton Studies in History series)
A pioneer study, which deals also with trade between the Near East and the Far East.

LEWIS, Bernard. *Historians of the Middle East.* Ed. Bernard Lewis and P. M. Holt. London, New York, Toronto, Oxford University Press, 1962 (School of Oriental and African Studies, University of London: Historical Writing on the Peoples of Asia series)

An outstanding collection of papers presented to a study conference at the School of Oriental and African Studies, University of London. Leading scholars describe and discuss the work of both Middle Eastern and Western historians of the region from the 7th century to the present.

*LEWIS, Bernard. *The Middle East and the West*. London, Weidenfeld; Bloomington, Indiana University Press, 1964; 1968 P (Indiana University International Studies series)
   A very readable description of the impact of the West on the Middle East. Essential background reading for an understanding of the current problems.

*LONGRIGG, Stephen Hemsley. *The Middle East: a social geography*. 2nd ed., incorporating new material by James Jankowski. London, Duckworth, 1970
   A well-balanced survey of the region, including much relevant historical, political, and economic material.

MANTRAN, Robert. *L'expansion musulmane, (viie-xie siècles)*. Paris, Presses Universitaires de France, 1969 (Collection Nouvelle Clio)
   In the 7th to 9th centuries Islam was a dynamic and expanding religious, military, and cultural force. A sound historian reviews the present state of historical knowledge of this period and discusses problems awaiting further research.

MAUDŪDĪ, Abul A'lā. *The Islamic law and constitution*. Tr. & ed. Khurshid Ahmad. [2nd ed.] Lahore, Islamic Publications, 1960
   A leading educated Pakistani conservative Muslim theologian's views on the place of Islamic law in an Islamic state and the nature of the constitution of the ideal Islamic state.

*MIQUEL, André. *L'Islam et sa civilisation, viie-xxe siècle*. Paris, Colin, 1968 (Collection Destins du Monde)
   A good general history, with an emphasis on "great currents." Good bibliographies and indexes.

MONTEIL, Vincent. *Le monde musulman*. Paris, Horizons de France, 1963 (Collection Hommes et Civilisations)
   Fine picture book, consisting mainly of evocative photos, with a short sociologically oriented text.

The Muslim world: a historical survey. Translated from the German by F. R. C. Bagley. 4 parts. Leiden, Brill, 1960-
   A valuable combination of concentrated students' textbook and reference book, by Bertold Spuler and other scholars. Part 1: *The age of the caliphs* (7th to mid-13th centuries); Part 2: *The Mongol period* (from the 13th century); Part 3: *The last great Muslim empires* (Ottoman Empire, Iran,

Central Asia, Moghul India); Part 4: (In preparation) *Modern times* (i.e. since the end of the 18th century).

ORGELS, Bernard. *La terre et les hommes dans le monde musulman.* Bruxelles, Centre pour l'Étude des Problemes du Monde Musulman Contemporain, 1964 (Collection Correspondance d'Orient. Le Monde Musulman Contemporain: Initiations)
> The human geography of the Middle East.

PATAI, Raphael. *Golden river to golden road: society, culture, and change in the Middle East.* 3rd ed. Philadelphia, University of Pennsylvania Press; London, Oxford University Press, 1969
> A penetrating examination of basic human and cultural factors in the changing societies of the Middle East. Anthropological orientation.

PIRENNE, Henri. *Mahomet et Charlemagne.* Paris, Club du Meilleur Livre, 1961 (repr. of 3rd ed., 1937)
> A Belgian historian's famous theory that the Arab conquests and the expansion of Islam were leading factors in the economic decline of Europe.

PIRENNE, Henri. *Mohammed and Charlemagne.* [Tr. Bernard Miall.] London, Allen & Unwin, 1939 (and repr.); New York, Barnes & Noble, 1955 (repr. of 1939 ed.); Cleveland, Meridian (World), 1957 P
> See preceding note.

PLANHOL, Xavier de. *Les fondements géographiques de l'histoire de l'Islam.* Paris, Flammarion, 1968 P
> A more detailed treatment of the same subject as the book below.

PLANHOL, Xavier de. *Le monde islamique: essai de géographie religieuse.* Paris, Presses Universitaires de France, 1957 (Collection Mythes et Religions)
> An excellent brief discussion of the geographical factors in Islamic history and society.

PLANHOL, Xavier de. *The world of Islam.* Ithaca, Cornell University Press; London, Routledge, 1959
> See preceding note.

*SAUNDERS, John J. *A history of medieval Islam.* London, Routledge; New York, Barnes & Noble, 1965
> A sound introduction for non-specialists to the history of the heartlands of Islam (i.e. excluding Spain, India, etc.) from the 7th to the mid-13th century. Informative annotated bibliographies at the end of the chapters.

SAUNDERS, John J. *The Muslim world on the eve of Europe's expansion.* Englewood Cliffs, N.J., Prentice-Hall, 1966 C&P (Spectrum Books)

Extracts from works by scholars and travellers from the 16th century to the present, describing the various parts of the Muslim world in the 16th century.

*SCHACHT, Joseph. *Esquisse d'une histoire du droit musulman*. Traduit de l'anglais par Jeanne et Félix Arin. Paris, Besson, 1953
   The best outline in French; from the earliest times to the modern period.

*SCHACHT, Joseph. *An introduction to Islamic law*. Oxford, Clarendon Press; Toronto, New York, Oxford University Press, 1964
   A masterly fundamental work.

*SOURDEL, Dominique. *La civilisation de l'Islam classique*. Par D. et J. Sourdel. Paris, Arthaud, 1968 (Collection Les Grandes Civilisations)
   A very attractively illustrated general cultural history, with excellent bibliography for further reading. The best book of its kind in French.

STEWART-ROBINSON, James (ed.) *The traditional Near East*. Englewood Cliffs, N.J., Prentice-Hall, 1966 P (Spectrum Books)
   The eight articles by various authors which compose this book were originally selected as introductory readings for a college Asian Studies course. They survey major characteristics of Islamic civilization until the end of the 18th century.

VON GRUNEBAUM, Gustave Edmund. *Medieval Islam: a study in cultural orientation*. 2nd ed. Chicago, University of Chicago Press, 1953 (and repr.); 1961 P (and repr.). (Phoenix Books)
   Excellent scholarly essays showing how mediaeval Muslims saw themselves and the world.

VON GRUNEBAUM, Gustave Edmund. *L'Islam médiévale: histoire et civilisation*. Tr. Odile Mayot. Paris, Payot, 1962 P (Collection Bibliothèque Historique)
   See preceding note. The French translation is not always reliable.

2 ARABS, ARAB LANDS

a/General Works

ABEL, Armand (ed.) *Le monde arabe et musulman*. Bruxelles, Meddens, 1968
   A lavishly illustrated general introductory work, mainly about the classical period, with emphasis on thought, art, and letters. Persian and Turkish matters are inadequately treated.

ALEM, Jean-Pierre. *Juifs et arabes: 3000 ans d'histoire*. Paris, Grasset, 1968
   Although the author sees the roots of the Arab-Israeli conflict in antiquity,

nine-tenths of this book is a good survey of the development of Jewish and Arab nationalisms since the 19th century.

ANTONIUS, George. *The Arab awakening: the story of the Arab national movement.* New York, Putnam, 1961; New York, Capricorn, 1965 P (repr. of 1939 ed.)

A classic presentation of the Arab nationalist interpretation of World War I diplomacy, first published in 1939.

BERQUE, Jacques. *L'ambivalence dans la culture arabe.* Par J. Berque, J.-P. Charnay, [et al.]. Paris, Anthropos, 1967 P

Sociological studies.

BERQUE, Jacques. *Les Arabes.* Paris, Delpire, 1959 (Collection Encyclopédie Essentielle)

A very general short popular work of "atmosphere," not of "facts"; describes "currents" rather than kings and dates. Excellent illustrations.

BERQUE, Jacques. *Les Arabes d'hier à demain.* 3ᵉ éd. Paris, Seuil, 1969

A subjective, but very interesting, interpretation of the past and present of the Arabs and, in particular, the impact of western culture on traditional Arab norms. Highly personal, often opinionated, and sometimes brilliant.

BERQUE, Jacques. *The Arabs: their history and future.* Tr. [from the 2nd French ed.] by Jean Stewart. London, Faber; New York, Praeger, 1964 (and repr.)

See preceding note.

GABRIELI, Francesco. *The Arabs: a compact history.* Tr. Salvator Attanasio. New York, Hawthorn; Toronto, McClelland & Stewart, 1963 [The same as: *A short history of the Arabs.* Tr. S. Attanasio. London, Hale, 1965]

A useful, somewhat over-simplified survey, mainly political. Transliteration inadequately adapted from the Italian.

GABRIELI, Francesco. *Les Arabes.* Traduit de l'italien par Marie de Wasmer. Paris, Buchet-Chastel, 1963

See preceding note.

*GOITEIN, Solomon Dov. *Jews and Arabs: their contacts through the ages.* [2nd ed.] New York, Schocken, 1964 P

A fascinating and level-headed survey of social and cultural life, written in lively style by the acknowledged master of this subject. Deals mostly with the pre-modern period, but the final chapter discusses the "new confrontation" of Arab nationalism and Zionism. Excellent select bibliography.

*GOITEIN, Solomon Dov. *Juifs et Arabes*. Paris, Editions de Minuit, 1958 (Collection Aleph)
    See preceding note.

GOITEIN, Solomon Dov. *A Mediterranean society: the Jewish communities of the Arab world as portrayed in the documents of the Cairo Geniza*. Berkeley, University of California Press; London, Cambridge University Press, 1967-
    Vol. 1: *The economic foundations*. An excellent work, the first of three projected volumes. Lucid and readable descriptions of social and economic life in the Islamic world during the 10th to 13th centuries. The book is based on Jewish documents of the period, but embraces also the Muslim and Christian communities. Specimen chapter subsections under "The working people": (1) Social classes, (2) Craftsmen, (3) Wage earners, (4) Industries, (5) Agriculture, (6) Professions of women, (7) Slaves.

GROUSSET, René. *L'épopée des croisades*. Paris, Périn, 1968 (repr. of 1939 ed.)
    A balanced and readable general history, based on both Arabic and western sources.

HAIM, Sylvia G. (ed.) *Arab nationalism: an anthology*. Berkeley, University of California Press, 1962
    Writings of 20 representative leaders of the Arab nationalist movement of various periods and places, which show the development of its ideology since its beginnings in the late 19th century. Evaluation in an excellent introductory essay by the editor.

HITTI, Philip Khuri. *The Arabs: a short history*. 5th ed. London, Macmillan; New York, St. Martin's, 1968 (and repr.)
    A condensed version of his *History of the Arabs*.

HITTI, Philip Khuri. *Précis d'histoire des Arabes*. Tr. M. Planiol. Paris, Payot, 1950 P (Collection Bibliothèque Historique)
    See preceding note.

*HITTI, Philip Khuri. *History of the Arabs, from the earliest times to the present*. 9th ed. London, Toronto, Macmillan; New York, St. Martin's, 1967 P
    The best available general survey, but somewhat superficial; cultural and economic as well as political. The last four centuries are only sketchily covered.

HITTI, Philip Khuri. *Makers of Arab history*. New York, St. Martin's; London, Toronto, Macmillan, 1968
    Biographies of 13 notable mediaeval Muslims, seven of them "religious and political" (from Muhammad to Saladin), and six "intellectuals" (e.g. Avicenna).

HOTTINGER, Arnold. *The Arabs: their history, culture and place in the modern world.* London, Thames & Hudson; Berkeley, University of California Press, 1963 (Past in the Present series)
A good general popularization by a Swiss journalist.

KALISKY, René. *Le monde arabe.* 2 vols. Verviers (Belgique), Gérard; Québec, Kasan; Paris, Inter, 1968 P (Collection Marabout Université)
Tome 1, *L'essor et le déclin d'un empire,* is a useful digest of standard histories to the Ottoman conquest. Tome 2, *Le reveil et la quête de l'unité,* is a more detailed, mainly political, account of the 19th and 20th centuries, over half discussing the Arab world from the establishment of Israel (1948) to the third Arab-Israeli war (1967). Thoughtful journalism.

*LEWIS, Bernard. *The Arabs in history.* 4th ed. London, Toronto, Hutchinson, 1966; New York, Harper, 1966 P (Harper Torchbooks)
An excellent, concise, and readable sketch, with emphasis on economic factors. Deals mainly with the period before the 16th century.

*LEWIS, Bernard. *Les Arabes dans l'histoire.* Tr. Annie Mesritz. Bruxelles, Office de Publicité; Neuchâtel, La Baconnière, 1958
See preceding note.

MONTAGNE, Robert. *La civilisation du désert: nomades d'Orient et d'Afrique* Paris, Hachette, 1947 (Collection Le Tour du Monde)
An important description of Bedouin life in all its aspects.

NUSEIBEH, Hazem Zaki. *The ideas of Arab nationalism.* Ithaca, Cornell University Press; London, Oxford University Press, 1956
A relatively detached investigation into the origin and development of Arab nationalist ideals. For more illustrative material, see Sylvia Haim's *Arab nationalism* (above).

RISLER, Jacques C. *La civilisation arabe.* Paris, Payot, 1962 P (Collection Petit Bibliothèque Payot)
A short general survey, up to about the 15th century.

ROUX, Jean Paul. *L'Islam au Proche-Orient: Égypte, Arabie, Palestine, Syrie, Liban, Jordanie, Irâq.* Paris, Payot, 1960 P (Collection Bibliothèque Historique)
A general outline of the main trends in the Islamic history of the Arab lands, particularly in modern times.

b/Syria, Lebanon, Jordan, Iraq

FEDDEN, Robin. *Syria and Lebanon.* 3rd ed. London, Murray, 1965
The monuments of Syria left by successive generations from prehistoric times to the present, described in their historical setting.

GLUBB, John Bagot. *Syria, Lebanon, Jordan.* London, Thames & Hudson, 1967 (New Nations and Peoples series)
> Very over-simplified and full of doubtful generalizations, yet informative for the beginner. Half the book is devoted to history, and half to culture, manners, and customs.

HAÏK, Farjallah. *Liban.* Notices géographiques, historiques et archéologiques de R. Boulanger. Photographies d'A. Raccah. Paris, Hachette, 1958 (Collection Les Albums des Guides Bleus)
> Notable photographs with brief explanatory text.

HAÏK, Farjallah. *Lebanon.* Photographs by A. Raccah. Translated from the French by Margaret Case. Paris, Hachette; New York, Hastings House, 1958 (Hachette World Albums series)
> See preceding note.

HITTI, Philip Khuri. *History of Syria, including Lebanon and Palestine.* London, New York, Macmillan, 1951
> A detailed account for laymen.

HITTI, Philip Khuri. *Lebanon in history, from the earliest times to the present.* 3rd ed. London, Toronto, Macmillan; New York, St. Martin's, 1967
> A detailed work.

HITTI, Philip Khuri. *A short history of Lebanon.* London, Toronto, Macmillan; New York, St. Martin's, 1965
> A useful outline.

HITTI, Philip Khuri. *Syria: a short history.* London, Toronto, Macmillan; New York, St. Martin's, 1959; New York, Collier, 1961 P
> An extremely compressed abridgement of Hitti's *History of Syria* (above).

ISMĀʿĪL, Ādil. *Le Liban: histoire d'un peuple.* Par Adel Ismail. Beyrouth, Dar al-Makchouf, 1965
> A very summary, unsophisticated, general history from antiquity to the present.

LONGRIGG, Stephen Hemsley. *Four centuries of modern Iraq.* Oxford, Clarendon Press, 1925; repr. Farnborough, Gregg, 1969
> A standard work, now a little dated, but still very useful.

LONGRIGG, Stephen Hemsley. *Syria and Lebanon under French mandate.* London, Toronto, New York, Oxford University Press (for the Royal Institute of International Affairs), 1958
> The most important work on the period from the First World War to the end of the Second.

NANTET, Jacques. *Histoire du Liban.* Paris, Editions de Minuit, 1963 (Collection Grands Documents)
>A good general history, with greater detail on the period since World War II.

*SALIBI, Kamal S. *The modern history of Lebanon.* London, Weidenfeld; New York, Praeger, 1965
>Mainly 19th and 20th century history of a unique country inhabited chiefly by Muslims, Christians, and Druzes.

THUBRON, Colin. *Mirror to Damascus.* London, Heinemann, 1967; Boston, Toronto, Little Brown, 1968
>An excellently written and well-informed account of this ancient city's past and present. Sympathetic yet critical; just right for the armchair traveller.

TIBAWI, Abdul Latif. *A modern history of Syria, including Lebanon and Palestine.* London, Toronto, Macmillan; New York, St. Martin's, 1969
>Informative, although somewhat tendentious.

c/Arabia, Yemen

BERREBY, Jean Jacques. *La péninsule arabique: terre sainte de l'Islam, patrie de l'arabisme et empire du pétrole.* Paris, Payot, 1958 P (Collection Bibliothèque Historique)
>A well-written study, with emphasis on the impact of oil.

BURTON, Richard Francis. *Personal narrative of a pilgrimage to al-Medinah and Meccah.* Ed. Isabel Burton. 2 vols. New York, Dover; Toronto, General; London, Constable, 1964 P (repr. of 1893 ed.)
>The exciting adventures of a remarkably gifted and eccentric Englishman who made the pilgrimage in disguise. First published 1855.

DOUGHTY, Charles Montague. *Travels in Arabia Deserta.* An abridgment by Edward Garnett. London, Cape, 1937 (and repr.) C&P; Garden City, N.Y., Doubleday, 1955
>A 19th century classic of travel literature.

DOUGHTY, Charles Montague. *Arabia deserta.* Textes choisis par E. Garnett, tr. Jacques Marty. Préface de T. E. Lawrence. Paris, Payot, 1950 P (Collection Bibliothèque Historique)
>See preceding note.

LANDEN, Robert Geran. *Oman since 1856: disruptive modernization in a traditional society.* Princeton, Princeton University Press, 1967
>A detailed scholarly study, based largely on Arabic texts and British government material. Mainly political and economic and mostly 19th century.

LAWRENCE, Thomas E. *The seven pillars of wisdom.* London, Cape, 1935 (and repr.); Harmondsworth, Penguin, 1962 (and repr.) P
Lawrence of Arabia's romanticized account of the 1916 Arab revolt, originally published 1926.

LAWRENCE, Thomas E. *Les sept piliers de la sagesse.* Paris, Payot, (n.d.) P
See preceding note.

MACRO, Eric. *Yemen and the western world, 1571-1964.* London, Hurst; New York, Praeger, 1968
Mainly political and mostly 20th century; the earlier period is only sketchily covered.

PHILLIPS, Wendell. *Oman: a history.* London, Longmans, 1967
The first modern general history of this mainly desert state, occupying the southeast corner of Arabia, whose ruling family has been in power continuously since the 18th century.

PHILLIPS, Wendell. *Unknown Oman.* London, Longmans, 1966
Notable modern travel book by a well-known archaeologist, explorer, and oilman.

PIRENNE, Jacqueline. *A la découverte de l'Arabie: cinq siècles de science et d'adventure.* Paris, Le Livre Contemporain, Nizet, 1958
A history of exploration in Arabia, with extracts from the works of the travellers and explorers.

WINDER, R. Bayly. *Saudi Arabia in the nineteenth century.* London, Toronto, Macmillan; New York, St. Martin's, 1965
A documented history of a little-known period.

d/Egypt

ABDEL-MALEK, Anouar. *Idéologie et renaissance nationale: l'Égypte moderne.* Paris, Anthropos, 1969 P
An expert study of the "classical" period of the development of nationalist and modernist movements in 19th century Egypt.

BERQUE, Jacques. *L'Égypte: impérialisme et révolution.* Paris, Gallimard, 1967
A sociologist's examination of Egypt from 1880 to the present with particular attention to the period 1919-52.

COLLINS, Robert O. *Egypt & the Sudan,* by Robert O. Collins [and] Robert L. Tignor. Englewood Cliffs, N.J., Prentice-Hall, 1967 (Spectrum Books)
A good short introduction to modern Egyptian history.

*HOLT, Peter M. *Egypt and the Fertile Crescent, 1516-1922: a political history.*
London, Longmans; Ithaca, Cornell University Press, 1966
   The best work on the Arab lands under Ottoman rule

HUSAYN, Taha. *The future of culture in Egypt.* By Taha Hussein. Tr. Sidney
Glazer. Washington, American Council of Learned Societies, 1954
   A work of great interest, rather inadequately summarized (rather than
   translated) in English.

*LANE, Edward W. *The manners and customs of the modern Egyptians.* London, Dent; New York, Dutton, 1908 (repr. 1954) (Everyman's Library series)
   First published in 1836, this is a very readable account of traditional, pre-
   westernized Islamic urban society by an Englishman who "went native."
   Contains excellent illustrations by the author.

MARLOWE, John. *Anglo-Egyptian relations, 1800-1956.* 2nd ed. London,
Cass, 1965. [U.S. title:] *A history of modern Egypt and Anglo-Egyptian rela-
tions, 1800-1956.* 2nd ed. Hamden, Conn., Archon, 1965
   The rise and fall of British influence: a political history by a British scholar.

POUTHAS, Charles H. (ed.) *Histoire de l'Égypte depuis la conquête ottomane
(1517-1937).* Paris, Hachette, 1948
   A useful textbook.

*SAFRAN, Nadav. *Egypt in search of political community. An analysis of the
intellectual and political evolution of Egypt, 1804-1952.* Cambridge, Mass.,
Harvard University Press, 1961 (Harvard Middle Eastern Studies series)
   A thoroughly researched study which interprets the causes of the instabil-
   ity in recent Egyptian and Arab history.

STEWART, Desmond. *Cairo: 5500 years.* New York, Crowell, 1968. [British
edition:] *Great Cairo, mother of the world.* London, Hart-Davis, 1969
   An enjoyably written "biography" of the city, laced with quotations by
   travellers from various epochs.

VATIKIOTIS, Panayiotis J. *The modern history of Egypt.* London, Weidenfeld; New York, Praeger, 1969 (Asia-Africa series)
   Intended to inform the layman of Egypt's development in the past 150
   years, but often highly specialized and detailed on political history. Inadequate treatment of social and cultural matters.

e/North Africa

i/General Works

BERQUE, Jacques. *Le Maghreb entre deux guerres.* Paris, Seuil, 1962
   A social and economic rather than political study of North Africa, showing
   keen psychological insight — but difficult reading at times.

BERQUE, Jacques. *French North Africa: the Maghrib between two wars*. Tr.
Jean Stewart. London, Faber; New York, Praeger, 1967
    See preceding note.

*BOUSQUET, Georges Henri. *Les Berbères: histoire et institutions*. 2ᵉ éd. Paris,
Presses Universitaires de France, 1961 P (Collection "Que sais-je?")
    The best reliable short book covering this neglected field.

*CHOURAQUI, André. *Between East and West: a history of the Jews of North
Africa*. Tr. Michael M. Bernet. Philadelphia, Jewish Publication Society, 1968
    The most accessible and readable work on its subject, covering the period
    from before the Christian era to the sudden virtual dissolution of the Jew-
    ish communities of Morocco, Algeria, and Tunisia in the 1950s and 1960s,
    with the resettlement of North African Jews in Israel and elsewhere.

CHOURAQUI, André. *Marche vers l'Occident: les Juifs d'Afrique du Nord*.
Paris, Presses Universitaires de France, 1952
    An important work on the history of the Jews in Morocco, Algeria, and
    Tunisia, and their way of life and culture around 1950.

GAUTIER, Émile-Félix. *Le passé de l'Afrique du Nord: les siècles obscurs*.
Paris, Payot, 1964 P (Collection Petit Bibliothèque Payot)
    A standard work on mediaeval North Africa.

*GALLAGHER, Charles F. *The United States and North Africa: Morocco, Al-
geria, and Tunisia*. Cambridge, Mass., Harvard University Press, 1963 (American Foreign Policy Library series)
    A good book with a misleading title. It is mainly about the history, poli-
    tics, and social structure of North Africa, not about US relations with the
    area.

*JULIEN, Charles-André. *Histoire de l'Afrique du Nord: Tunisie, Algérie, Maroc,
de la conquête arabe à 1830*. 3ᵉ éd. 2 vols. Paris, Payot, 1964 P (Collection
Bibliothèque Historique)
    A standard work. Vol. 1 revised by Christian Courtois; vol. 2 revised by
    Roger Le Tourneau.

MARÇAIS, Georges. *La Berberie musulmane et l'Orient au Moyen Age*. Paris,
Montaigne, 1946 (Collection Les Grandes Crises de l'Histoire)
    A sound history of the 10th to 12th centuries.

PEYROUTON, Marcel. *Histoire générale du Maghreb. Algérie, Maroc, Tunisie,
des origines à nos jours*. Paris, Albin Michel, 1966
    A fair synthesis based on other works and the experience of the author, a
    Frenchman who held the highest administrative posts in each of the three
    countries. Nine-tenths of the book deals with the pre-nationalist period.

ii/Algeria, Libya

AGERON, Charles Robert. *Histoire de l'Algérie contemporaine (1830-1966)*. 2e éd. Paris, Presses Universitaires de France, 1966 P (Collection "Que sais-je?")
> A brief up-to-date outline.

*BOURDIEU, Pierre. *Sociologie de l'Algérie*. [2e éd.] Paris, Presses Universitaires de France, 1961
> An excellent sociological survey of the heterogeneous elements that make up Algeria and its culture.

*BOURDIEU, Pierre. *The Algerians*. Tr. Alan C. M. Ross. Boston, Beacon; Toronto, Saunders, 1962
> Translation of the preceding book.

BOYER, Pierre. *La vie quotidienne à Alger à la veille de l'intervention française*. Paris, Hachette, 1963
> An interesting social survey of Algiers about the beginning of the 19th century.

JUIN, Alphonse. *Histoire parallèle: la France en Algérie, 1830-1962*. [Par] Alphonse Juin [et] Amar Naroun. Paris, Perrin, 1963
> Separate accounts of the same events, one by Marshal Juin, an Algerian-born Frenchman, the other by an Algerian Muslim politican. An interesting experiment in "bifocal history."

JULIEN, Charles-André. *Histoire de l'Algérie contemporaine*. Paris, Presses Universitaires de France, 1964-   [in progress]
> Tome 1: *La conquête et les débuts de la colonisation (1827-1871)*. 1964.
> A detailed standard work.

*MOUILLESEAUX, Louis (ed.) *Histoire de l'Algérie*. Paris, Productions de Paris, 1962
> A readable illustrated survey, brightly written for non-specialists.

WRIGHT, John. *Libya*. London, Benn; Toronto, General; New York, Praeger, 1969 (Nations of the Modern World series)
> A general, though mainly political, history. Two-thirds of the book is devoted to Libya in the 20th century.

ZIADEH, Nicola A. *The modern history of Libya*. London, Weidenfeld; New York, Praeger, 1968 (Asia-Africa series)
> From the 16th century to the present.

iii/Morocco

AYACHE, Albert. *Le Maroc: bilan d'une colonisation.* Paris, Éditions Sociales, 1956
> A review of Morocco at the end of 44 years of French rule, from a Marxist viewpoint. Heavy stress on economic and social matters.

LE TOURNEAU, Roger. *Fez in the age of the Marinides.* Translated from the French by Besse Alberta Clement. Norman, University of Oklahoma Press, 1961 (Centers of Civilization series)
> Excellent little book describing all aspects of life in an important mediaeval Muslim city.

*LE TOURNEAU, Roger. *La vie quotidienne à Fès en 1900.* Paris, Hachette, 1965
> A reconstruction of life in Fez before the modernization, based on interviews and the author's experience. Presents a good picture of pre-modern urban Muslim life in the Maghreb.

SEFRIOUI, Ahmed. *Maroc.* Photographies de Jacques Belin et Gabriel Gillet. Notices géographiques, historiques et archéologiques de Jean Besancenot. Paris, Hachette, 1956 (Collection Les Albums des Guides Bleus)
> Mainly attractive photographs and brief explanatory text.

SEFRIOUI, Ahmed. *Morocco.* Photographs by Jacques Belin and Gabriel Gillet. Geographical, historical and archaeological notes by Jean Besancenot. Paris, Hachette, 1956 (Hachette World Albums series)
> See preceding note.

TERRASSE, Henri. *Histoire du Maroc.* 2 vols. Casablanca, Editions Atlantides, 1949-50
> A basic general history, down to the establishment of the French protectorate.

f/Spain (Islamic Period and Heritage)

HOYLE, Edwin. *Andalus: Spain under the Muslims.* London, Hale, 1958
> A sound and readable general work.

*LEVI-PROVENÇAL, Évariste. *La civilisation arabe en Espagne: vue générale.* Paris, G.-P. Maisonneuve, 1961 (Collection Islam d'Hier et d'Aujourd'hui)
> Three valuable lectures by an outstanding expert.

LEVI-PROVENÇAL, Évariste. *Islam d'Occident: études d'histoire médiévale.* Paris, G.-P. Maisonneuve, 1948 (Collection Islam d'Hier et d'Aujourd'hui)
> Eleven articles on the Muslim history and literature of Spain and North Africa.

SORDO, Enrique. *Moorish Spain: Cordoba, Seville, Granada.* Photographs by Wim Swaan. London, Elek, 1963
Descriptions of three historic cities, with outstanding photographs of the architecture.

SORDO, Enrique. *L'Espagne mauresque: Cordoue, Séville, Grenade.* Photographies de Wim Swaan. Tr. Claude Couffon. Paris, Albin Michel, 1964
See preceding note.

TERRASSE, Henri. *Islam d'Espagne: une rencontre de l'Orient et de l'Occident.* Paris, Plon, 1958 (Collection Civilisations d'Hier et d'Aujourd'hui)
A sound general survey, which is especially good on art and archaeology.

WATT, William Montgomery. *A history of Islamic Spain.* Edinburgh, Edinburgh University Press; Chicago, Aldine, 1965; Garden City, N.Y., Doubleday, 1967
The most useful short treatment in English, attractively illustrated.

3 PERSIA (IRAN), THE KURDS

L'Âme de l'Iran. Par Georges Contenau, J. Duchesne-Guillemin [et al.] [Sous la direction de René Grousset, Louis Massignon, Henri Massé] Paris, Albin Michel, 1951
A series of nine good essays on various aspects of Iranian/Persian culture (art and archaeology, literature, and religion) from prehistoric times to the present.

*ARBERRY, Arthur John (ed.) *The legacy of Persia.* Oxford, Clarendon Press; Toronto, New York, Oxford University Press, 1953 (and repr.)
A useful survey of some of the main facets of Persian civilization and culture, in the form of essays by different scholars. Subjects include history, language, literature, arts, science.

ARFA, Hassan. *The Kurds: an historical and political study.* London, Toronto, New York, Oxford University Press, 1966
On the Kurds in Turkey, Iran, and Iraq, by an Iranian general and diplomat.

BERREBY, Jean Jacques. *Le golfe persique: mer de légende, reservoir de pétrole.* Paris, Payot, 1959 P (Collection Bibliothèque Historique)
How the region was affected by the discovery of oil and the clash of international interests in exploiting it.

BOSWORTH, Clifford Edmund. *The Ghaznavids: their empire in Afghanistan and eastern Iran.* Edinburgh, Edinburgh University Press; Chicago, Aldine, 1963

The Ghaznavids were a well-known dynasty (999-1040) which can be taken as representative of the many other military dynasties that arose in the Muslim world. This book is particularly good in its description of social, economic, and cultural factors.

BOULANGER, Robert. *Iran.* Texte et photographies de Robert Boulanger. Paris, Hachette, 1956 (Collection Les Albums des Guides Bleus)
A small book consisting mainly of attractive photographs with brief explanatory text.

BROWNE, Edward Granville. *A year amongst the Persians. Impressions as to the life, character, and thought of the people of Persia, received during twelve month's residence in that country in the years 1887-1888.* 3rd ed. London, Black; New York, Macmillan, 1950 (and repr.)
A fine travel book by a keen, sympathetic observer.

The Cambridge History of Iran. Cambridge, New York, Cambridge University Press, 1968-   [in progress]
Vol. 1: *The land of Iran.* Ed. W. B. Fisher, 1968. Vol. 5: *The Saljuq and Mongol periods.* Ed. J. A. Boyle, 1968. The new standard detailed history, a collective work by experts. Vol. 1 is a masterly detailed treatment of geography and vol. 5 a history of the 11th to 13th centuries.

La Civilisation iranienne (Perse, Afghanistan, Iran extérieur). Préface de Henri Massé, introduction de René Grousset. Paris, Payot, 1952 P (Collection Bibliothèque Historique)
A useful but very summary survey of many aspects of the civilization of Iran (in its broad sense) from prehistoric times to the present. Consists of numerous short sections, each written by an expert.

COSTA, A., photographer. *Persia:* 105 pictures in photogravure, 5 colour plates. Introductory essay and notes by L. Lockhart. London, Thames & Hudson; Toronto, Longmans, 1957; New York, Praeger, 1958
Persia's cultural and artistic heritage and people are shown in excellent photographs, with interesting commentary.

ELWELL-SUTTON, Laurence Paul. *A guide to Iranian area study.* Ann Arbor, Mich., American Council of Learned Societies, 1952
A very useful descriptive bibliography. Deserves bringing up to date.

*FRYE, Richard N. *The heritage of Persia.* Cleveland, World; London, Weidenfeld, 1963; Toronto, New York, New American Library, 1966 P (Mentor Books)
An excellent summary of all aspects of the pre-Islamic civilizations of Iran and their survival up to the 10th century.

*FRYE, Richard N. *Persia*. [3rd ed.] London, Allen & Unwin, 1968 C&P
A handy little introduction to Iran, particularly its history. Useful bibliographical chapter at the end of the book.

FURON, Raymond. *L'Iran: Perse et Afghanistan*. 2nd ed. Paris, Payot, 1951 P
(Collection Bibliothèque Géographique)
A fair historical outline to 1950, with emphasis on geography. Neglects
many recent scholarly works.

*GHIRSHMAN, Roman. *L'Iran, des origines à l'Islam*. Paris, Payot, 1951 P (Collection Bibliothèque Historique)
An excellent survey of pre-Islamic Iran, providing a useful background for
later Persian history and culture.

*GHIRSHMAN, Roman. *Iran, from the earliest times to the Islamic conquest*.
Tr. Margaret Munn-Rankin. Harmondsworth, Baltimore, Penguin, 1954 P
See preceding note.

KINNANE, Derk. *The Kurds and Kurdistan*. London, Toronto, New York, Oxford University Press (for the Institute of Race Relations), 1964
A short account of Kurdish history and society, especially in the last few
years.

LOCKHART, Laurence. *The fall of the Safavi dynasty and the Afghan occupation of Persia*. Cambridge, Cambridge University Press, 1958
A well-written historical study of a complicated and interesting period —
the end of the 17th and the early 18th centuries.

LOCKHART, Laurence. *Persian cities*. London, Luzac; Chester Springs, Pa.,
Dufour, 1960
Historic panorama of 23 cities.

MORIER, James. *The adventures of Hajji Baba of Ispahan*. With an introduction by Richard Jennings. London, Cresset, 1949 (and repr.); Chester Springs,
Pa., Dufour, 1960
An excellent picaresque novel of traditional Persian life — closely observed,
slightly satirical, and often very funny. First published in 1824 and frequently reprinted.

NIKITINE, Basile. *Les Kurdes: étude sociologique et historique*. Paris, Klincksieck, 1956
An important scholarly work.

RAMAZANI, Rouhollah K. *The foreign policy of Iran, 1500-1941: a developing
nation in world affairs*. Charlottesville, Va., University Press of Virginia, 1966

An interesting examination; in spite of the title, deals mainly with the 20th century.

STEVENS, Roger. *The land of the Great Sophy.* London, Methuen, 1962
A superior travel book, with emphasis on archaeology and architecture.

SYKES, Percy Molesworth. *A history of Persia.* 2 vols. 3rd ed. London, Macmillan; New York, St. Martin's, 1930, repr. 1969
An out-of-date but not yet superseded general history.

*WILBER, Donald Newton. *Iran: past and present.* 6th ed. Princeton, Princeton University Press, 1967
A handy and informative factual introduction to many aspects of Iran's history and culture from antiquity to the present day. Its sweeping generalizations are perhaps unavoidable in so short a book.

4 TURKEY AND THE OTTOMAN EMPIRE

ALLEN, William Edward David. *Problems of Turkish power in the sixteenth century.* London, Central Asian Research Centre, 1963
The Ottoman Empire was the most powerful Muslim state of its period and at the zenith of its power in the 16th century. This well-informed booklet shows how it dealt with its political and economic problems.

BABINGER, Franz. *Mahomet II le Conquérant et son temps (1432-1481): la grande peur du monde au tournant de l'histoire.* Tr. H. E. del Medico. Paris, Payot, 1954 P (Collection Bibliothèque Historique)
A somewhat controversial biography of the great Turkish sultan who conquered Istanbul in 1453 and greatly extended Ottoman power in both Asia and Europe.

BERKES, Niyazi. *The development of secularism in Turkey.* Montreal, McGill University Press, 1964
An excellent study of "the transformation of Turkey from a traditional Islamic society to a secular national state," from the 18th century until 1939.

BIRGE, John Kingsley. *A guide to Turkish area study.* Washington, American Council of Learned Societies, 1949
Still a useful guide to many aspects of Turkish history and culture, though limited to works in European languages (mainly English) published before 1947. Reprint to appear "shortly."

BUSBECQ, Ogier Ghiselin de. *The Turkish letters* of Ogier Ghiselin de Busbecq, Imperial ambassador at Constantinople 1554-1562. Translated from the Latin

by Edward Seymour Forster. London, Toronto, New York, Oxford University Press, 1969 (repr. of 1927 ed.)
The Ottoman Empire at its zenith excellently and acutely described by the Holy Roman Empire's ambassador. From the 16th to the 18th century this book was one of the main sources of popular knowledge of Turkey for Europeans.

CAHEN, Claude. *Pre-Ottoman Turkey: a general survey of the material and spiritual culture and history, c. 1071-1330.* Translated from the French by J. Jones-Williams. London, Sidgwick; New York, Taplinger, 1968
A well-balanced work by a noted scholar; includes a special illustrated section on Turkish art and architecture, and a detailed bibliography to each chapter.

COLES, P. H. *The Ottoman impact on Europe.* London, Thames & Hudson; New York, Harcourt, 1968 C&P (Library of European Civilisation series)
Over-emphasis on military aspects, but useful as a general guide. Copious illustrations.

*CREASY, Edward S. *History of the Ottoman Turks.* With a new introduction by Zeine N. Zeine. Beirut, Khayat, 1961 (Oriental Reprints series)
A reprint of a useful history of the Ottoman Empire, written a century ago. The best one-volume history available, out of date but not yet superseded. Mainly political. A really good modern history of the Ottoman Empire is still a desideratum.

DAVISON, Roderic Hollett. *Reform in the Ottoman Empire, 1856-76.* Princeton, Princeton University Press, 1963
A very good detailed study.

GABRIEL, Albert. *En Turquie.* [2nd ed.] Paris, Hartmann, 1962
Notable photographs of the "unchanging" aspects of Turkey, mainly architecture and landscape; no factories, modern urban housing, or power stations shown, although these are sources of great pride to modern Turks.

GABRIEL, Albert. *Turkey in pictures.* 194 photographs, with an introduction and notes. Tr. Barbara Comerford. London, Duckworth, 1962
See preceding note.

*GIBB, Hamilton Alexander Rosskeen. *Islamic society and the West: a study of the impact of western civilization on Moslem culture in the Near East.* By Sir Hamilton Gibb and Harold Bowen. 2 vols. London, Toronto, New York, Oxford University Press, 1950-57 (and repr.)
The two volumes so far published are numbered "Vol. 1, pts. 1-2: *Islamic society in the 18th century.*" An important study (based largely on ori-

ginal Turkish and Arabic sources) of the Ottoman Empire as it was in the
period just preceding the major movements of westernization.

HÜRLIMANN, Martin. *Istanbul.* London, Thames & Hudson; New York, Viking, 1958 (and repr.)
    A hundred fine photographs of historic Istanbul, with short historical in-
    troduction.

HÜRLIMANN, Martin. *Istanbul, Constantinople.* Version française de Simone
Runacher. Paris, Braun, 1958
    See preceding note.

KINGLAKE, Alexander William. *Eothen.* London, Dent; New York, Dutton,
1908, repr. 1954 (Everyman's Library series)
    An excellently observed and entertaining travel book, showing the Otto-
    man Empire (including the Arab world) in pre-modern times. First pub-
    lished 1844.

*KINROSS, Lord (Balfour, Patrick, baron Kinross). *Atatürk: the rebirth of a
nation.* London, Weidenfeld, 1964; New York, Morrow, 1966
    The best biography based on primary sources. Essential and fascinating
    reading for those interested in modern Turkey.

LAMB, Harold. *Suleiman the Magnificent, Sultan of the East.* Garden City,
N.Y., Doubleday, 1951; London, Hale, 1953
    An enjoyable romanticized popular biography.

LAMOUCHE, Léon. *Histoire de la Turquie, depuis les origines jusqu'à nos
jours.* Nouvelle [2e] éd., complétée par J. P. Roux. Paris, Payot, 1953 P (Collection Bibliothèque Historique)
    A serviceable survey, in rather greater detail than Mantran's *Histoire de la
    Turquie* (below).

*LEWIS, Bernard. *The emergence of modern Turkey.* [2nd ed.] London, New
York, Toronto, Oxford University Press (for the Royal Institute of International Affairs), 1968 P
    A first-class study of the development of Turkey from the beginning of
    westernization at the end of the 18th century until 1950. The best work
    of its kind. Demonstrates incidentally how sound scholarship is enhanced
    by a fine literary style.

LEWIS, Bernard. *Istanbul and the civilization of the Ottoman Empire.* Norman,
University of Oklahoma Press, 1963 (Centers of Civilization series)
    A word picture of life in Istanbul in the heyday of the Ottoman Empire;
    made up of quotations from contemporary Turkish and western works,
    linked by a good modern text.

MANTRAN, Robert. *Histoire de la Turquie.* [2e éd.] Paris, Presses Universitaires de France, 1961 (Collection "Que sais-je?")
A handy but very brief outline.

MANTRAN, Robert. *Turquie.* Photographies d'Émile Daher et E. Boudot-Lamotte. Paris, Hachette, 1955 (Collection Les Albums des Guides Bleus)
A guide-sized book of 72 attractive photographs and explanatory text.

MANTRAN, Robert. *Turkey.* Photographs by Émile Daher and Emmanuel Boudot-Lamotte. Paris, Hachette, 1955 (Hachette World Albums series)
See preceding note.

MANTRAN, Robert. *La vie quotidienne à Constantinople au temps de Soliman le Magnifique et de ses successeurs, XVIe et XVIIe siècles.* [Paris], Hachette, 1965
An interesting social study of the capital of the Ottoman Empire in its golden age; particularly useful for laymen.

MARDIN, Şerif. *The genesis of Young Ottoman thought: a study in the modernization of Turkish political ideas.* Princeton, Princeton University Press, 1962 (Princeton Oriental Studies series)
An excellent study of the intellectual leaders of Turkish political thought in the 19th century.

OTTIN, Merry. *Terre des empereurs et des sultans. Les grands siècles d'Asie mineure.* Paris, Éditions du Pont Royal, 1962
A beautifully produced picture book illustrating the history of Turkey from ancient to modern times, accompanied by an outline historical text.

OTTIN, Merry. *Land of emperors and sultans: the forgotten cultures of Asia Minor.* Tr. Mervyn Savill. London, Souvenir Press; Toronto, Ryerson, 1964
See preceding note.

PETERS, Richard F. *Histoire des Turcs: de l'empire à la démocratie.* Traduit de l'allemande par Lucien Piau. Paris, Payot, 1966 P (Collection Bibliothèque Historique)
Rather superficial and misinterprets many details but does give information. More than half deals with Republican Turkey (since 1923).

RAMSAUR, Ernest Edmondson. *The Young Turks: prelude to the revolution of 1908.* Princeton, Princeton University Press, 1957; repr. Beirut, Khayat, 1965
A sound work.

SCHWOEBEL, Robert. *The shadow of the crescent: the Renaissance image of the Turk (1453-1517).* New York, St. Martin's, 1967

An interesting study of western views on the Turks near their zenith, with many quotations from contemporary European sources.

WITTEK, Paul. *The rise of the Ottoman Empire.* London, Royal Asiatic Society, 1938, repr. 1958.
This is the fundamental study of the subject and analyses the psychological foundations of the Ottoman Empire.

5 MUSLIM INDIA AND PAKISTAN

*AHMAD, Aziz. *An intellectual history of Islam in India.* Edinburgh, [Edinburgh] University Press; Chicago, Aldine, 1969
A good but highly compressed historical survey of the Muslim cultural impact on India. Includes theology and mysticism, education, literature (in Arabic, Persian, Chagatay Turkish, Urdu, and other languages), and the arts generally.

AZIZ, Khursheed Kamal. *The making of Pakistan: a study in nationalism.* London, Chatto; Toronto, Clarke Irwin, 1967
A historical study by a Pakistani political scientist.

BOLITHO, Hector. *Jinnah: creator of Pakistan.* London, Murray, 1954; New York, Macmillan, 1955
A sympathetic biography of the architect of modern Pakistan.

HARDY, Peter. *Historians of medieval India: studies in Indo-Muslim historical writing.* London, Luzac, 1960
On the methodology of traditional Muslim historians of India.

HOLLISTER, John N. *The Shia of India.* London, Luzac, 1953
The history and present state of the Shi'ite branch of Islam, particularly its Ismā'īlī subdivision.

IKRAM, S. M. (ed.) *The cultural heritage of Pakistan.* Ed. S. M. Ikram and Percival Spear. Karachi, Toronto, London, New York, Oxford University Press, 1955
Articles by several scholars outlining major aspects of the cultural legacy of Muslim India and Pakistan.

*IKRAM, S. M. *Muslim civilization in India.* Ed. Ainslie T. Embree. New York, London, Columbia University Press, 1964
An excellent comprehensive interpretation of religious and cultural history, 712-1858.

MUJEEB, Mohammed. *The Indian Muslims.* London, Allen & Unwin; Montreal, McGill University Press, 1967
    A broad sociological study of the whole period of Indian Islam, containing some debatable generalizations. Read in conjunction with Aziz Ahmad, *Studies in Islamic culture in the Indian environment* (section F1 below).

NIZAMI, Khaliq Ahmad. *Some aspects of religion and politics in India during the thirteenth century.* Aligarh, Muslim University, 1961
    An excellent study based on original sources.

PRASAD, Ishwari. *A short history of Muslim rule in India, from the advent of Islam to the death of Aurangzeb.* 2nd ed. Allahabad, Indian Press, 1965
    A standard text used in Indian universities.

*QURESHI, Ishtiaq Husain. *The Muslim community of the Indo-Pakistan subcontinent (610-1947): a brief historical analysis.* 's-Gravenhage, Mouton, 1962 (Columbia University, Publications in Near and Middle East Studies series)
    A readable historical review of Islam's place in Hindu India through the ages.

SAYEED, Khalid B. *Pakistan: the formative phase, 1857-1948.* 2nd ed. London, New York, Toronto, Oxford University Press, 1968
    A political scientist's scholarly examination of the Muslim separatist movement and how it led to the creation of Pakistan.

6 ISRAEL, PALESTINE

ABRAMSKY, Samuel. *Ancient towns in Israel.* Jerusalem, Youth and Hechalutz Department of the World Zionist Organization, 1963
    Historical surveys of 32 towns and regions up to the 18th century, with emphasis on their Jewish history. The word "ancient" in the title means "pre-modern."

BEN-GURION, David (ed.) *The Jews in their land.* [Translated from the Hebrew by Mordechai Nurock and Misha Louvish.] London, Aldus Books; Garden City, N. Y., Doubleday, 1966
    A lavishly illustrated popular history of Jewish Palestine from antiquity to the present, from a Zionist viewpoint. The editor, who wrote the chapter on Zionism and Israel, is the former prime minister of Israel.

BEN-GURION, David (ed.) *Destins d'Israël.* Par David Ben-Gourion. Paris, Hachette, 1967
    See preceding note.

*BEN-ZVI, Itzhak. *The exiled and the redeemed.* Translated from the Hebrew by Isaac A. Abbady. [2nd ed.] Philadelphia, Jewish Publication Society; London, Vallentine Mitchell, 1961 (and repr.)

Very interesting accounts of the major ancient communities of oriental Jews of Asia and North Africa, their histories and present situation. The late author was a keen student of oriental Jewish history and ethnography before he became president of Israel.

BENTWICH, Norman. *Mandate memories, 1918-1948.* [By] Norman and Helen Bentwich. London, Hogarth Press; Toronto, Clarke Irwin; New York, Schocken, 1965

An interesting picture of Palestine in the British period, drawn from a combination of contemporary letters and later reminiscences. The author was a government official for most of this period.

BENTWICH, Norman. *The new-old land of Israel.* London, Allen & Unwin, 1960

A popular work, describing Israel's rich archaeological heritage in the context of the modern state.

BERLIN, Isaiah. *Chaim Weizmann.* London, Weidenfeld; New York, Farrar, 1958

An illuminating biographical essay by a noted historian and long-time friend of Weizmann.

CHOURAQUI, André. *Théodore Herzl.* Paris, Seuil, 1964
An over-dramatic, rather unreliable, but popularly written biography.

COHEN, Israel. *A short history of Zionism.* London, Muller, 1951
A standard summary.

COHEN, Israel. *Theodore Herzl: founder of political Zionism.* London, New York, Yoseloff, 1959
A standard short biography.

DAYAN, Shmuel. *The promised land: memoirs.* Introduced, edited and arranged by Yaël Dayan. Translated from the Hebrew by Sidney Lightman. London, Routledge, 1961

The autobiography of a veteran kibbutznik (the father of General Moshe Dayan), provides an inside view of the ideas and actions which led to the development of the state of Israel.

EBAN, Abba. *My people: the story of the Jews.* New York, Behrman; Toronto, Random House, 1968

Eloquently written history, from the viewpoint of a leading Israeli statesman. About half the book is devoted to the period since the rise of Zionism and the establishment of Israel. Gives an insight into Israeli thinking.

GLUECK, Nelson. *Rivers in the desert: a history of the Negev.* New York, Farrar; Toronto, Ambassador, 1959; New York, Norton; Toronto, McLeod, 1968 P
A noted archaeologist describes his outstanding discoveries in the Negev desert of southern Israel.

GRAYZEL, Solomon. *A history of the contemporary Jews from 1900 to the present.* Philadelphia, Jewish Publication Society, 1960; New York, Harper, 1965 P (Harper Torchbooks)
A short history, which sets the Zionist movement and the state of Israel in perspective.

HALPERN, Ben. *The idea of the Jewish state.* 2nd ed. Cambridge, Mass., Harvard University Press; London, Oxford University Press, 1969
An analysis of the rise of Zionism in the context of the condition of the Jews of the 19th century.

HERZBERG, Arthur (ed.) *The Zionist idea: a historical analysis and reader.* New York, Harper; Garden City, N.Y., Doubleday, 1959 C&P; repr. Westport, Conn., Greenwood Press, 1970
Compilation of extracts from the words of 19th century Zionist leaders of many shades of opinion. The editor's analysis is sometimes challengeable. Read in conjunction with Ben Halpern, *The idea of the Jewish state* (above) and contrast with S. Haim, *Arab nationalism* (section C2a above).

LITVINOFF, Barnet. *To the house of their fathers: a history of Zionism.* New York, Praeger, 1965. The same as: *Road to Jerusalem: Zionism's imprint on history.* London, Weidenfeld, 1966
A journalistic account, to 1948.

ORNI, Efraim. *Geography of Israel.* By Efraim Orni and Elisha Efrat. 2nd ed. Jerusalem, Israel Program for Scientific Translations; New York, Daniel Davey, 1966
A standard work.

PEARLMAN, Moshe. *Historical sites in Israel.* By Moshe Pearlman and Yaacov Yannai. London, W. H. Allen, 1964
A well-illustrated review, in non-technical language, of the historical background to the important sites of antiquity.

STRIZOWER, Schifra. *Exotic Jewish communities.* London, New York, Yoseloff, 1962 C&P (Popular Jewish Library series)
A chatty description, partly at first hand, of the past and present of three

ancient oriental Jewish communities (Yemenites, Bene Israel of India, and Cochin Jews) and two schismatic groups (Karaites and Samaritans).

*SYKES, Christopher. *Cross roads to Israel.* London, Collins; Cleveland, World, 1965; New York, New American Library; London, New English Library, 1967 P (Mentor Books)
   A well-written and thorough study of history and politics of the years 1917 to 1948, which preceded the establishment of the state of Israel; based on documents and acquaintance with the principals, British, Arab, and Jewish.

WEIZMANN, Chaim. *Trial and error: the autobiography of Chaim Weizmann.* London, Hamish Hamilton; New York, Harper, 1949; New York, Schocken, 1966 P
   Weizmann was a major figure in Zionist history and became first president of Israel. This book is important for an understanding of both psychological and political factors.

YAARI, Avraham. *The goodly heritage.* Memoirs describing the life of the Jewish community of Eretz Yisrael from the seventeenth to the twentieth centuries. Abridged and translated by Israel Schen. Jerusalam, Youth and Hechalutz Department of the [World] Zionist Organization, 1958
   Twenty-nine extracts, some very interesting, from contemporary accounts. The majority date from the 19th and early 20th century.

7 CENTRAL ASIA, AFGHANISTAN, AND OTHER MUSLIM REGIONS

ALLWORTH, Edward (ed.) *Central Asia: a century of Russian rule.* New York, London, Columbia University Press, 1967
   An informative series of articles dealing with the history and culture of the Turkic- and Iranian-speaking Muslim peoples of Central Asia since the middle of the 19th century (Karakalpak, Kazakh, Kirgiz, Tajik, Turkmen, Uygur, and Uzbek).

*BARTOL'D, Vasiliĭ Vladimirovich. *Histoire des Turcs d'Asie centrale.* Par W. Barthold. Adaptation française par M. Donskis. Paris, A.-Maisonneuve, 1945 (Collection Initiation à l'Islam)
   Still the most important general work on the subject.

BELENITSKY, Aleksandr. *Central Asia.* Translated from the Russian by James Hogarth. Geneva, Nagel; London, Barrie, 1969 (Ancient Civilizations series)
   A leading archaeologist describes the great series of civilizations, from prehistoric times to the Arab conquests (8th century). Rather brief notebook style, redeemed by excellent and plentiful illustrations.

CAROE, Olaf. *The Pathans, 550 B.C.–A.D. 1957.* London, Macmillan; New York, St. Martin's, 1958 P
A notable history of a warlike people on the Afghan-Pakistan frontier region.

CAROE, Olaf. *Soviet empire: the Turks of Central Asia and Stalinism.* 2nd ed. London, Toronto, Macmillan; New York, St. Martin's, 1967 P
A study of Soviet policies in Muslim Central Asia, with a useful historical introduction.

DUNLOP, Douglas M. *The history of the Jewish Khazars.* Princeton, Princeton University Press; London, Oxford University Press, 1954; New York, Schocken, 1967 P (Princeton Oriental Studies series)
An interesting, original study of the large Jewish-Turkic state of Khazaria in southern Russia between the 8th and 10th centuries.

FLETCHER, Arnold. *Afghanistan: highway of conquest.* Ithaca, Cornell University Press, 1965
A useful political history, somewhat negative on the role of the British.

*FRASER-TYTLER, William Kerr. *Afghanistan: a study of political developments in central and southern Asia.* Rev. M. C. Gillett. 3rd ed. London, Toronto, New York, Oxford University Press, 1967
An important standard work on the history and politics of the area, especially relations with Britain, Persia, Russia, and India.

FRYE, Richard Nelson. *Bukhara: the medieval achievement.* Norman, University of Oklahoma Press, 1965 (Centers of Civilization series)
An evocation of the culture of Bukhara a millennium ago: a composite of Iranian revivals, Islam, and Turkish traditions.

GREGORIAN, Vartan. *The emergence of modern Afghanistan: politics of reform and modernization, 1880-1946.* Stanford, Stanford University Press, 1969
A detailed political treatment.

GREKOV, Boris D. *La Horde d'Or. La domination tatare au XIIIe et au XIVe siècle, de la Mer Jaune à la Mer Noire.* Par B. D. Grekov et A. I. Iakoubovski. Tr. F. Thuret. 2nd ed. Paris, Payot, 1961 P (Collection Bibliothèque Historique)
The history of the huge state in Central Asia founded by the Mongols of the steppes.

GROUSSET, René. *Le conquérant du monde: vie de Gengis-Khan.* [2nd ed.] Paris, Albin Michel, 1961

A very readable biography of Chingis Khan, the great Mongol conqueror (d. 1227).

GROUSSET, René. *Conqueror of the world.* Tr. Marian McKellar and Denis Sinor. New York, Orion, 1966
See preceding note.

*GROUSSET, René. *L'empire des steppes: Attila, Gengis-Khan, Tamerlan.* 5ᵉ éd. Paris, Payot, 1959 P (Collection Bibliothèque Historique)
An accessible history of the nomadic peoples of Central Asia.

*HAMBIS, Louis. *La Haute-Asie.* Paris, Presses Universitaires de France, 1953 P (Collection "Que sais-je?")
A short popular account of the history and present state of the peoples of Central Asia, mainly Turkic and Mongol.

*HEISSIG, Walther. *A lost civilization: the Mongols rediscovered.* [Translated from the German by D. J. S. Thomson.] London, Thames & Hudson; New York, Basic Books, 1966
A history of the world-conquering people of Chingis Khan, Hulagu and Kublai Khan, covering the 13th to 20th centuries. Strong emphasis on information gained from recent archaeological discoveries.

LAMB, Harold. *Genghis Khan: the conqueror, emperor of all men.* New York, Grosset, 1963 P
A vivid, somewhat romanticized biography of the great conqueror (first published in 1927).

MONTEIL, Vincent. *Les musulmans soviétiques.* Paris, Seuil, 1957 P (Collections Esprit, "Frontière Ouverte")
A useful survey for the general reader.

PHILLIPS, Eustace Dockray. *The Mongols.* London, Thames & Hudson; New York, Praeger, 1969 (Ancient Peoples and Places series)
A useful popular short general history, beginning with a description of nomadism in northeastern Asia, but devoted mainly to Chingis Khan and his successors.

PHILLIPS, Eustace Dockray. *The royal hordes: nomad peoples of the steppes.* London, Thames & Hudson; New York, McGraw-Hill, 1965
Archaeological-historical emphasis.

PRAWDIN, Michael. *Genghis Khan.* Tr. A. Cogniet. Paris, Payot, 1938 P (and repr.) (Collection Bibliothèque Historique)
A semipopular biography.

PRAWDIN, Michael. *The Mongol empire: its rise and legacy.* Tr. Eden and Cedar Paul. London, Allen & Unwin, 1940 (and repr.); 2nd ed. New York, Barnes & Noble, 1964; New York, Macmillan, 1967 P
Readable popularization, though somewhat out of date.

*SINOR, Denis. *Inner Asia: history, civilization, languages – a syllabus.* Bloomington, Indiana University Press; The Hague, Mouton, 1969 P (Indiana University Publications, Uralic and Altaic series)
Clearly written, short and non-technical; an excellent introduction to Central Asia, with particular emphasis on history. Useful notes on further reading given at chapter ends.

SPULER, Bertold. *Les Mongols dans l'histoire.* Paris, Payot, 1961 P (Collection Bibliothèque Historique)
An outline from the time of Chingis Khan (late 12th century), dealing largely with the relations of the Mongols with their neighbours.

VERNADSKY, George. *The Mongols and Russia.* New Haven, Yale University Press, 1953
Mainly on the impact of the Mongols on Russia, not on the Mongols for their own sake, but contains much useful information.

*WHEELER, Geoffrey. *The modern history of Soviet Central Asia.* London, Weidenfeld; New York, Praeger, 1964 (and repr.)
An excellent short history, largely on social and cultural life since the western impact.

D LITERATURE: HISTORY AND CRITICISM OF LITERATURE

1 GENERAL WORKS

ROSENTHAL, Franz. *A history of Muslim historiography.* Leiden, Brill, 1952
An excellent study of the Muslim concept of history and history-writing
with several large extracts in English translation.

2 ARABIC

*ABD-EL-JALIL, Jean M. *Brève histoire de la littérature arabe.* 3ᵉ éd. Paris,
G.-P. Maisonneuve, 1960 P
A sound didactic general survey, followed by a brief anthology of trans-
lated extracts.

*BLACHÈRE, Régis. *Histoire de la littérature arabe, des origines à la fin du XVᵉ
siècle de J.-C.* 3 vols. Paris, A.-Maisonneuve, 1952-66
A first-class major work, including important general essays; not just a catalogue of names.

CHEJNE, Anwar G. *The Arabic language: its role in history.* Minneapolis, University of Minnesota Press; Toronto, Copp Clark; London, Oxford University
Press, 1969
Describes the development of Arabic from a local language into a great
international cultural force.

*GIBB, Hamilton Alexander Rosskeen. *Arabic literature: an introduction.* 2nd
ed. Oxford, Clarendon Press; Toronto, New York, Oxford University Press,
1963
The best brief outline for the general reader, but very short on modern literature. Includes a useful select listing of translations of Arabic works into
English.

KHATIBI, Abdelkébir. *Le roman maghrebin.* Paris, Maspero, 1968 (Collection
Domaine Maghrebin)

MEMMI, Albert (ed.) *Bibliographie de la littérature nord-africaine d'expression
française, 1945-62.* [Par Jacqueline Arnaud, Abdelkébir Khatibi, Jean Déjeux,
Arlette Roth. Publié sous la direction d'Albert Memmi.] Paris, Mouton, 1965
(École Pratique des Hautes Études-Sorbonne: 6ᵉ section)
Lists over 500 novels, short stories, poems, plays, and writings of or on lit-
erature or acculturation, by natives of North Africa writing in French; also
French translations of Arabic works by these writers. No annotations, un-
fortunately.

*NICHOLSON, Reynold Alleyne. *A literary history of the Arabs.* [2nd ed.]
Cambridge, Cambridge University Press, 1930, repr. 1966; 1969 P
    The best work of its kind for the interested layman who wants more infor-
    mation than is available in H. A. R. Gibb's little book (above). An excellent
    introduction to classical Arabic literature, until about the 14th century.

PELLAT, Charles. *Langue et littérature arabes.* Paris, Colin, 1952
    A useful review, from the Arabic classical period to the present.

RIKABI, Jawdat. *La poésie profane sous les ayyûbides et ses principaux rep-
résentants.* Paris, G.-P. Maisonneuve, 1949 P
    A study of Arab poetry in its social milieu during the 12th and 13th cen-
    turies. (Some parts are too technical for the general reader.)

WIET, Gaston. *Introduction à la littérature arabe.* Paris, G.-P. Maisonneuve,
1966 (Collection Unesco — Collection d'Introductions aux Littératures Orientales)
    A detailed review for non-specialists. Contains stimulating assessments of
    classical authors, but is inadequate on modern literature. Somewhat idio-
    syncratic.

3 PERSIAN

*ARBERRY, Arthur John. *Classical Persian literature.* London, Allen & Unwin;
New York, Macmillan, 1958
    A well-written historical treatment, going to the end of the 15th century.
    Illustrated by a large number of extracts translated by various hands.

*BROWNE, Edward G. *A literary history of Persia.* 4 vols. Cambridge, Cambridge University Press, 1902-24 (repr. 1964)
    The best work of its type; it also gives a real insight into Islamic culture in
    a broad sense. Covers pre-Islamic times to 1924. Includes many translated
    extracts from Persian literature.

KAMSHAD, Hassan. *Modern Persian prose literature.* Cambridge, New York,
Cambridge University Press, 1966
    A history of imaginative Persian prose in the past 60 years. The second half
    of the book is devoted to a detailed study of the leading Persian writer
    Ṣādiq Hidāyat (1903-51).

*LEVY, Reuben. *An introduction to Persian literature.* London, New York, Columbia University Press, 1969 (Unesco Introductions to Asian Literature series)
    Particularly suitable for those who want a brief conspectus of the main au-
    thors, works, and genres of poetry and prose. A fair proportion of the

book is given to translated excerpts from Persian authors. (A French edition is in preparation.)

REZVANI, Medjid. *Le théâtre et la danse en Iran.* Paris, G.-P. Maisonneuve, 1962 P
A somewhat erratic work on a neglected field; includes information on pre-Islamic, classical Islamic, folk, regional, and religious "theatre," dance, and folk song.

*RYPKA, Jan. *History of Iranian literature.* By Jan Rypka, in collaboration with O. Klima, V. Kubícková, [and others]. Ed. Karl Jahn. Translated from the German by P. van Popta-Hope and revised. Dordrecht (Holland), Reidel, 1967; New York, Humanities Press, 1968
A first-class work in considerable detail, covering ancient Persian, Islamic Persian to the present time, Tajik, Persian literature in India, folk literature, and Judaeo-Persian literature.

VIROLLEAUD, Charles. *Le théâtre persan: ou le drame du Kerbéla.* Paris, A.-Maisonneuve, 1950
Shi'ite Islam's religious drama, corresponding in some respects to the "Passion plays" of Christianity.

4 TURKISH

AND, Metin. *A history of theatre and popular entertainment in Turkey.* Ankara, Forum Yayinlari, 1964
The only work of its kind in English, dealing with both traditional and modern forms. Rather "cataloguish" in its style. Well illustrated.

*BOMBACI, Alessio. *Histoire de la littérature turque.* Tr. I. Mélikoff. Paris, Klincksieck, 1968 P ([Collection de l'] Institut d'Études Turques de l'Université de Paris)   ·
Excellent; the only adequate general work for the layman. Covers not only Ottoman and modern Turkish to World War I, but also pre-Islamic Central Asian Turkish and Chagatay (the classical Islamic Turkic literature of Central Asia). [An enlarged edition in English, translated by Kathleen Burrill, is in active preparation and will appear in the series "Publications in Near and Middle East Studies," Columbia University, New York (The Hague, Mouton, publishers).]

CHADWICK, Nora Kershaw. *Oral epics of Central Asia.* [By] Nora K. Chadwick and Victor Zhirmunsky. Cambridge, [Cambridge] University Press, 1969
A pioneer work which paraphrases and analyses some major epics. Technical at times.

GIBB, Elias John Wilkinson. *A history of Ottoman poetry.* 6 vols. London, Luzac, 1900-9, repr. 1958-63

> The standard detailed survey; the numerous translations reflect both English and Turkish tastes at the end of the 19th century. Vol. 1 is an excellent general outline of the conventions common to all Islamic poetry.

5 URDU

*SADIQ, Muhammad. *A history of Urdu literature.* London, Toronto, New York, Oxford University Press, 1964

> A lively readable survey, making comparisons with English literature.

VAHID, Syed Abdul. *Iqbal, his art and thought.* London, Murray, 1959

> A perceptive literary study of the great poet of Pakistan.

VAHID, Syed Abdul. *Studies in Iqbal.* Lahore, Ashraf, 1967

> In this more advanced work, a distinguished Pakistani scholar makes some fruitful comparisons between Iqbal and both Islamic and European poets. The many citations from Iqbal are translated into English.

6 HEBREW (MODERN)

BAND, Arnold J. *Nostalgia and nightmare: a study in the fiction of S. Y. Agnon.* Berkeley, University of California Press, 1968

> An analysis of the work of the Nobel Prize-winner for Literature (1966), with particular attention to autobiographical and psychological aspects.

HALKIN, Simon. *Modern Hebrew literature: trends and values.* New York, Schocken, 1950

> Not a history of literature, but rather a study of the social and historical forces that produced it. An interesting book.

RABINOVICH, Isaiah. *Major trends in modern Hebrew fiction.* Tr. Murray Roston. Chicago, London, University of Chicago Press, 1968

> The work of 12 writers of fiction forms the basis of this notable critical study of the "older" period of modern Hebrew literature, from the 1880s to the late 1940s.

*RIBALOW, Menachem. *The flowering of modern Hebrew literature: a volume of literary evaluation.* Ed. & tr. Judah Nadich. New York, Twayne; London, Vision, 1959

> An excellent review of 10 leading figures and an evaluation of trends; illustrated by many translations.

WALLENROD, Reuben. *The literature of modern Israel.* New York, Abelard-Schuman, 1957

A fair critical survey and analysis of the major trends in Israeli literature.

E LITERATURE: TEXTS IN TRANSLATION†

1 GENERAL WORKS

*KRITZECK, James (comp.) *Anthology of Islamic literature from the rise of Islam to modern times.* With an introduction and commentaries. New York, Holt, 1964; London, Penguin, 1964 P (and repr.); Toronto, New York, New American Library, 1966 P (Mentor Books)
> A convenient introduction to classical Islamic literature through texts, chiefly Arabic and Persian, with a few Turkish. Consists mainly of extracts from existing translations; some genres of literature are hardly represented. The notes of the original translations have unfortunately been suppressed.

KRITZECK, James (comp.) *Modern Islamic literature, from 1800 to the present.* With an introduction and commentaries. New York, Holt, 1970
> A sequel to the work above and in the same general style, but covering a wider geographical area – from West Africa to Indonesia. A pioneer anthology of its type.

SCHROEDER, Eric (comp. & tr.) *Muhammad's people: a tale by anthology.* Portland, Maine, Bond Wheelright; Toronto, Burns & MacEachern, 1955
> Subtitled: *The religion and politics, poetry and violence, science, ribaldry, and finance of the Muslims, from the Age of Ignorance before Islam and the Mission of God's Prophet to sophistication in the eleventh century; a mosaic translation.* A good impressionistic survey of Islamic civilization, made up entirely of excerpts from a wide variety of Muslim sources.

SHAH, Idries. *Tales of the dervishes: teaching stories of the Sufi masters over the past thousand years.* Selected from the Sufi classics and oral tradition ... in many countries. London, Cape, 1967
> Pleasant reading.

WIET, Gaston (ed.) *Grandeur de l'Islam: de Mahomet à François Ier.* Paris, La Table Ronde, 1961 P
> A selection of Arabic, Persian, and Turkish texts of historical interest, translated by various hands and linked by brief editorial passages. Useful conspectus of Islamic history-writing for the western general reader.

2 ARABIC

a/Anthologies

*DERMENGHEM, Émile (comp.) *Les plus beaux textes arabes.* Paris, La Colombe, 1951

---

†Including original works in English or French by Asian writers.

A good large anthology from the 6th to 20th centuries, covering most genres but excluding the Koran, philosophical and theological, scientific and legal texts. Brief biographies of authors.

b/Classical and Traditional Literature

i/History and Travel

GABRIELI, Francesco (comp. & tr.) *Arab historians of the Crusades.* Selected and translated from the Arabic sources. Translated from the Italian by E. J. Costello. Los Angeles, University of California Press, 1968; London, Routledge, 1969
The Crusades, vividly described from the Muslim side.

IBN BAṬṬŪTAH, Muḥammad ibn 'Abd Allāh. *Ibn Battúta's travels in Asia and Africa, 1325-1354.* Translated and selected by H. A. R. Gibb. London, Routledge, 1929, repr. 1957
A selection of the reminiscences of a remarkable 14th century Moroccan world traveller.

IBN IYĀS. *Journal d'un bourgeois du Caire: chronique d'Ibn Iyas.* Tr. G. Wiet. 2 vols. Paris, Colin, 1955-60 (Collection Bibliothèque Générale)
A 16th century diary of the end of the Mamluk and beginning of the Ottoman periods.

IBN AL-QALĀNISĪ. *Damas de 1075 à 1154.* Traduction annoté [par Roger Le Tourneau] d'un fragment de l'histoire de de Damas d'Ibn al-Qalānisī. Damas, Institut Français, 1952
Local history, including the Crusades, described from the "other side" by a reliable Arab eyewitness.

IBN AL-QALĀNISĪ. *The Damascus Chronicle of the Crusades (from A.D. 1097-1159).* Extracted and translated from the Chronicles of Ibn al-Qalanisi by H. A. R. Gibb. London, Luzac, 1967 (repr. of 1932 ed.) (University of London Historical series)
Contemporary Arab account of the Crusades, well translated.

IBN JUBAYR, Muḥammad ibn Aḥmad. *The Travels of Ibn Jubayr: being the chronicle of a mediaeval Spanish Moor concerning his journey to the Egypt of Saladin, the Holy Cities of Arabia, Baghdad the city of the Caliphs, the Latin Kingdom of Jerusalem, and the Norman Kingdom of Sicily.* Translated from Arabic by R. J. C. Broadhurst. London, Cape, 1952
An interesting 12th century travel diary.

IBN JUBAYR, Muḥammad ibn Aḥmad. *Voyages [d']Ibn Jobair.* Tr. Maurice Gaudefroy-Demombynes. Parties 1-3. Paris, Geuthner, 1949-56 (Collection

Documents Relatifs à l'Histoire des Croisades)
See preceding note. Good full translation and notes.

USĀMAH IBN MUNQIDH. *Memoirs of an Arab-Syrian gentleman, or an Arab knight in the period of the Crusades: Memoirs of Usāmah ibn-Munqidh (Kitāb al-i'tibār).* Tr. Philip K. Hitti. [Repr.] Beirut, Khayat, 1964
Memoirs of a Muslim eyewitness of the Crusades. (Originally published under the title *An Arab-Syrian gentleman and warrior in the period of the Crusades.*)

ii/Ethics, Philosophy, and Politics

BAHYĀ BEN JOSEPH IBN PAQŪDA. *Duties of the heart.* Translated from Arabic into Hebrew by Jehuda ibn Tibbon ... Hebrew text, with English translation by Moses Hyamson. 2 vols. Jerusalem, Boys' Town Press, 1962 (repr. of New York, 1925-47 ed.)
A famous Jewish ethical work of the mediaeval period, which retains its popularity to this day.

al-FARĀBĪ. *Fuṣūl al-madani. Aphorisms of the statesman.* Edited with English translation, introduction and notes by D. M. Dunlop. Cambridge, Cambridge University Press, 1961
The work of an important mediaeval Islamic political philosopher (d. 950).

al-GHAZZĀLĪ. *Ghazali's Book of counsel for kings (Naṣīhat al-mulūk).* Tr. F. R. C. Bagley. London, Toronto, New York, Oxford University Press, 1964 (University of Durham Publications series)
A great 11th century thinker's manual of kingship. Chapters on faith; on qualities required by kings, ministers, secretaries; on intelligence and women. Each is illustrated by anecdotes. Other Islamic works of this interesting genre include al-Jāhiz, *Le livre de la couronne* (below, section iii), Kay Kā'ūs, *Mirror for princes,* and Niẓām al-Mulk, *Book of government* (both below, section 3).

IBN HAZM, 'Ali ibn Ahmad. *Epître morale (Kitāb al-ahlāq wa-l-siyar).* Introduction et texte établi, traduit et annoté par Nada Tomiche. Beyrouth, Commission Internationale pour la Traduction des Chefs-d'Oeuvre, 1961 (Collection Unesco d'Oeuvres Représentatives − Série Arabe)
Philosophical and psychological observations by a famous 11th century theologian and thinker of Muslim Spain.

IBN KHALDŪN. *An Arab philosophy of history: selections from the Prolegomena of Ibn Khaldun of Tunis.* Tr. Charles Issawi. London, Murray; New York, Paragon, 1950 (and repr.) (Wisdom of the East series)
Quotations from a remarkable Arabic work of the 14th century by a thinker much ahead of his time. Arranged under such headings as historical meth-

od, geography, economics, society and the state, religion and politics, knowledge, teaching methods.

*IBN KHALDŪN. *The Muqaddimah: an introduction to history.* Tr. Franz Rosenthal, abridged by N. J. Dawood. London, Routledge; Princeton, Princeton University Press, 1967; 1969 P
> A handy abridgement of this interesting work. (The full translation by Franz Rosenthal was published in 3 vols.: New York, Pantheon, 1958.)

IBN KHALDŪN. *Discours sur l'histoire universelle (al-Muqaddima).* Traduction nouvelle, préface et notes par Vincent Monteil. 3 vols. Beyrouth, Commission Internationale pour la Traduction des Chefs d'Oeuvre, 1967-68 (Collection Unesco d'Oeuvres Représentatives – Série Arabe)
> A full but fluent scholarly translation of the remarkable 14th century work embodying his philosophy of history.

*IBN KHALDŪN. *Les textes sociologiques et économiques de la Mouqaddima ...* Classés, traduits et annotés par G.-H. Bousquet. Paris, Rivière, 1965

al-RĀZĪ, Muhammad ibn Zakariyā. *The spiritual physick of Rhazes.* Translated from the Arabic by A. J. Arberry. London, Murray; New York, Paragon, 1950 (Wisdom of the East series)
> This great Persian thinker and physician (864-925) was popular in mediaeval scholastic circles in Europe through translations of his medical works into Latin. In this little book he discusses the psychological, ethical, and physical health of man.

iii/Poetry and Artistic Prose

ARBERRY, A. J. (ed. & tr.) *Arabic poetry: a primer for students.* Cambridge, Cambridge University Press, 1965
> Thirty-one poems, 6th to 20th centuries, in fairly literal translation. Helpful short introduction.

al-HAMADHĀNĪ, Badī' al-Zamān. *Maqāmāt (Séances),* choisies et traduites de l'arabe, avec une étude sur le genre, par Régis Blachère et Pierre Masnou. Paris, Klincksieck, 1957 P (Collection Études Arabes et Islamiques – Textes et Traductions)
> The "maqāmah" is a brilliant and original literary form created by this 10th century author to recount picaresque tales.

al-HARĪRĪ. *Les séances de Harīrī.* Traduction française par Venture de Paradis. Édition critique avec introduction et notes par Attia Amer. Stockholm, Almqvist 1964 P (Acta Universitatis Stockholmiensis, Stockholm Oriental Studies)

al-Ḥarīrī (11th century) was the best "maqāmah" writer after al-Hamadhānī (see preceding entry). This selection was translated by an 18th century French orientalist.

IBN ḤAZM, 'Alī ibn Ahmad. *The ring of the dove: a treatise on the art and practice of Arab love.* Tr. A. J. Arberry. London, Luzac, 1953
An 11th century theologian's popular textbook on the theory of courtly love, illustrated by apt anecdotes.

IBN HAZM, 'Alī ibn Ahmad. *Le collier du pigeon, ou, de l'amour et des amants.* Texte et traduction par Léon Bercher. Alger, Carbonel, 1949
See preceding note.

IBN AL-MUQAFFA'. *Le livre de Kalila et Dimna.* Traduit de l'arabe par André Miquel. Paris, Klincksieck, 1957 P (Collection Études Arabes et Islamiques – Textes et Traductions)
This 8th century literary adaptation of the Indian *Fables of Bidpai* is one of the first major pieces of Arabic prose.

IBN SAʿĪD AL-MAGHRIBĪ, 'Alī ibn Mūsā. *Moorish poetry: a translation* [*by A. J. Arberry*] *of the Pennants, an anthology compiled in 1243 by the Andalusian Ibn Saʿid.* Cambridge, Cambridge University Press, 1953
A metrical translation.

al-JĀḤIZ, 'Amr ibn Baḥr. *Le livre des avares de Ǧāḥiẓ.* Tr. Charles Pellat. Paris, G.-P. Maisonneuve, 1951 P (Collection Islam d'Hier et d'Aujourd'hui) (Collection Unesco d'Oeuvres Représentatives – Série Arabe)
A readable collection of entertaining anecdotes showing psychological insight, by a 9th century polymath who was the greatest essayist of classical Arabic literature.

al-JĀḤIZ, 'Amr ibn Baḥr. *Le livre de la couronne, sur les règles de conduite des rois* (Kitāb at-Tāǧ fī aḥlāq al-mulūk), *attribué à Ǧāḥiẓ.* Tr. Charles Pellat. Paris, Les Belles Lettres, 1954 (Collection Unesco d'Oeuvres Représentatives – Série Arabe)
Another work of the popular genre of advice for rulers.

MU'ALLAQAT. *The seven odes: the first chapter in Arabic literature.* Tr. A. J. Arberry. London, Allen & Unwin; New York, Macmillan, 1957
These ancient Arabic poems, written before the 7th century, have always been looked upon by Arabs as a high point in their poetry.

al-MUTANABBĪ, Abū al-Tayyib Aḥmad ibn al-Ḥusayn. *Poems of al-Mutanabbi: a selection* with introduction, translation and notes by A. J. Arberry. Cambridge, Cambridge University Press, 1967

Twenty-six poems by a man widely considered to be the finest Arabic poet (915-965). Translations fairly literal.

iv/Popular Literature

*ARABIAN NIGHTS. *Scheherezade: tales from the thousand and one nights.* Tr. A. J. Arberry. London, Allen & Unwin, 1953; New York, Toronto, New American Library, 1955 P (Mentor Books)
Aladdin and three other tales, vividly translated into a modern idiom (e.g. "crazy about him," "bigwigs") as an attempt to reproduce the colloquial flavour of the original. In spite of its popularity among Europeans, the Arabian Nights is not considered "literature" by educated Arabs.

ARABIAN NIGHTS. *The Arabian nights' entertainments, or the Book of a thousand and one nights.* A selection of the most famous and representative of these tales from the ... translations by Richard F. Burton ... chosen ... by Bennet A. Cerf. Introductory essay by Ben Ray Redman. New York, Modern Library; Toronto, Random House, 1932 (and repr.)
A "frank" translation of selected portions by an eccentric 19th century man of action and scholar.

ARABIAN NIGHTS. *Aladdin and other tales.* Tr. N. J. Dawood. Harmondsworth, Montreal, Baltimore, Penguin, 1957 P
This book and the next are readable modern unexpurgated translations of portions of the Arabian Nights.

ARABIAN NIGHTS. *The thousand and one nights: the Hunchback, Sindbad and other tales.* Tr. N. J. Dawood. Harmondsworth, Montreal, Baltimore, Penguin, 1954 P (and repr.)
See preceding note.

*ARABIAN NIGHTS. *Les mille et une nuits.* Contes arabes traduits par Antoine Galland, préface de Armand Abel. 2 vols. Verviers (Belgique), Gérard; Québec, Kasan; Paris, Inter, 1963 P (Collection Marabout Géant)
This edition and the two below are reprints of the enjoyable classic version of Antoine Galland (originally published in 1704-17), which first introduced the Arabian Nights to Europe.

ARABIAN NIGHTS. *Les mille et une nuits.* Contes arabes traduits par Galland. [Édition revue et préfacée par Gaston Picard.] 2 vols. Paris, Garnier, 1960 P

ARABIAN NIGHTS. *Les mille et une nuits.* Contes arabes traduits par Antoine Galland. Introduction par Jean Gaulmier. 3 vols. Paris, Garnier-Flammarion, 1965 P

ARABIAN NIGHTS. *Les mille et une nuits.* Traduction nouvelle et complète faite directement sur les manuscrits par René R. Khawam. 4 vols. Paris, Albin Michel, 1965-67
A modern scholarly translation.

NOY, Dov (comp.) *Moroccan Jewish folktales, with an introduction and notes.* New York, Herzl Press, 1966
A selection from the rich folk literature of North African Jewry.

c/Modern Literature

i/Anthologies

*Anthologie de la littérature arabe contemporaine. 3 vols. Paris, Seuil, 1964-67
Tome 1: *Le roman et la nouvelle.* Choix et présentation de Raoul Makarius. Tome 2: *Les essais.* Choix, présentation, traduction et introduction par Anouar Abdel-Malek. Tome 3: *La poésie.* Choix, présentation et traduction par Luc Norin et Edouard Tarabay. A very valuable selection of characteristic texts, which clearly bring out the interests and concerns of contemporary Arab writers. The texts in vol. 1 are chosen according to the countries of origin of the writers; those in vol. 2 by subject; those in vol. 3 by style. Much of the translation is very successful.

MEMMI, Albert (ed.) *Anthologie des écrivains maghrébins d'expression française.* Sous la direction de Albert Memmi. 2ᵉ éd. Paris, Présence Africaine, 1965
Contains specimens of good literary work by North African authors, above all from the period 1945-63. Most of the writers originate from Algeria, but Morocco and Tunisia are also represented.

MONTEIL, Vincent (ed.) *Anthologie bilingue de la littérature arabe contemporaine.* Beyrouth, Imprimerie Catholique, 1961
A representative selection of prose passages (novel, short story, play) by leading modern writers of Lebanon, Iraq, Egypt, Syria, Tunisia, and Morocco, with brief biographical introductions. Most of the passages were written in the 1950s. The anthology is preceded by a helpful article by the compiler, "Les grands courants de la littérature arabe contemporaine."

ii/Novel and Short Story

BAALBAKI, Leïla. *Je vis!* Traduit de l'arabe par Michel Barbot. Paris, Seuil, 1961 (Collection Méditerranée)
A best-selling novel in Arabic by a twenty-year-old Lebanese girl, expressing the revolt of the young generation against the traditional mores of the Arab East.

CHARHADI, Driss ben Hamed. *A life full of holes:* a novel. Tr. Paul Bowles. New York, Grove, 1964
>An oral Arabic novel, vivid and full of local colour, recently created by an illiterate North African, and tape-recorded by an American.

CHARHADI, Driss ben Hamed. *Une vie pleine de trous.* Texte receuilli et transcrit par Paul Bowles, traduit de l'anglais par Céline Zins. Paris, Gallimard, 1965 P (Collection du Monde Entier)
>See preceding note.

CHRAÏBI, Driss. *Le passé simple.* Paris, Denoël, 1954
>A notable novel in French by a Moroccan writer, which illustrates the problems of westernization and acculturation to European (French) civilization.

DIB, Mohammed. *La grande maison.* Paris, Seuil, 1953 (Collection Méditerranée)
>A best-selling novel of Algerian life in 1939, which won the Fénélon prize for literature.

DIB, Mohammed. *L'incendie.* [2ᵉ éd.] Paris, Seuil, 1954 (Collection Méditerranée)
>A realistic novel of social protest, set amongst the poor Muslim peasantry of Algeria.

FERAOUN, Mouloud. *La terre et le sang.* Paris, Seuil, 1953 (Collection Méditerranée)
>A representative novel by a distinguished Algerian writer, set in Kabylia (Algeria).

GHĀNIM, Fathī. *The man who lost his shadow.* By Fathy Ghanem. Translated from the Arabic by Desmond Stewart. London, Chapman; Boston, Houghton, 1966
>An Egyptian novel about the life of an ambitious journalist in modern Cairo.

al-ḤAKĪM, Tawfīq. *L'oiseau d'Orient.* [Par] Tewfik el Hakim. Paris, Nouvelles Éditions Latines, 1960 P
>A notable novel by the famous Egyptian writer.

al-ḤAKĪM, Tawfīq. *Souvenirs d'un magistrat-poète.* [Par] Tewfik el Hakim. Paris, Nouvelles Éditions Latines, 1961 P (Collection Les Maîtres Étrangèrs)
>A noted social novel, in the form of a diary on the administration of justice in rural Egypt.

ḤUSAYN, Ṭaha. *Adīb; ou l'aventure occidentale.* [Par] Taha Hussein. Tr. Amina et Moenis Taha-Hussein. Le Caire, Dar al-Maaref, 1960

The author of this and the following works is widely considered the greatest modern Egyptian writer (b. 1889) — a blind village boy who became a scholar, novelist, literary critic, and, above all, the master of a remarkably simple neo-classical style.

ḤUSAYN, Ṭaha. *L'appel du Karaouan.* [Par] Taha Hussein. Tr. Raymond Francis. Beyrouth, Dar al-Maaref, 1961

ḤUSAYN, Ṭaha. *L'arbre de la misère.* Par Taha Hussein. Tr. Gaston Wiet. Le Caire, Dar al-Maaref, 1964
   A novel of country life in Egypt at the end of the 19th and beginning of the 20th century.

ḤUSAYN, Ṭaha. *Le livre des jours.* [Par] Taha Hussein. Tr. Jean Lecerf et Gaston Wiet. Paris, Gallimard, 1947 P
   The autobiography of a remarkable man.

*JOHNSON-DAVIES, Denys (ed. & tr.) *Modern Arabic short stories.* London, Toronto, New York, Oxford University Press, 1967
   A well-chosen selection on a wide range of themes, in a variety of styles. The writers are mainly Egyptian, Lebanese, Syrian, and Iraqi.

*KHAWAM, René (ed. & tr.) *Nouvelles arabes,* choisies et traduites sur le texte arabe. Paris, Seghers, 1964
   Interpreting "nouvelle" in a very broad sense, the translator has given interesting examples of the different genres of the Arabic "short story" from authors writing between the 9th and 20th centuries.

MAḤFŪZ, Najīb. *Midaq alley, Cairo.* [By] Naguib Mahfouz. Tr. Trevor Le Gassick. Beirut, Khayat, 1966
   A best-selling novel about the people living in a small Cairo street. The book mirrors the changes taking place in Arab life.

MEMMI, Albert. *La statue de sel.* [2ᵉ éd.] Paris, Gallimard, 1966 P
   An interesting, partly autobiographical, novel by a well-known Tunisian Jewish writer in French. The work reflects his conflicts of identification.

MEMMI, Albert. *The pillar of salt.* Tr. E. Roditi. New York, Criterion, 1955; London, Elek, 1956; New York, Grossman, 1963
   See preceding note.

TAYMUR, Maḥmūd. *The call of the unknown.* By Mahmoud Teymour. Tr. Hume Horan. Beirut, Khayat, 1965 P
   An adventure, by a leading Egyptian writer.

iii/Poetry and Drama

GIBRAN, Kahlil. *Nymphs of the valley.* Translated from the Arabic by H. M. Nahmad. New York, Knopf; Toronto, Random House; London, Heinemann, 1948 (and repr.)

This work and the following ones are representative of the mystical prose, parable, and poetry of the distinguished Lebanese-American poet Jibran Khalil Gibran (1883-1931), who has not inaptly been compared to the English poet William Blake.

GIBRAN, Kahlil. *Spirits rebellious.* Translated from the Arabic by H. M. Nahmad. New York, Knopf, 1948; London, Heinemann, 1949 (and repr.)

See preceding note.

GIBRAN, Kahlil. *A tear and a smile.* Translated from the Arabic by H. M. Nahmad. New York, Knopf; Toronto, Random House; London, Heinemann, 1950 (and repr.)

See previous note.

al-ḤAKĪM, Tawfīq. *Théâtre arabe.* Traduction de l'arabe par A. Khédry, N. Costandi et Sami Gabra. Paris, Nouvelles Éditions Latines, 1950 P

The author is a pioneer of the play in Arabic. This collection of 10 plays includes several of his best, such as *La caverne des songes, Schéhérazade, Salomon le Sage, Pygmalion.*

al-ḤAKĪM, Tawfīq. *Théâtre multicolore: politique, burlesque, tragique.* [Traduction de l'arabe par A. Khédry et al.] Paris, Nouvelles Éditions Latines, 1954 P

Eleven more plays.

al-ḤAKĪM, Tawfīq. *The tree climber.* [By] Tewfik al-Hakim. Tr. Denys Johnson-Davies. London, Toronto, New York, Oxford University Press, 1966 P (Three Crowns Books)

A contemporary play.

*KHAWAM, René R. *La poésie arabe, des origines à nos jours.* Paris, Seghers, 1960; Verviers (Belgique), Gérard; Québec, Kasan, 1967 P (Collection Unesco d'Oeuvres Représentatives – Série Arabe) (Collection Marabout Université)

An anthology of the various styles, with a useful introduction on the history and techniques of Arabic poetry. The selections are mainly from classical poetry although there are a few from the 19th and 20th centuries. The translations are simple and quite effective.

3 PERSIAN AND TAJIK

AINI, Sadriddin. *Boukhara.* [Par] Sadriddine Aïni. Traduit du tadjik par S. Borodine et P. Korotkine. Paris, Gallimard, 1956 P (Collection Littératures Soviétiques)

Aini (1878-1954) was the founder of modern (i.e. Soviet) Tajik literature, breaking it away from traditional Persian literature. He has strongly influenced all modern Tajik writing, as well as the neighbouring Uzbek literature.

ARBERRY, Arthur John (ed.) *Persian poems: an anthology of verse translations.* London, Dent; New York, Dutton, 1954 (Everyman's Library series)
Classical and modern poems in translations ranging from the 18th to the 20th century.

'AṬṬĀR, Farīd al-Dīn. *Le Livre divin (Elahi-nameh).* Tr. Fuad Rouhani. Paris, Albin Michel, 1961 P (Collection Spiritualités Vivantes) (Collection Unesco d'Oeuvres Représentatives – Série Persane)
A long religio-philosophical poem, interspersed with apt anecdotes, by a major Persian mystic (d. 1230).

*'AṬṬĀR, Farīd al-Dīn. *Muslim saints and mystics: episodes from the Tadhkirat al-Auliyā.* Tr. A. J. Arberry. London, Routledge, 1965; Chicago, University of Chicago Press, 1966 (Unesco Collection of Representative Works – Persian Series)
A classic with an illuminating introduction showing the author's place in Islamic mysticism.

BOWEN, John Charles Edward (ed. & tr.) *Poems from the Persian.* [3rd ed.] London, Baker, 1964
A pleasant introduction to classical Persian poetry, in the form of elegant verse translations of 50 poems by famous poets.

ELWELL-SUTTON, Laurence P. *Persian proverbs.* London, Murray, 1954 (Wisdom of the East series)
450 Persian proverbs and sayings. Many which seem cryptic turn out to be the punch-lines of anecdotes, which the compiler explains.

*FIRDAWSĪ. *The epic of the kings: Shah-Nama, the national epic of Persia by Ferdowsi.* Tr. Reuben Levy. London, Routledge; Chicago, University of Chicago Press, 1967 (Persian Heritage series) (Unesco Collection of Representative Works – Persian Series)
An agreeable prose translation (with some omissions) of the great 10th century epic poem which marks the real beginning of modern Persian literature (10th century). Parts of this poem have had an influence on English literature (e.g. *Sohrab and Rustam*).

GURGĀNĪ, Fakhr al-Dīn As'ad. *Le roman de Wîs et Râmîn,* [par] Gorgâni. Tr. Henri Massé. Paris, Les Belles Lettres, 1959 (Collection Unesco d'Oeuvres Représentatives – Série Persane) (Traductions de Textes Persans publiées sous la direction de l'Association Guillaume Budé)
An 11th century Persian parallel of "Tristan et Iseut."

ḤĀFIẒ. *Fifty poems of Ḥāfiẓ*. Texts and translations collected and made by Arthur J. Arberry. Cambridge, New York, Cambridge University Press, 1947, repr. 1962
Verse translations by various hands, with a very informative introduction. This little book is a good initiation to Ḥāfiẓ (d. 1389), the most popular of Persian lyric poets.

*HIDĀYAT, Ṣādiq. *The blind owl*. [By] Sadegh Hedayat. Translated from the Persian by D. P. Costello. London, Calder; New York, Fernhill, 1957; New York, Grove, 1969 P
A novel by the leading Persian writer of the 20th century (1903-51).

*HIDĀYAT, Ṣādiq. *La chouette aveugle*. Traduit du persan par Roger Lescot. Paris, Corti, 1953
See preceding note.

JAMĀLZĀDAH, Muḥammad 'Alī. *Choix de nouvelles (par) Djamalzadeh*. Traduit du persan par Stella Corbin et Hassan Lotfi. Paris, Les Belles Lettres, 1959 (Traductions de Textes Persans publiées sous le patronage de l'Association Guillaume Budé) (Collection Unesco d'Auteurs Contemporains — Série Persane)
Eight short stories by one of the foremost contemporary Persian writers.

JUVAYNĪ, 'Alā al-Dīn 'Aṭā Malik. *The history of the World-Conqueror*. By 'Ala ad-Din Ata-Malik Juvaini. Translated from the Persian by John Andrew Boyle. 2 vols. Manchester, Manchester University Press; Cambridge, Mass., Harvard University Press, 1958 (Unesco Collection of Representative Works — Persian Series)
The 13th century was marked by the rise and expansion of Mongol power, beginning with the invasions of the civilized world, from the Middle East to China, by Chingis Khan ("the World Conqueror"). This is a nearly contemporary account.

KAY KĀ'ŪS IBN ISKANDAR. *A mirror for princes: the Qābūs nāma*. Translated from the Persian by Reuben Levy. London, Cresset; New York, Dutton, 1951; repr. Chester Springs, Pa., Dufour, 1964
Sage advice by a mediaeval Persian prince to his son on many subjects, including human relations, love, marriage, child-rearing, business, and kingship.

KHAYYAM, Omar. *Rubaiyat of Omar Khayyam*. Translated from Persian into English verse by Edward Fitzgerald. Boston, International Pocket Library, [n.d.] P
Many of Fitzgerald's quatrains were "inspired by" rather than translations of Khayyam's originals. There are numerous editions on the market; this is an inexpensive one, containing the texts of Fitzgerald's 1st and 5th editions, and the variants in the 3rd edition.

*KHAYYAM, Omar. *Omar Khayyam: a new version based upon recent discoveries.* By Arthur John Arberry. London, Murray; New Haven, Yale University Press, 1952

A verse translation, which is far from literal, yet rather more faithful in content than Edward Fitzgerald's famous paraphrases. Arberry, who bases his version on an early manuscript of the *Rubā'īyāt*, writes an entertaining and informative introduction, giving a history of Khayyam studies and comparing some of Fitzgerald's renderings with literal translations.

KHAYYAM, Omar. *A new selection from the Rubaiyat of Omar Khayyam.* Rendered into English verse by John Charles Edward Bowen. Literal translation of each Persian quatrain by A. J. Arberry. Persian script by Sharafuddin Khorasani Sharaf. London, Unicorn Press, 1964

KHAYYAM, Omar. *The Rubaiyyat of Omar Khayaam.* A new translation with critical commentaries by Robert Graves and Omar Ali-Shah. London, Toronto, Cassel, 1967

This translation is more accurate than Fitzgerald's, but lacks his charm. The introduction is a full-scale attack on the "Fitz-Omar cult." Some of the scholarship is doubtful.

KHAYYAM, Omar. *Les quatrains.* Nouvelle traduction littérale, suivie de notes ..., par M. Fouladvand. Paris, G.-P. Maisonneuve, 1960

243 of the famous quatrains in a rather literal translation.

*MASSÉ, Henri. *Anthologie persane (XIe-XIXe siècle).* Paris, Payot, 1950 P (Collection Bibliothèque Historique)

One of the most useful anthologies available in French, covering all the major forms of Persian literature, including brief extracts from the works of some 150 authors, with bibliographical information about editions and translations.

NIZĀM AL-MULK. *The Book of Government, or Rules for Kings: the Siyāsatnāma or Siyar al-Mulūk.* Translated from the Persian by Hubert Darke. London, Routledge; New Haven, Yale University Press, 1960 (Unesco Collection of Representative Works – Persian Series)

Advice for rulers and leaders by a famous 11th century vezir.

NIZĀMĪ. *The story of Layla and Majnun.* [Translated from the Persian and edited by R. Gelpke. English version in collaboration with E. Mattin and G. Hill.] Oxford, Cassirer, 1966

The newest prose translation of one of the greatest Persian love epics (12th century). (A French translation by Henri Massé of another of his epic poems entitled *Le Roman de Chosroès et Chirin* is being prepared for publication by G.-P. Maisonneuve.)

NIẒĀMĪ 'ARŪẒĪ. *Revised translation of the Chahár Maqála, the Four discourses* ... by Edward G, Browne. London, Luzac, 1921, repr. 1955 (E. J. W. Gibb Memorial Series)

Four essays on the functions of the ideal royal (1) secretary, (2) poet, (3) astrologer, and (4) physician with numerous interesting anecdotes in support. This well-known Persian treatise was composed by a court poet in Central Asia in the 12th century.

NIẒĀMĪ 'ARŪẒĪ. *Les quatre discours.* Tr. I. de Gastines. Paris, G.-P. Maisonneuve, 1968 (Collection Unesco d'Oeuvres Représentatives — Série Persane)

See preceding note.

RŪMĪ, Jalāl al-Dīn. *Discourses of Rūmī.* [Ed. & tr.] A. J. Arberry. London, Murray, 1961

Prose utterances and anecdotes of great interest and mystical insight by the leading mystic poet of Islam (1207-73).

RŪMĪ, Jalāl al-Dīn. *Mystical poems of Rūmī.* First selection: poems 1-200. Tr. A. J. Arberry. Chicago, London, University of Chicago Press, 1968 (Unesco Collection of Representative Works — Persian Series)

Arberryesque translations.

RŪMĪ, Jalāl al-Dīn. *Roubâ'yât [de] Mevlânâ Djelâl-Eddîn-i-Roûmî.* Traduits de persan par Assaf Hâlet Tchelebi. Paris, A.-Maisonneuve, 1950 P

A rather literal translation of 276 of Rūmī's quatrains.

RŪMĪ, Jalāl al-Dīn. *Rūmī, poet and mystic (1207-1273).* Selections from his writings, translated from the Persian with introduction ... by Reynold A. Nicholson. London, Allen & Unwin, 1950 (and repr.); New York, Macmillan, 1956 (Ethical and Religious Classics of East and West)

Aptly described by the translator as "a book of translations illustrating Sufi doctrine and experience as depicted by the greatest of Iranian mystical poets."

RŪMĪ, Jalāl al-Dīn. *Tales from the Masnavi.* [Tr.] A. J. Arberry. London, Allen & Unwin, 1961 (Unesco Collection of Representative Works — Persian Series)

The "Masnavi" is THE great religious poem in Persian. Among its 25,000 verses on the mystical life and doctrine (Sufism) many anecdotes are told to illustrate its main themes. One hundred of these are included in this book and the rest are contained in the work below. Readable translation into "rhythmic prose."

RŪMĪ, Jalāl al-Dīn. *More tales from the Masnavi.* [Tr.] A. J. Arberry. London, Allen & Unwin; New York, Hillary, 1963 (Unesco Collection of Representative Works — Persian series).

The remaining anecdotes. See preceding note.

*SA'DĪ. *The Gulistan, or Rose Garden.* Tr. Edward Rehatsek, edited with a preface by W. G. Archer, introduction by G. M. Wickens. London, Allen & Unwin, 1964

A complete translation of one of the most famous and popular books in Persian literature; "timeless wisdom" in the form of entertaining anecdotes, by the famous 13th century poet. Informative introduction on the author's life and the *Gulistan*'s place in literature.

SA'DĪ. *Le jardin de roses – Gulistan* par Sheikh Muslihuddîn Saadi Shirazi. Tr. Omar Ali Shah. Paris, Albin Michel, 1966 (Collection Spiritualités Vivantes – Série Islam)

A prose and verse translation which emphasizes the mystical interpretation.

SA'DĪ. *Kings and beggars, the first two chapters of Sa'di's Gulistān.* Translated into English by A. J. Arberry. London, Luzac, 1945

A good initiation into the *Gulistan.*

*ṢAFĀ, Ẓabīḥ Allāh (ed.) *Anthologie de la poésie persane, XIᵉ-XXᵉ siècle.* Textes choisis par Z. Safa. Tr. G. Lazard, R. Lescot et H. Massé. Paris, Gallimard, 1964 (Collection Unesco d'Oeuvres Représentatives – Série Persane)

The best anthology in French translation, giving representative examples of the works of the classical poets but excluding the new style of poetry which began about 1930 and broke with the classical tradition. The introduction reviews the development of traditional poetry and describes its various genres.

ṬĀHIR, of Hamadān. *The Rubáiyyát of Bábá Táhir Oryán of Hamadán.* Rendered from Persian verse into English verse by Mehdi Nakosteen. Boulder, University of Colorado Press, 1967

An interesting translation, with a slight Fitzgeraldian flavour, of quatrains by a contemporary of Omar Khayyam.

ṬŪSĪ, Naṣīr al-Dīn. *The Nasirean ethics* by Naṣīr al-Dīn Ṭūsī. Translated from the Persian by G. M. Wickens. London, Allen & Unwin, 1964 (Unesco Collection of Representative Works – Persian Series) [Available from Orientalia Inc., New York]

This work of a 13th century Persian philosopher, scientist, and statesman was for centuries one of the most popular ethical treatises of the Islamic world, revealing its moral and intellectual preoccupations. It is an example of the mediaeval Islamic blend of Greek, Muslim, and other elements. Good introduction by the translator.

[VARĀVĪNĪ] *Tales of Marzuban.* Tr. Reuben Levy. London, Thames & Hudson; Bloomington, Indiana University Press, 1959 (Unesco Collection of Representative Works – Persian Series) [Available from Greenwood Press, Westport, Conn.]

Mediaeval fables ... "shrewd practical wisdom in a wrapping of entertainment."

4 TURKISH AND OTHER TURKIC

AKHUNDOV, Fath 'Alī. *Comédies*. Par Mirza Fath-Ali Akhundov. Traduit de l'azerbaïdjanais par Louis Bazin. Paris, Gallimard, 1967 P (Collection Caucase) (Collection Unesco d'Oeuvres Représentatives – Série Azerbaïdjanaise)

Azeri or Azerbaijani is a language of the Turkish family spoken in eastern Turkey, northern Persia, northern Iraq, and the adjoining regions of the Soviet Union. The author (1812-78), who has been called "the Azerbaijani Molière," wrote the first native modern-style plays to be performed in the Muslim world in a Muslim language on subjects of local and national interest. They are still much admired.

AKSAN, Akil (ed. & tr.) *Anthologie de la nouvelle poésie turque*. Introduction, traduction, notices par Akil Aksan. Monte Carlo, Editions Regain, 1966 P (Les Cahiers des Poètes de Notre Temps)

A representative selection of poems by recent and contemporary poets; fair translation.

ARZIK, Nimet (ed. & tr.) *Anthologie de la poésie turque, XIIIᵉ-XXᵉ siècle*. Paris, Gallimard, 1968 P

A selection of poems or parts of poems from the 13th to the 20th centuries. Divided by types: (1) popular, (2) Divan (classical court), (3) syllabic poetry of the 19th and 20th centuries, and (4) free verse. The selections are sometimes scrappy; the translations are very free though often quite pleasant. The notes preceding the pieces are inadequate and often inaccurate.

AVEZOV, Mukhtar. *Abaï,* par Moukhtar Aouezov. Traduit du kazakh par Antoine Vitez. Paris, Gallimard, 1960 P (Collection Littératures Soviétiques)

This work and the one below constitute a historical novel by a recent leading Kazakh literary figure (d. 1961), based on the life of Abai, a noted 19th century Kazakh intellectual and innovator.

AVEZOV, Mukhtar. *La jeunesse d'Abaï,* par Moukhtar Aouezov. Traduit du kazakh par Léonide Sobolev et Antoine Vitez. Paris, Gallimard, 1959 P (Collection Littératures Soviétiques)

See preceding note.

DAḠLARCA, Fazıl Hüsnü. *Selected poems: Seçme şiirler*. Tr. Talât Sait Halman. Introduction by Yaşar Nabi Nayır. Pittsburgh, University of Pittsburgh Press, 1969

A representative selection of work by an original and prolific poet who has achieved wide recognition for his writing in many genres and styles for more than one-third of a century. He is regarded by many as Turkey's greatest living poet. Serviceable translations.

EMRE, Yunus. *Le divan [de] Younous Emre.* Traduit du turc et préfacé par Yves Régnier. Paris, Gallimard, 1963 P (Collection Métamorphoses)
The beautiful yet simple hymns of this 14th century poet and saint have maintained their popularity to the present day among Turks of all classes.

ER-TÖSHTÜK. *Aventures merveilleuses sous terre et ailleurs de Er-Töshtük, le géant des steppes. Épopée du cycle Manas.* Traduit du kirghiz par Pertev Boratav. Paris, Gallimard, 1965 P (Collection Caucase) (Collection Unesco d'Oeuvres Représentatives — Série Kirghize)
A good representative of the epic tradition of Central Asian Turkic literature.

FAIK, Sait. *Un point sur la carte.* [Par] Sait Faik Abasıyanık. Choix et traduction Sabri Esat Siyavuşgil. Leyde, Sythoff, 1962 P
Forty-one short stories by one of the most widely read modern writers (d. 1954). His themes are often timeless and his writing always informed with sympathy.

GÜNTEKIN, Reşat Nuri. *The autobiography of a Turkish girl.* Tr. Wyndham Deedes. London, Allen & Unwin, 1949
Written in 1922, this Turkish novel, about a woman teacher who serves in a Turkish village and brings the "enlightenment of modern attitudes," had a great effect and remained a best seller for many years.

HIKMET, Nazim. *Anthologie poétique.* Paris, Editeurs Français Réunis, 1964 P
This well-known communist poet (d. 1963) spent most of his life in exile, yet his distinctive powerful style has greatly influenced Turkish poets for the last 30 years. This collection contains 147 poems translated with irregular skill by various hands.

HIKMET, Nazim. *Selected poems.* Translated from Turkish by Taner Baybars. London, Cape, 1967 P
A little book containing fairly effective translations of 28 pieces in free verse.

KĀTIB ÇELEBI. *The balance of truth,* by Kātib Chelebi. Tr. G. L. Lewis. London, Allen & Unwin, 1957 (Ethical and Religious Classics of East and West series)
Twenty-one short essays by a famous 17th century Ottoman Turkish polymath, on a variety of subjects, including singing, tobacco, coffee, pilgrimage.

KEMAL, Yaşar. *Anatolian tales.* By Yashar Kemal. Translated from the Turkish by Thilda Kemal. New York, Dodds, 1969
Seven stories which give a vivid impression of the problems of Turkish village life.

KEMAL, Yaşar. *Memed, my hawk.* By Yashar Kemal. Translated from the Turkish by Edouard Roditi. London, Collins; New York, Pantheon, 1961
A powerful prize-winning novel of the Anatolian countryside, brigandage, and a Turkish Robin Hood.

KEMAL, Yaşar. *Memed le mince.* Traduit du turc par Guzine Dino. Paris, Del Duca, 1961 (Collection Le Roman Mondial Alcyon) (Collection Unesco d'Auteurs Contemporains)
See preceding note.

KEMAL, Yaşar. *Le pilier.* [Par] Yachar Kemal. Traduit du turc par Guzine Dino. Paris, Gallimard, 1966 P (Collection Du Monde Entier)
Another novel set in the author's native region, southeastern Anatolia.

KEMAL, Yaşar. *The wind from the plain.* By Yashar Kemal. Translated from the Turkish by Thilda Kemal. New York, Harvill, 1963; London, Toronto, Collins, 1964

*MAKAL, Mahmut. *A village in Anatolia.* Translated from the Turkish by Wyndham Deedes. London, Vallentine Mitchell, 1954
The peasantry of the 40,000 villages of Turkey found their first real voice in Mahmut Makal, a village schoolmaster. This book of his "notes," first published in 1950, revealed to townsmen the conditions of life among the peasants. The shock generated had an important effect on the national elections in 1950. Interesting also for its "new" literary style, which is very close to colloquial Turkish.

*MAKAL, Mahmut. *Un village anatolien.* Récit d'un instituteur paysan. Par Mahmout Makal. Textes rassemblés et presentés par Guzine Dino; traduit du turc par O. Ceyrac et G. Dino. Paris, Plon, 1963 (Collection Terre Humaine)
See preceding note.

NASREDDIN HOCA. *Les bonnes histoires de Mollah.* [Receuillis en Perse par] Jean Dj. Bader. Neuchâtel, La Baconnière, 1962
A representative collection of humorous anecdotes about the classical character of Islamic, and particularly Turkish, folk humour.

NASREDDIN HOCA. *Tales of the Hodja.* Retold by Charles Downing. London, Oxford University Press, 1964
Another good selection.

NASREDDIN HOCA. *Tales of Mullah Nasir-ud-Din: Persian wit, wisdom and folly.* [Tr.] Eric Daenecke. New York, Exposition Press, 1960
Ninety-one of the numerous anecdotes, translated from the Persian version. Turks, Arabs, and Persians all regard the Hoca as one of themselves.

NAVĀ'Ī, 'Alī Shīr. *Muḥākamat al-lughatain.* By Mīr 'Alī Shīr Navā'ī. Introduction, translation and notes by Robert Devereux. Leiden, Brill, 1966
An interesting attempt by the major literary figure of Chaghatay Turkish (the Eastern Turkic literary language of Central Asia) to show that it was a beautiful and fitting vehicle for literature and superior to Persian. Navā'ī (1441-1501) was also a master of Persian. The translation is frequently erroneous, but the general sense of the treatise remains clear.

*WALKER, Warren S. *Tales alive in Turkey.* [By] Warren S. Walker and Ahmet E. Uysal. Cambridge, Mass., Harvard University Press, 1966
A very good collection of living Turkish folk tales of all kinds.

5 INDIAN MUSLIM

ALI, Ahmed (ed. & tr.) *The bulbul and the rose: an anthology of Urdu poetry.* Translated with an introduction. Karachi, Talim-i-Milli, 1960
Fair verse translations of poems by 11 traditional Urdu poets of the 18th and 19th centuries; preceded by a useful introduction to the history of Urdu poetry.

BOWEN, John Charles Edward (ed. & tr.) *The golden pomegranate: a selection from the poetry of the Mogul Empire in India, 1526-1858.* London, Baker; Chester Springs, Pa., Dufour, 1966
Engaging verse translations of 35 poems originally in Persian, Urdu, and Pushtu.

GHĀLIB. *Ghalib, 1797-1869.* Tr. & ed. Ralph Russell and Khurshidul Islam. London, Allen & Unwin, 1969- (Unesco Collection of Representative Works – Indian Series). Vol. 1. *Life and letters.*
Ghālib is one of the two greatest Urdu poets (the other is Iqbāl). These excellently selected and translated letters, together with the editor's comments, give a good conspectus of his life, character, and gifts.

HOSAIN, Shahid (ed.) *First voices: six poets from Pakistan.* London, Toronto, New York, Oxford University Press, 1965
The work of young poets.

IQBĀL, Muḥammad. *Javid-nama.* Translated from the Persian, with introduction and notes, by A. J. Arberry. London, Allen & Unwin; New York, Hillary, 1966 (Unesco Collection of Representative Works – Pakistan Series)

This poem, somewhat akin to Dante's *Divine Comedy*, is widely regarded as the greatest work of Iqbāl (1873-1938), the "spiritual father of Pakistan," a notable philosopher, religious thinker, and poet. Iqbāl wrote most of his poetry in Persian, which was the principal literary language of India's Muslims.

IQBĀL, Muḥammad. *Le livre de l'éternité, Djavid-Nama.* Tr. Eva Meyerovitch et Mohammad Mokri. Paris, Albin Michel, 1962 (Collection Spiritualités Vivantes — Série Islam) (Collection Unesco d'Oeuvres Représentatives — Série Pakistanaise)
  See preceding note.

IQBĀL, Muḥammad. *Message de l'Orient* [*Payâm-i Mashriq*]. Tr. Eva Meyerovitch et Mohammad Achena. Paris, Les Belles-Lettres, 1956 (Collection Unesco d'Oeuvres Représentatives — Série Pakistanaise)
  Iqbal's "reply" in Persian poetry to Goethe's *Westöstlicher Diwan.*

IQBĀL, Muḥammad. *The mysteries of selflessness: a philosophical poem.* Translated [from the Persian] by A. J. Arberry. London, Murray; New York, Paragon, 1953 (Wisdom of the East series)
  On the ideal (Islamic) society and the position of the individual in it.

IQBĀL, Muḥammad. *Persian psalms* [*Zabūr-i 'Ajam*]. Pts. 1 and 2. Translated into English verse from the Persian by A. J. Arberry. Lahore, Ashraf, 1949 (and repr.)
  Iqbal's message in the form of lyric poems.

IQBĀL, Muḥammad. *Poems from Iqbal.* Ed. & tr. V. G. Kiernan. London, Murray; New York, Paragon, 1955 (Wisdom of the East series)
  The poems in this selection were chiefly written in Urdu and cover a wide variety of Iqbal's favourite themes.

JASIM UDDIN. *Gipsy wharf (Sojan badiar ghat).* Translated from the Bengali by Barbara Painter and Yann Lovelock. London, Allen & Unwin, 1969 (Unesco Collection of Representative Works — Pakistan Series)
  The disintegration of a society under religious and economic pressure is revealed in the treatment of a Romeo and Juliet theme.

MUJEEB, Mohammed. *Ghalib.* New Delhi, Sahitya Akademi, 1969 (Makers of Indian Literature series)
  A good short introduction to the poet in the context of his time and of Urdu literature. Almost half this 80-page book consists of translations of selected couplets of Ghalib's poetry.

RUSSELL, Ralph (ed. & tr.) *Three Mughal poets: Mir, Sauda, Mir Hasan.* By Ralph Russell and Khurshidul Islam. Cambridge, Mass., Harvard University

Press; London, Allen & Unwin, 1969 (Unesco Collection of Representative Works — Indian Series)

> A welcome interpretative introduction to three different types of 18th century Urdu poetry. Sauda is particularly interesting as an observer and satirist of his society.

RUSWA, Mirza Mohammad Hadi. *Courtesan of Lucknow (Umrao Jan Ada).* Translated from the Urdu by Khushwant Singh and M. A. Husaini. Calcutta, Orient-Longmans, 1961 (Unesco Collection of Representative Works — Indian Series)

> This "biography of a courtesan" in 19th century India is interesting in its descriptions of life a century ago.

SORLEY, Harold Tower. *Shāh Abdul Latīf of Bhīt: his poetry, life and times.* A study of the literary, social and economic conditions in eighteenth century Sind. Lahore, Oxford University Press, Pakistan Branch, 1966 (repr. of 1940 ed.)

> The work of the outstanding mystical Sindhi poet, discussed and translated into rather old-fashioned English.

WALIULLAH, Syed. *Tree without roots.* Translated from the Bengali by Qaisar Saeed, Anne-Marie Thibaud, and others. London, Chatto; Toronto, Clarke Irwin, 1967 (Unesco Collection of Representative Works — Pakistan Series)

> A novel of faith and imposture in a Bengali village, by a leading Pakistani journalist and novelist.

WALIULLAH, Syed. *L'arbre sans racines.* Tr. Anne-Marie Thibaud. Paris, Seuil, 1963 (Collection Unesco d'Oeuvres Représentatives — Série Pakistanaise)

> See preceding note.

6 HEBREW (MEDIAEVAL AND MODERN)

AGNON, Samuel Joseph. *The bridal canopy.* Tr. I. M. Lask. New York, Schocken; London, Gollancz, 1967

> Agnon (1888-1969), who won the Nobel Prize for Literature in 1966, was a master stylist unique in modern Hebrew literature. His simple, classical, but highly allusive style loses a great deal in any translation, however skilful. Most of his works are imbued with symbolism. This work and those below are representative.

AGNON, Samuel Joseph. *A guest for the night.* Translated from the Hebrew by Misha Louvish. [Ed. Naftali C. Brandwein and Allen Mandelbaum.] New York, Schocken, 1968

A moving novel which explores the discontinuity in perspective between the intensive Jewish life of the small town in Eastern Europe, which the author knew in his youth, and the modern generation in Israel. Partly autobiographical.

AGNON, Samuel Joseph. *In the heart of the seas:* a story of a journey to the land of Israel. Tr. I. M. Lask. New York, Schocken, 1966; London, Gollancz, 1967
    The adventures of immigrants travelling from Poland to the Holy Land a century and a half ago.

AGNON, Samuel Joseph. *Two tales: Betrothed, and Edo and Enam.* Translated from the Hebrew by Walter Lever. New York, Schocken; London, Gollancz, 1966

AMICHAI, Yehuda. *Not of this time, not of this place.* New York, Harper, 1968
    An Israeli novel.

AMICHAI, Yehuda. *Poems.* Translated from the Hebrew by Assia Gutmann. New York, Harper; Toronto, Fitzhenry, 1969
    Forty-six short poems by a powerful Israeli poet (born 1924), notably translated.

BLOCKER, Joel (ed. & tr.) *Israeli stories: a selection of the best contemporary Hebrew writing.* Introduced by Robert Alter. New York, Schocken, 1962; 1968 P [subtitled: *a selection of the best writing in Israel today*]
    A representative choice.

*BURNSHAW, Stanley (ed.) *The modern Hebrew poem itself, from the beginnings to the present: 69 poems in a new presentation.* Ed. Stanley Burnshaw, T. Carmi, Ezra Spicehandler. New York, Holt, 1965; New York, Schocken, 1966 P
    Works by 24 poets, from the late 19th century to the present, translated and discussed in an unusual way, which is particularly helpful in enabling those who do not know Hebrew to get close to the spirit of the originals.

COHEN, Israel (ed.) *An anthology of Hebrew essays.* Selected by Israel Cohen and B. Y. Michali. 2 vols. Tel Aviv, Institute for the Translation of Hebrew Literature and Massada, 1966
    An interesting selection, devoted both to Hebrew and to general literature, and drawing many fruitful comparisons. Grouped under these subject headings: Biblical topics; On literature; the Writer and society; Philosophical themes.

GOLDSTEIN, David (ed. & tr.) *Hebrew poems from Spain*. London, Routledge, 1965
> Fair translations of many different types of poetry by 13 major Jewish poets and scholars of Muslim Spain in the period between the 9th and 13th centuries.

al-ḤARĪZĪ, Judah ben Solomon. *The Tahkemoni*. An English translation by Victor Emanuel Reichert. Vol. I. Jerusalem, Raphael Haim Cohen's Press, 1965
> A medley of imaginative prose and poetry, literary criticism, and general information. The author's purpose was to show the vitality and versatility of Hebrew when Arabic had become the main Jewish literary language of the Middle East. The 13th century author was well versed in classical Arabic. The translation contains 15 of the 51 chapters.

HAZAZ, Hayim. *Mori Saʾid*. Translated from the Hebrew by Ben Halpern. New York, Abelard-Schuman; Toronto, Nelson Foster, 1956
> In this novel of three generations, the impact of modern life on the Yemenite Jewish community of Israel is explored by a leading Israeli writer of the old school.

IBN GABIROL, Solomon ben Judah. *The kingly crown*. Translated with introduction and notes by Bernard Lewis. London, Vallentine Mitchell, 1961
> This meditation by a famous 11th century Spanish Jewish philosopher and poet ("Avicebron") is a fine example of mediaeval Hebrew religious poetry. The translation is distinguished yet simple.

IBN GABIROL, Solomon ben Judah. *La couronne royale* (Kether malcouth). Introduction, traduction et notes de Paul Vuillaud. Paris, Dervy, 1953 P (Collection: Les Classiques de l'Hermétisme et de le Mystique)
> A straightforward translation, explaining some of the allusions.

*JUDAH HA-LEVI. *Selected poems of Jehudah Halevi*. Tr. Nina Salaman. Philadelphia, Jewish Publication Society of America, 1924, repr. 1946
> Fine translations from the Hebrew poetry of one of the greatest Jewish poets and thinkers of Muslim Spain (12th century). The poem beginning "My heart is in the East, and I in the uttermost West" opens the section of odes to Zion; subsequent sections are entitled Love and Bridal Songs, Poems of Friendship, and Devotional Poems.

KAHN, Sholom Jacob (ed.) *A whole loaf: stories from Israel*. New York, Vanguard; Toronto, Copp Clark, 1962
> Stories by leading writers who mirror the range of traditions that meet in contemporary Israel.

MEGGED, Aharon. *The living on the dead.* Tr. Misha Louvish. London, Cape, 1970 (Unesco Collection of Representative Works – Israel Series)
A prizewinning novel about the would-be biographer of a national hero and how and why he failed to produce the required work.

*MINTZ, Ruth Finer (ed. & tr.) *Modern Hebrew poetry: a bilingual anthology.* Berkeley, University of California Press; London, Cambridge University Press, 1966 C&P
Sensitive translations of poems by 28 leading poets of the 20th century.

NOY, Dov (ed.) *Folktales of Israel.* Tr. Gene Baharav. Chicago, University of Chicago Press; London, Routledge, 1963
Seventy-one folk tales, mostly gathered from Jews originating outside Europe. The most numerous tales in this book are from Iraq, Afghanistan, Turkey, and the Yemen, in that order.

PENUELI, S. Y. (ed.) *Anthology of modern Hebrew poetry.* Selected by S. Y. Penueli and A. Ukhmani. 2 vols. Jerusalem, Institute for the Translation of Hebrew Literature, 1966
From Bialik (1873-1934) to poets now in their fifties; translations vary in quality, but some are very good.

*PENUELI, S. Y. (ed.) *Hebrew short stories: an anthology.* Selected by S. Y. Penueli and A. Ukhmani. 2 vols. Tel-Aviv, Institute for the Translation of Hebrew Literature, 1965
A good representative anthology. Useful biographical and critical notes.

RABIKOVITZ, Dalia (ed.) *The new Israeli writers: short stories of the first generation.* New York, Funk and Wagnalls, 1969
Fourteen stories (some good) by as many writers, most in their thirties or forties. The writing is representative of the interests and skills esteemed by the Hebrew-reading public.

SHAMIR, Moshe. *David's stranger.* Tr. Margaret Benaya. London, New York, Abelard-Schuman, 1964
This book, about an event in the life of King David, and the following one, set in the Hasmonean period, are examples of popular Israeli historical novels.

SHAMIR, Moshe. *The king of flesh and blood.* Translated from the Hebrew by David Patterson. London, East and West Library, 1958
See preceding note.

7 OTHER LITERATURES

FAROOKI, Nasir Ahmad (ed. & tr.) *A selection of contemporary Pakistani short stories.* Lahore, Ferozsons, 1955
> Mainly rather poor love stories, representative of recent popular taste in Pakistan.

KHŪSHḤĀL KHĀN KHATTAK. *Poems from the Divan of Khushal Khan Khattak.* Translated from the Pashto by D. N. Mackenzie. London, Allen & Unwin, 1965 (Unesco Collection of Representative Works — Pakistan Series)
> The author, who was a 17th century Pathan chieftan on the frontiers of present-day Afghanistan and Pakistan, is regarded as the father of Pashto poetry.

LAOUST, Emile (ed. & tr.) *Contes berbères du Maroc.* Avec traduction et annotations. 2 vols. Paris, Larose, 1950 (Publications [de l'] Institut des Hautes Études Marocaines, Rabat)

F RELIGION AND IDEAS

1 GENERAL WORKS

ABD-EL-JALIL, Jean-M. *Aspects intérieurs de l'Islam.* 2ᵉ éd. Paris, Seuil, 1962
Thoughtful articles by a Catholic author on Muslim traditional and modern thought, piety and prayer, and on the relationship between the Islamic and Christian communities.

AHMAD, Aziz. *Studies in Islamic culture in the Indian environment.* Oxford, Clarendon; Toronto, New York, Oxford University Press, 1964
A series of excellent essays which require some preliminary general knowledge for full appreciation.

CHARNAY, Jean-Paul (ed.) *Normes et valeurs de l'Islam contemporain.* Paris, Payot, 1966 P (Collection Bibliothèque Scientifique)
Various aspects of Islamic civilization, and particularly its ambivalent attitude to western civilization, discussed in articles by Muslim and non-Muslim authors.

DANIEL, Norman. *Islam and the West: the making of an image.* Edinburgh, Edinburgh University Press; Chicago, Quadrangle, 1960
An important study of mediaeval Europe's concept of Islam.

DANIEL, Norman. *Islam, Europe and empire.* Edinburgh, Edinburgh University Press; Chicago, Aldine, 1966 (Edinburgh University Publications, Language and Literature series)
This thoroughly documented study of European attitudes to Islam and its civilization in the 19th century is a sequel to the same author's *Islam and the West* (above).

GARDET, Louis. *Connaître l'Islam.* Paris, Fayard, 1958 P (Collection "Je sais, je crois")
A good survey of Islam as a religion and civilization. The last third of the book discusses contemporary Islam, in its relationship to such currents as nationalism and socialism.

GARDET, Louis. *L'Islam: religion et communauté.* Paris, Desclée, 1967 (Collection Bibliothèque Française de Philosophie)
An excellent scholarly presentation, by a distinguished Catholic philosopher, of the religious values which are "lived" by Muslims. Some attention is also given to contemporary problems.

*GIBB, Hamilton Arthur Rosskeen (ed.) *Shorter Encyclopaedia of Islam.* Edited on behalf of the Royal Netherlands Academy by H. A. R. Gibb and J. H.

Kramers. Leiden, Brill; London, Luzac, 1953 (and repr.); Ithaca, Cornell University Press, 1957 (and repr.)

A very useful reference book. Consists of all articles dealing with religion and law in Islam which appeared in the original edition of the *Encyclopaedia of Islam,* 1913-38.

*LAOUST, Henri. *Les schismes dans l'Islam.* Introduction à une étude de la religion musulmane. Paris, Payot, 1965 P (Collection Bibliothèque Historique)

An excellent pioneer study of the doctrines and history of the main sects of Islam up to the present time.

MACDONALD, Duncan Black. *Development of Muslim theology, jurisprudence and constitutional theory.* Beirut, Khayat, 1965 (repr. of 1908 ed.)

A good, though somewhat dated, outline.

PADWICK, Constance E. *Muslim devotions: a study of prayer-manuals in common use.* London, S.P.C.K., 1961

Translations of prayers used by the Muslim masses, which give a real picture of what Islam means to the "man in the street," together with illuminating introductions to Muslim prayer and its categories.

*ROSENTHAL, Erwin Isak Jakob. *Judaism and Islam.* London, New York, Yoseloff 1961 P (Popular Jewish Library series).

Consists of two parts: (1) "Judaism in Islam," showing the great influence of Judaism on Islam in its formative period, and (2) "Judaism under Islam," describing in some detail Jewish civilization in the Muslim world in the mediaeval period. An absorbing book written for non-specialists, though occasionally assuming some prior knowledge by the reader.

*SÉROUYA, Henri. *La pensée arabe.* Paris, Presses Universitaires de France, 1960 P (Collection "Que sais-je?")

A more accurate title would be "La pensée islamique." A competent outline of Islam as a religion, a description of major Muslim philosophical schools, and short sketches of several famous mediaeval philosophers.

SOUTHERN, Richard William. *Western views of Islam in the Middle Ages.* Cambridge, Mass., Harvard University Press; London, Oxford University Press, 1962

Three readable lectures covering the period 700-1460, from the "age of ignorance" to the "moment of vision." A much fuller, thoroughly documented account is given by Norman Daniel, *Islam and the West* (above).

2 OUTLINES OF ISLAM AND
GENERAL INTRODUCTORY WORKS

BOUSQUET, Georges Henri. *Les grandes pratiques rituelles de l'Islam*. Paris, Presses Universitaires de France, 1949 (Collection Mythes et Religions)
> A handy introduction to the basic Muslim rituals of prayer, fasting, and pilgrimage.

CRAGG, Kenneth. *The call of the minaret*. New York, Toronto, London, Oxford University Press, 1956; 1964 P (Galaxy Books)
> An explanation of what Islam means to a Muslim, and an investigation of mutual religious understanding between Christians and Muslims.

DERMENGHEM, Émile. *Mahomet et la tradition islamique*. Paris, Seuil, 1957 (Collection Maîtres Spirituels)
> A sketchy description of Muhammad's life and work, and the basics of Islam as a religion. The second part of the book consists of translated extracts from the Koran and Muslim religious literature. Very attractive illustrations, largely from Islamic manuscripts.

DERMENGHEM, Émile. *Muhammad and the Islamic tradition*. Tr. Jean M. Watt. London, Longmans; New York, Harper, 1958 (and repr.) P (Men of Wisdom series)
> See preceding note.

*GIBB, Hamilton Arthur Rosskeen. *Mohammedanism: an historical survey*. 2nd ed. (with revisions). London, Oxford University Press, 1961 (and repr.); New York, Oxford University Press, 1962 P
> Perhaps the best short introduction to Islam. This is an excellently written authoritative survey with a useful annotated bibliographical guide to further reading.

GUILLAUME, Alfred. *Islam*. [2nd ed.] London, Cassell; New York, Barnes, 1964; [1st ed.] Harmondsworth, Montreal, Baltimore, Penguin, 1954 P (and repr.) (Pelican Books)
> A handy descriptive outline, a little patronizing at times.

HAMIDULLAH, Muhammad. *Introduction to Islam*. [2nd ed.] Paris, Centre Culturel Islamique, 1959
> A standard apologia by a modern Muslim.

[HAMIDULLAH, Muhammad]. *Initiation à l'Islam*. Paris, Imprimerie de Carthage [for Centre Culturel Islamique], 1966 P
> French version of the above work.

*JEFFERY, Arthur (ed.) *Islam: Muhammad and his religion.* New York, Liberal Arts Press; Indianapolis and New York, Bobbs-Merrill, 1958 P (The Library of Liberal Arts)

A good textbook. Selection of passages from standard Muslim texts illustrating the orthodox Muslim teaching about Islam; excludes modernist interpretations.

*LAMMENS, Henri. *L'Islam: croyances et institutions.* 2ᵉ éd. rev. et augm. Beyrouth, Imprimerie Catholique, 1941; repr. 1964

A classic general introduction.

*LAMMENS, Henri. *Islam: beliefs and institutions.* Tr. E. Denison Ross. London, Methuen, 1929; New York, Barnes & Noble, repr. 1968

See preceding note.

MASSÉ, Henri. *L'Islam.* 7ᵉ éd. Paris, Colin, 1957

A satisfactory short introduction to Islam as a religion.

MASSÉ, Henri. *Islam.* Tr. Halide Edip. Beirut, Khayat, 1967 (repr. of 1938 ed.)

See preceding note.

MAUDŪDĪ, Abul Aʻlā. *Towards understanding Islam.* Tr. & ed. Khurshid Ahmad. Lahore, Islamic Publications, 1966 C&P

Written as a textbook for Indo-Pakistani school children, this is described by the translator as "a simple, understandable and unsophisticated interpretation." The author is a leading modern conservative Muslim theologian.

MOUBARAC, Youakim. *L'Islam.* Tournai (Belgique), Casterman, 1962 P (Collection Eglise Vivante)

A useful general presentation prepared originally for Catholic students, and paying special attention to Muslim-Christian relationships. Covers early, mediaeval and modern periods.

*RAHMAN, Fazlur. *Islam.* London, Weidenfeld, 1966; New York, Holt, 1967 (History of Religion series)

An outstanding work, which, however, assumes at least a basic knowledge (such as can be obtained from works like those by H. A. R. Gibb or A. Guillaume, above). This is a historical, descriptive, and partly interpretative account. The problems of Islam in modern times are well discussed in the final chapters.

*SCHUON, Frithjof. *Comprendre l'Islam.* Paris, Gallimard, 1961 P

The author's aim is not so much to describe Islam as to explain why Muslims believe in it. He succeeds excellently.

*SCHUON, Frithjof. *Understanding Islam*. Tr. D. M. Matheson. London, Allen & Unwin, 1963 (and repr.); New York, Roy, 1964
  See preceding note.

WATT, William Montgomery. *What is Islam?* London, Longmans, 1968 (Arab Background series)
  A theological examination of the Koran and the development of Islam; includes a study of the relationship of Islam to Christianity.

*WILLIAMS, John Alden (ed.) *Islam*. New York, Braziller, 1961; Washington Square Press, 1963 P
  A well-chosen selection of passages from the Koran and classical Muslim authors on various aspects of Islam. The result is a good picture of Islam as seen "from the inside." Sympathetic introductions and linking commentary enhance the book's value as an introduction to understanding the Muslim way of life.

3 KORAN (QUR'ĀN), MUHAMMAD, THE RISE OF ISLAM

*ANDRAE, Tor. *Mohammed: the man and his faith*. Tr. Theophil Menzel. New York, Barnes & Noble, 1955 (and repr.); London, Allen & Unwin, 1956; New York, Harper, 1960 P (Harper Torchbooks)
  A standard short biography (first published in 1936) which shows exceptional religious and psychological insight.

*ANDRAE, Tor. *Mahomet, sa vie et sa doctrine*. Tr. Jean Gaudefroy-Demombynes. Paris, A.-Maisonneuve, 1945 P (Collection Initiation à l'Islam)
  See preceding note.

ANDRAE, Tor. *Les origines de l'Islam et le Christianisme*. Tr. J. Roche. Paris, A.-Maisonneuve, 1955 P (Collection Initiation à l'Islam)
  An important study of the Christian aspects of the Arabian environment at the time of the rise of Islam.

ARNOLD, Thomas W. *The preaching of Islam: a history of the propagation of the Muslim faith*. Lahore, Ashraf, 1961
  A very sympathetic account of the rise of Islam and its spread in all parts of the world, until the 19th century. (Reprinted from the 2nd ed., 1913.)

BELL, Richard. *Introduction to the Qur'ān*. Edinburgh, Edinburgh University Press, 1953 (and repr.) (Edinburgh University Publications, Language and Literature series)
  An important study, intelligible to the non-specialist.

*BLACHÈRE, Régis. *Le Coran.* Paris, Presses Universitaires de France, 1966 P (Collection "Que sais-je?")

An excellent brief survey of the text, its main themes, and the Muslim "sciences" which developed from the study of the Koran and its place in Muslim life.

BLACHÈRE, Régis. *Introduction au Coran.* 2ᵉ éd. Paris, G.-P. Maisonneuve, 1959

An important work for those who wish for a deeper insight. Partly technical.

al-BUKHĀRĪ, Muḥammad ibn Ismāʿīl. *L'authentique tradition musulmane: choix de h'adîths.* Traduction, introduction et notes par G.-H. Bousquet. Paris, Grasset, 1964

This collection of traditions concerning the Prophet's sayings and deeds was compiled from the reports of witnesses. Next to the Koran, it is probably the most influential work in Islamic practice and law, by which Muslims are guided in their private and public lives. Clear translation.

*GABRIELI, Francesco. *Mahomet.* Paris, Albin Michel, 1965 (Collection Le Mémorial des Siècles)

Muhammad as seen by Muslims. Consists mainly of selections from standard classical Arabic works and traditions, but one chapter is devoted to quotations about him by westerners from Dante to Victor Hugo.

GABRIELI, Francesco. *Muhammad and the conquests of Islam.* Tr. Virginia Luling and Rosamund Linell. London, Weidenfeld; New York, Toronto, McGraw-Hill, 1968 C&P (World University Library series)

An attempt to explain the success of Islam and its early conquests of minds and territories.

GABRIELI, Francesco. *Mahomet et les grandes conquêtes arabes.* Texte français de Claude Carme. Paris, Hachette, 1967 P (Collection L'Univers des Connaissances)

See preceding note.

*GAUDEFROY-DEMOMBYNES, Maurice. *Mahomet.* Paris, Albin Michel, 1957 (Collection L'Évolution de l'Humanité)

A good detailed biography and description of Muhammad's teachings.

HAMIDULLAH, Muhammad. *Le Prophète de l'Islam.* 2 vols. Paris, Vrin, 1959

Tome 1: *Sa vie*; tome 2: *Son oeuvre.* A biography by a modern Muslim.

IBN HISHĀM, ʿAbd al-Malik. *The life of Muhammad: a translation of* [Ibn Hishām's abridgement of Ibn] *Ishāq's Sīrat Rasūl Allāh,* with an introduction

and notes by A. Guillaume. London, Toronto, New York, Oxford University Press, 1955 P (and repr.)
An early standard reverent biography, translated from the Arabic.

KORAN
The Holy Book of Islam is regarded by Muslims as divine revelation, which is by its very nature untranslatable both as to content and as to style. Its rhythm has moved Muslims for nearly 14 centuries and the meaning of its words has been the subject of countless commentaries. Each translation has its virtues and defects. Several English and French versions, both by Muslims and by non-Muslims, have therefore been cited here.

*KORAN. *The Koran interpreted.* [Tr.] A. J. Arberry. London, Allen & Unwin; New York, Macmillan, 1955 (and repr.); London, Toronto, New York, Oxford University Press, 1964 (The World's Classics series)
An eloquent translation, which makes an attempt at "imitating the rhetorical and rhythmical patterns" of the original. Preceded by a short history of previous translations, with examples from them.

*KORAN. *The Meaning of the glorious Koran.* An explanatory translation by Mohammed Marmaduke Pickthall. London, Allen & Unwin, 1930, repr. 1957; New York, New American Library, 1953, repr. 1961 P (Mentor Books)
The modern orthodox interpretation, translated in a style reminiscent of the King James' (Authorized) version of the Bible.

KORAN. *The Koran.* Translated into English from the original Arabic, with explanatory notes taken from the most approved commentators ... by George Sale. London, New York, Warne, [many repr.]
A very serviceable version, somewhat old-fashioned in style – the translator died in 1736. Both his translation and notes reflect accurately the views of the standard classical Arabic commentaries; they do not suffer from the apologetics of modern Muslim versions, or from the liberties often taken by other Christian translators.

*KORAN. *Le Coran.* Traduction français par Régis Blachère. Paris, G.-P. Maisonneuve, 1957, repr. 1966
The most scientific, though rather literal, French version, adapted for the non-specialist from the translator's own scholarly edition.

*KORAN. *Le Coran.* Introduction, traduction et notes par Denise Masson. Paris, Gallimard, 1967
The most readable French translation, in a style which slightly echoes the original. Excellent introduction.

KORAN. *Le Coran.* Traduction intégrale et notes de Muhammad Hamidullah, avec la collaboration de Michel Léturmy. Nouvelle éd., Club Français du Livre, 1966

A rather literal modern Muslim translation with helpful notes, giving interpretation from a modern traditionalist, slightly apologetic viewpoint.

MASSON, Denise. *Le Coran et la révélation judéo-chrétienne.* 2 vols. Paris, A.-Maisonneuve, 1958
An interesting comparative study.

RODINSON, Maxime. *Mahomet.* Paris, Club Français du Livre, 1961 (Collection Portraits de l'Histoire)
A sympathetic biography which reflects a consensus of rationalist orientalist opinion on the life and work of Muhammad.

*WATT, William Montgomery. *Muhammad, prophet and statesman.* London, Toronto, Oxford University Press, 1961 (and repr.); 1964 P
A sympathetic, though not uncritical, popular biography with particular attention to the social and economic environment of Arabia at the time of the rise of Islam. Sound on facts, but the interpretations are not always uncontested. This work is essentially an abridgement of Watt's detailed and documented works, *Muhammad at Mecca,* and *Muhammad at Medina* (Oxford University Press, 1953 and 1956 respectively).

*WATT, William Montgomery. *Mahomet, prophète et homme d'état.* Tr. Odile Mayot. Paris, Payot, 1962 P (Collection Petit Bibliothèque Payot)
See preceding note. Essentially an abridgement of Watt's *Mahomet à la Mecque* and *Mahomet à Médine* (Paris, Payot, 1958 and 1959 respectively).

4 THEOLOGY, PHILOSOPHY, ETHICS (INCLUDING CLASSICAL ISLAMIC WORKS)

AFNAN, Soheil Muhsin. *Avicenna: his life and works.* London, Allen & Unwin; New York, Macmillan, 1958
A general study of the famous philosopher and scientist (980-1037).

ARBERRY, Arthur John. *Revelation and reason in Islam.* London, Allen & Unwin; New York, Macmillan, 1957 (and repr.)
A review of the attempts made over the centuries by Muslim theologians, philosophers, and mystics to establish the relationship between revelation and reason.

AVERROES. *Averroes on the harmony of religion and philosophy: a translation ... of Ibn Rushd's Kitāb faṣl al-maqāl.* By George F. Hourani. London, Luzac, 1961 (E. J. W. Gibb Memorial series, New series) (Unesco Collection of Great Works — Arabic Series)

A classic 12th century treatise dealing with the conflict between religion and philosophy. Important introduction by the translator.

AVERROES. *Traité décisif,* Façl el-maqâl, *sur l'accord de la religion et de la philosophie, suivi de l'appendice,* Dhamîma. Tr. L. Gauthier. Alger, Carbonel, 1948
   See preceding note.

AVICENNA. *Avicenna on theology.* Tr. A. J. Arberry. London, Murray; New York, Grove, 1951
   Passages chosen from the great 11th century philosopher-scientist's work.

AVICENNA. *Le livre des directives et remarques* (Kitāb al-Išārāt wa 'l-tanbīhāt). Tr. A. M. Goichon. Beyrouth, Commission Internationale pour la Traduction des Chefs d'Oeuvre; Paris, Vrin, 1951 (Collection Unesco d'Oeuvres Représentatives – Série Arabe)
   One of his major philosophical works, translated by a distinguished specialist.

BOER, Tjitze J. de. *The history of philosophy in Islam.* Tr. E. R. Jones. London, New York, Dover, 1967; Mystic, Conn., Verry, 1967 P (repr. of 1903 ed.)
   The major mediaeval systems are described.

*CORBIN, Henry. *Histoire de la philosophie islamique.* Paris, Gallimard, 1964- (Collection Idées)
   Tome 1: *Des origines jusqu'à la mort d'Averroes (1198).* Two further volumes of this masterly work will deal with the later period.

DONALDSON, Dwight M. *Studies in Muslim ethics.* London, S.P.C.K.; Napierville, Ill., Allenson, 1953
   Useful.

GARDET, Louis. *Introduction à la théologie musulmane.* Par Louis Gardet et G.-C. Anawati. Paris, Vrin, 1948 (Collection Études de Philosophie Mediévale)
   An important work, but rather technical.

GAUTHIER, Léon. *Ibn Rochd (Averroès).* Paris, Presses Universitaires de France, 1948 (Collection Les Grands Philosophies)
   A scholarly study of the famous philosopher (d. 1198).

al-GHAZZĀLĪ. *The faith and practice of al-Ghazālī.* Tr. W. Montgomery Watt. London, Allen & Unwin; New York, Macmillan, 1953 (and repr.)
   The spiritual autobiography (entitled "Deliverance from errors") of perhaps the major Islamic religious personality of mediaeval times (d. 1111).

al-GHAZZĀLĪ. *al-Munqiḏ min aḏlāl: Erreur et délivrance.* Texte arabe et traduction française avec introduction par Farid Jabre. Beyrouth, Commission Internationale pour la Traduction des Chefs-d'Oeuvre, 1959 P (Collection Unesco d'Oeuvres Représentatives — Série Arabe)
See preceding note.

al-GHAZZĀLĪ. *Lettre au disciple (Ayyuhā l-walad)* [Par] al-Ġazzālī. Traduction française par Toufic Sabbagh. 2ᵉ éd. Beyrouth, Commission Internationale pour la Traduction des Chefs-d'Oeuvre, 1959 P (Collection Unesco d'Oeuvres Représentatives — Série Arabe)
On the essential meaning of religion in the life of the individual, by the great Islamic thinker.

GIBB, Hamilton Arthur Rosskeen. *La structure de la pensée religieuse de l'Islam.* Traduit de l'anglais par Jeanne et Félix Arin. Paris, Larose, 1950 (Institut des Hautes Études Marocaines, Collection Notes et Documents)

GOICHON, Amélie-Marie. *La philosophie d'Avicenne et son influence en Europe.* 2ᵉ éd. Paris, A.-Maisonneuve, 1951 P
Particularly illuminating in tracing Avicenna's influence on European philosophers.

GOLDZIHER, Ignaz. *Le dogme et la loi de l'Islam.* Repr. Paris, Geuthner, 1958
A basic work.

LERNER, Ralph. *Medieval political philosophy: a sourcebook.* Ed. Ralph Lerner and Muhsin Mahdi. Toronto, Collier-Macmillan; New York, Free Press of Glencoe, [1963]
Contains a serviceable selection of texts translated from leading mediaeval Muslim and Jewish philosophers of the Middle East.

MAHDI, Muhsin. *Ibn Khaldūn's philosophy of history: a study in the philosophic foundation of the science of culture.* London, Allen & Unwin, 1957; Chicago, University of Chicago Press, 1964 P (Phoenix Books)
On the work of the outstanding Arab philosopher of history (14th century).

*MOSES BEN MAIMON. *The guide of the perplexed* [by] Maimonides. An abridged edition with introduction and commentary by Julius Guttmann. Translated from the Arabic by Chaim Rabin. London, East and West Library, 1952 (Philosophia Judaica series)
A selection addressed to the layman. Good introduction on the major Jewish scholar of the mediaeval Islamic world (1135-1204).

MOSES BEN MAIMON. *The guide of the perplexed.* [By] Moses Maimonides. Translated with an introduction by Shlomo Pines. With an introductory essay by Leo Strauss. Chicago, University of Chicago Press, 1963 (and repr.)

An outstanding new translation of a great Jewish-Arabic philosophical classic of the Middle Ages. The two excellent introductions link it with mediaeval Islamic philosophy and theology.

MOSES BEN MAIMON. *Le guide des égarés.* Traité de théologie et de philosophie, par Moïse ben Maimon. Traduit et accompagné de notes par S. Munk. 3 vols. Paris, Besson, 1960 (repr. of 1856-1866 ed.)
The classic French translation, less accurate than that of Pines (above).

NASR, Seyyed Hossein. *Ideals and realities of Islām.* London, Allen & Unwin, 1966; New York, Praeger, 1967
Six valuable lectures, which look at basic Islamic attitudes and doctrines from a mystical and philosophical angle.

NASR, Seyyed Hossein. *Three Muslim sages: Avicenna, Suhrawardī, Ibn 'Arabī.* Cambridge, Mass., Harvard University Press, 1964 (Harvard Studies in World Religions)
An outstanding study of three major figures of mediaeval Islamic philosophy and mysticism, viewed in their historical context.

QUADRI, Goffredo. *La philosophie arabe dans l'Europe médiévale,* des origines à Averroès. Traduit de l'italien par Roland Huret. 2ᵉ éd. Paris, Payot, 1960 P (Collection Bibliothèque Scientifique)
A standard work, with particular emphasis on Averroes.

ROSENTHAL, Erwin Isak Jakob. *Political thought in medieval Islam: an introductory outline.* Cambridge, New York, Cambridge University Press, 1958; 1962 P
A good systematic introduction to the views of leading mediaeval thinkers on the relationship of politics, philosophy, law, and government.

ROTH, Leon. *The guide for the perplexed: Moses Maimonides.* London, New York, Hutchinson's University Library, 1948
A popular account of the life, work, and influence of Maimonides.

SA'ADIAH BEN JOSEPH, Gaon. *The book of beliefs and opinions,* [by] Sa'adiah Gaon. Translated from the Arabic and the Hebrew by Samuel Rosenblatt. New Haven, Yale University Press, 1948 (Yale Judaica series)
A complete translation of the earliest major philosophical-religious classic of the Jewish-Islamic world.

SA'ADIAH BEN JOSEPH, Gaon. *The book of doctrines and beliefs,* by Sa'adiah Gaon. Abridged edition, translated from the Arabic, with an introduction, by Alexander Altmann. Oxford, East and West Library, 1946; New Haven, Yale University Press, 1948 (Philosophia Judaica series)
A useful selection.

*WATT, William Montgomery. *Islamic philosophy and theology*. Edinburgh, Edinburgh University Press; Chicago, Aldine, 1962 (and repr.) (Islamic Surveys series)
>Except for its omission of the Koran from consideration, this is a good, clear survey with excellent annotated bibliographies after each chapter.

WATT, William Montgomery. *Muslim intellectual: a study of al-Ghazzali*. Edinburgh, Edinburgh University Press; Chicago, Aldine, 1963
>An understanding study of perhaps the greatest theologian of mediaeval Islam.

WENSINCK, Arent Jan. *La pensée de Ghazzālī*. Paris, A.-Maisonneuve, 1940 (and repr.)
>A thorough study of Ghazzalī's ideas, especially his mysticism, as expressed in his main writings.

5 MYSTICISM, SUFISM

ANAWATI, Georges C. *Mystique musulmane: aspects et tendances, expériences et techniques*. Par G.-C. Anawati et Louis Gardet. Paris, Vrin, 1961 (Collection Études Musulmanes)
>A standard descriptive analysis, containing specimen passages translated from the writings of Muslim mystics.

*ARBERRY, Arthur John. *Sufism: an account of the mystics of Islam*. London, Allen & Unwin, 1950 (and repr.); New York, Macmillan, 1951 (and repr.) (Ethical and Religious Classics of East and West)
>A good introduction to the subject, illustrated by translated extracts.

*ARBERRY, Arthur John. *Le soufisme: introduction à la mystique de l'Islam*. Tr. J. Gouillard. Paris, Cahiers du Sud, 1952
>See preceding note.

BURCKHARDT, Titus. *Introduction aux doctrines ésotériques de l'Islam*. Alger, Messerschmitt; Lyon, Derain, 1955 (Collection Soufisme)
>An outline of the basic metaphysics, showing unusual insight. Inadequate attention is given to the methods and cosmology of the numerous Sufi (mystical) orders.

BURCKHARDT, Titus. *An introduction to Sufi doctrine*. Tr. D. M. Matheson. Lahore, Ashraf, 1959
>A translation of the preceding work.

IBN 'ARABĪ. *La sagesse des prophètes (Fuçuç al-Hikam)*. Traduction et notes par Titus Burckhardt. Paris, Albin Michel, 1955

Part of a work by a major mystic (1165-1240) who preached the doctrine of the "Unity of Existence," a kind of pantheistic monism.

KHAWAM, René (ed. & tr.) *Propos d'amour des mystiques musulmans.* Choisis, présentés et traduits de l'arabe. Paris, Orante, 1960
  Short selections from writings of early mystics.

MOLÉ, Marijan. *Les mystiques musulmans.* Paris, Presses Universitaires de France, 1965 (Collection Mythes et Religions)
  Not a history, but a brief general survey of Sufism, with quotations from several representative mystical works.

*NICHOLSON, Reynold A. *The mystics of Islam.* London, Routledge, 1963 (reprint of 1914 ed.); Chester Springs, Pa., Dufour, 1965; Beirut, Khayat, 1966
  A very good brief introduction with translations of sample passages from Islamic mystics.

NICHOLSON, Reynold A. *Studies in Islamic mysticism.* Cambridge, Cambridge University Press, 1921; repr. London, Cambridge University Press, 1967
  A valuable work, more advanced than the book above.

RICE, Cyprian. *The Persian Ṣūfis.* London, Allen & Unwin, 1964
  A brief study of mediaeval Persian mysticism by a Catholic theologian.

6 ISLAMIC MODERNISM,
  MODERN ISLAMIC THOUGHT

'ABDUH, Muḥammad. *The theology of Unity.* Translated from the Arabic by Kenneth Cragg and Isḥāq Musa'ad. London, Allen & Unwin, 1966
  This basic work of modern Islamic apologetics was first published in 1897 and has since been reprinted 18 times in Arabic.

*AHMAD, Aziz. *Islamic modernism in India and Pakistan, 1857-1964.* London, Toronto, New York, Oxford University Press, 1967
  The development of both modernist and conservative religio-political thought in the Islam of the subcontinent, and a comparison with Islamic modernism in other lands. The most balanced work of its kind.

ALI, Syed Ameer. *The spirit of Islam: a history of the evolution and ideals of Islam, with a life of the Prophet.* London, Methuen, 1965 P (repr. of 1922 ed.)
  A notable apologia by a modernist of his period.

BENNABI, Malek. *La vocation de l'Islam.* Paris, Seuil, 1964
  A thoughtful book on Islam in the modern world by an Algerian Muslim modernist.

GIBB, Hamilton Arthur Rosskeen. *Modern trends in Islam.* Chicago, University of Chicago Press, 1947 (and repr.)
A lucid presentation of the effects of modern western ideas on Islamic orthodoxy.

GIBB, Hamilton Arthur Rosskeen. *Les tendences modernes d'Islam.* Tr. B. Vernier. Paris, G.-P. Maisonneuve, 1949 (Collection Islam d'Hier et d'Aujourd'hui)
See preceding note.

GÖKALP, Ziya. *Turkish nationalism and western civilization: selected essays.* Translated and edited with an introduction by Niyazi Berkes. London, Allen & Unwin; New York, Columbia University Press, 1959
The blend of Turkish nationalist, Islamic, and western ideas on which the Turkish Republic was founded, as formulated by its "spiritual father."

*HOURANI, Albert. *Arabic thought in the liberal age, 1798-1939.* London, Toronto, New York, Oxford University Press (for the Royal Institute of International Affairs), 1962; 1970 P
A perceptive study of Arab intellectual history under the influence of English and French liberal thought. Fine literary style.

IQBĀL, Muḥammad. *The reconstruction of religious thought in Islam.* London, Oxford University Press, 1934; repr. London, Luzac, 1958; Lahore, Ashraf, 1962
Sir Muḥammad Iqbāl (1876-1938) was a spiritual father of Pakistan. His ideas and his interpretation of Islam permeate his poetical works in Persian and Urdu, but are more systematically developed in this work, which greatly influenced his Muslim contemporaries and successors.

IQBĀL, Muḥammad. *Reconstruire la pensée religieuse de l'Islam.* Traduction et notes d'E. Meyerovitch. Paris, A.-Maisonneuve, 1955
See preceding note.

JOMIER, Jacques. *Introduction à l'Islam actuel.* Paris, Editions du Cerf, 1964
A balanced picture.

LAHBABI, Mohammed Aziz. *Le personnalisme musulman.* Paris, Presses Universitaires de France, 1964 (Collection Initiation Philosophique)
"Discussion de la definition et condition de la personne selon le Coran et les traditions du Prophète Muhammad."

MAUDŪDĪ, Abul A'lā. *Towards understanding Islam.* Tr. & ed. Khurshid Ahmad. [6th ed.] Lahore, Islamic Publications, 1960 (and repr.)
A leading Pakistani theologian's outline of the beliefs of Islam and its rational bases.

MORGAN, Kenneth William (ed.) *Islam – the straight path: Islam interpreted by Muslims.* New York, Ronald, 1958
Eleven contemporary Muslim scholars each contribute a chapter on an aspect of Islamic religion, thought, and culture. Not free of apologetics.

PROCTOR, J. Harris (ed.) *Islam and international relations.* New York, Praeger, 1965
Eight papers by specialists examining the relationship between Islam and modern international politics.

RISLER, Jacques C. *L'Islam moderne.* Paris, Payot, 1963 P (Collection Petit Bibliothèque Payot)
A fair outline of the present situation of Islam, with chapters on Islam in the two world wars, North Africa and France, the influence of petroleum politics, and current trends.

*RONDOT, Pierre. *L'Islam et les Musulmans d'aujourd'hui.* 2e éd. 2 vols. Paris, Orante, 1965
Tome 1: *La Communauté musulmane: ses bases, son état présent, son évolution;* Tome 2: *De Dakar à Djakarta: l'Islam en devenir.* An excellent detailed survey of the development of Islamic doctrines and institutions, with particular emphasis on modern developments in various parts of the Islamic world. Very good bibliographies of works in French for further reading.

ROSENTHAL, Erwin Isak Jakob. *Islam in the modern national state.* Cambridge, Cambridge University Press, 1965
A thoughtful study, with special reference to Pakistan and India, Malaya, Iran, Turkey, Tunisia, and Morocco; preceded by a survey of classic Islamic political thought and practice.

SMITH, Wilfred Cantwell. *Islam in modern history.* Princeton, Princeton University Press, 1957; New York, New American Library, 1959 P (and repr.) (Mentor Books)
This interesting work is notable for its penetrating analysis of the modern Islamic world in the light of its history, and especially for its examination of Indian Islam.

SMITH, Wilfred Cantwell. *L'Islam dans le monde moderne.* Préface et traduction de A. Guimbretière. Paris, Payot, 1962 P (Collection Bibliothèque Historique)
See preceding note.

TITUS, Murray Thurston. *Islam in India and Pakistan: a religious history of Islam in India and Pakistan.* [2nd ed.] Calcutta, Y.M.C.A., 1959
A balanced survey, including chapters on modern movements in Islam and "the new Muslim apologetic and polemic."

VON GRUNEBAUM, Gustave E. *Modern Islam: the search for cultural identity*. Berkeley, University of California Press, 1962; New York, Vintage, 1964 P [slightly revised]

Eleven notable essays on the intellectual and psychological problems of Islam in the modern world.

G ARTS AND CRAFTS, ARCHITECTURE, AND SCIENCE

1 GENERAL WORKS

AKURGAL, Ekrem. *Treasures of Turkey*. The earliest civilizations of Anatolia
by E. Akurgal; Byzantium, by C. Mango; the Islamic period, by R. Ettinghaus-
en. Geneva, Skira; Cleveland, World, 1966
    A sumptuously illustrated volume, with text by experts.

AKURGAL, Ekrem. *Les trésors de Turquie*. L'Anatolie des premiers empires,
par E. Akurgal; Byzance, par C. Mango; Les siècles de l'Islam, par R. Ettinghausen. Genève, Skira, 1966 (Collection Les Trésors du Monde)
    See preceding note.

DIMAND, Maurice S. *A handbook of Muhammadan art*. 3rd ed. New York,
Metropolitan Museum of Art, 1958
    A standard general review of all fields – pedestrian in style, but helpful.

*GODARD, André. *L'art de l'Iran*. Paris, Arthaud, 1962 (Collection Art et Pay-
sages)
    An excellent survey from the earliest times up to and including the Islamic
    period. Especially strong on architecture. Profusely illustrated.

*GODARD, André. *The art of Iran*. Tr. Michael Heron; ed. Michael Rogers. London, Allen & Unwin; New York, Praeger, 1965
    See preceding note.

*GRUBE, Ernst J. *The world of Islam*. New York, Toronto, McGraw-Hill; London, Hamlyn, 1967 (Landmarks of the World's Art series)
    An informative survey of Islamic art in its broad sense. Contains 200 excel-
    lent illustrations (half of them in colour). The best general book of its type
    in its price range.

*KÜHNEL, Ernst. *Islamic art and architecture*. Tr. Katherine Watson. London,
Bell; Ithaca, Cornell University Press, 1966
    A good manual, covering Islamic art from its beginning to the present day
    Particularly useful on applied arts and crafts. Excellent illustrations.

*KÜHNEL, Ernst. *Minor arts of Islam*. Tr. Katherine Watson. London, Bell;
Ithaca, Cornell University Press, 1970
    A comparatively short yet masterly conspectus of Islamic art in all its main
    centres from North Africa to India. "Minor arts" include the book arts
    (calligraphy and miniatures in manuscripts, bookbinding), ceramics, metal-
    work, glass, and carving in ivory, wood, and stone. Over 200 fine illustra-
    tions, some in colour.

LUKENS, Marie G. *Islamic art.* New York, Metropolitan Museum of Art, 1965 (The Metropolitan Museum of Art, Guide to the Collection)
> A brief but informative review of the whole field, with illustrations from the museum's rich collections.

MARÇAIS, Georges. *L'art musulman.* Paris, Presses Universitaires de France, 1962 P (Collection Les Neuf Muses)
> A useful, though over-compressed, general survey with 40 good illustrations.

MARÇAIS, Georges. *L'art de l'Islam.* Paris, Larousse, 1946 P (Collection Arts, Styles et Techniques)
> An excellent short survey, with special emphasis on architecture.

*OTTO-DORN, Katherina. *L'art de l'Islam.* Paris, Albin Michel, 1967 (Collection L'Art dans le Monde)
> A sound general historical outline, well illustrated in colour.

RICE, David Talbot. *Islamic art.* London, Thames & Hudson; New York, Praeger, 1965 C&P (World of Art series)
> Numerous excellent illustrations (many in colour) make this fairly inexpensive book worth buying; unfortunately the text is rather unreliable.

RICE, David Talbot. *L'art de l'Islam.* Paris, Larousse, 1967 C&P (Collection Le Monde de l'Art)
> See preceding note.

TAMUZ, Benjamin. *Art in Israel.* Ed. B. Tamuz and Max Wykes-Joyce. Painting: Yona Fisher. Sculpture: Mira Friedman. Architecture: Aviah Hashimshony. Crafts and design: John Cheney. Jerusalem, Massada, 1965; New York, International Publications Service, 1966; Philadelphia, Chilton, 1967
> Well-illustrated survey of all aspects of recent art and architecture in Israel.

2 PAINTING, MINIATURES, AND BOOK ARTS

*ARNOLD, Thomas W. *Painting in Islam: a study of the place of pictorial art in Muslim culture.* With a new introduction by B. W. Robinson. New York, Dover; Toronto, General, 1965 P (repr. of 1928 ed. of Clarendon Press, Oxford, with new introduction)
> Not a history of Islamic art, but an absorbing study of the position of painting in the social and religious context of Islamic civilization.

BARRETT, Douglas. *Persian painting of the fourteenth century.* London, Faber, 1952 P
> A few well-chosen miniatures.

ESIN, Emel. *Turkish miniature painting.* Rutland, Vt., Tuttle, 1960
> Some large colour plates, with notes and a short introduction for the layman.

*ETTINGHAUSEN, Richard. *Arab painting.* Geneva, Skira; Cleveland, World, 1962 (Treasures of Painting series)
> Outstanding text and illustrations covering the 7th to 14th centuries.

*ETTINGHAUSEN, Richard. *La peinture arabe.* Tr. Yves Rivière. Genève, Skira, 1962 (Collection Les Trésors de l'Asie)
> See preceding note.

ETTINGHAUSEN, Richard (ed.) *Turkey: ancient miniatures.* Preface [by] Richard Ettinghausen. Introduction [by] M. Ş. İpşiroğlu and S. Eyuboğlu. New York, New York Graphic Society by arrangement with Unesco, 1961 (Unesco World Art series)
> Thirty-two magnificent large colour plates of miniatures from several Turkish manuscripts dating from the 13th to the 18th centuries, with a short though useful general preface.

*ETTINGHAUSEN, Richard (ed.) *Turkish miniatures, from the thirteenth to the eighteenth century.* Introduction by Richard Ettinghausen. New York, Toronto, New American Library; London, Collins, 1965 P (Mentor-Unesco Art Books) (Fontana-Unesco Art Books)
> An inexpensive paperback containing 28 well-chosen miniatures reproduced from Turkish manuscripts, preceded by a useful 20-page introduction. A paperback bargain.

*ETTINGHAUSEN, Richard (ed.) *Miniatures turques.* Paris, Flammarion, 1965 P (Collection Le Grand Art en Edition de Poche; Collection Unesco)
> See preceding note.

FONDAZIONE "GIORGIO CINI," Venice. Centro di Cultura e Civiltà. Istituto Venezia e l'Oriente. *Muslim miniature paintings from the XIII to XIX century from collections in the United States and Canada.* Catalogue of the exhibition, by Ernst J. Grube. Venezia, Pozza, 1962
> This exhibition catalogue containing mainly black and white reproductions of 125 miniatures (several in colour) gives some idea of the outstanding examples to be found in North American collections. A half page or more of description accompanies each picture.

GRAY, Basil. *Persian miniatures from ancient manuscripts.* New York, New American Library; London, Fontana, 1962 P (Mentor-Unesco Art Books) (Fontana-Unesco Art Books)
> An attractive inexpensive pocketbook introducing Persian miniature painting. Twenty-eight colour plates of the 15th and 16th centuries with brief analysis and commentary on each plate.

GRAY, Basil. *Miniatures persanes.* Paris, Flammarion, 1962 P (Collection Le Grand Art en Livres de Poche; Collection Unesco)
> See preceding note.

*GRAY, Basil. *Persian painting.* Geneva, Skira; Cleveland, World, 1961
(Treasures of Asia series)
>An excellent choice of colour plates of miniatures covering the 13th to
>17th centuries, with good text.

*GRAY, Basil. *La peinture persane.* Tr. Yves Rivière. Genève, Skira, 1961 (Collection Les Trésors de l'Asie)
>See preceding note.

MEREDITH-OWENS, G. M. *Persian illustrated manuscripts.* London, British
Museum, 1965 P
>A helpful short introduction to Persian miniature painting, with a description of Persian artistic conventions. The 24 illustrations are from outstanding manuscripts in the British Museum.

MEREDITH-OWENS, G. M. *Turkish miniatures.* London, British Museum, 1963 P
>A useful brief historical survey of Turkish miniature painting, illustrated by 25 examples from the British Museum collection.

OXFORD, Bodleian Library. *Mughal miniatures of the earlier period.* Oxford,
Bodleian Library, 1953 P (Bodleian Picture Book series)
>Twenty-four black and white reproductions of miniatures from the period around 1600, with short introduction and notes.

ROBINSON, Basil William. *Persian drawings from the 14th through the 19th
century.* New York, Shorewood, 1965 (Drawings of the Masters series)
>Reproductions of 96 good miniature paintings (some in colour), with an elementary general introduction on styles, schools, and techniques, and individual descriptions of the miniatures shown.

ROBINSON, Basil William. *Persian paintings.* 2nd ed. London, Her Majesty's
Stationery Office [for Victoria and Albert Museum], 1965 P
>A booklet of 36 well-chosen miniatures from British and Irish collections by noted Persian artists, 15th to 18th centuries. Reproduction in black and white only, but good value at a very low price. Brief explanatory notes to each picture.

STCHOUKINE, Ivan. *Les peintures des manuscripts safavis de 1502 a 1587.*
Paris, Geuthner, 1959 (Institut Français d'Archéologie de Beyrouth)
>A thorough study of a great period in Persian art, with 88 plates (none in colour unfortunately).

SUGANA, Gabriele Mandel. *The life and times of Mohammed.* London, New
York, Toronto, Hamlyn, 1968 (Portraits of Greatness series)
>Beautiful colour illustrations, largely from Islamic miniature paintings of the last few hundred years. No comments on the paintings as art; the text concerning Muhammad's life is somewhat banal.

WILKINSON, James Vere Stewart. *Mughal painting*. London, Faber, 1948 (and repr.)

Ten excellent Mughal paintings of the 16th and 17th centuries with a sketchy introduction to Mughal painting in the 16th to 19th centuries.

3 ARCHITECTURE

BLUNT, Wilfrid. *Ispahan, pearl of Persia*. Photographs by Wim Swaan. London, Elek; Toronto, Ryerson; New York, Stein & Day, 1966

An excellently illustrated architectural history of a beautiful city.

BLUNT, Wilfrid. *Ispahan, perle de la Perse*. Tr. R. Latour. Paris, Albin Michel, 1967 (Collection Cités d'Art)

See preceding note.

CRESWELL, Keppel Archibald Cameron. *A short account of early Muslim architecture*. Harmondsworth, Baltimore, Penguin, 1958 P

An important standard work, somewhat technical, covering the first two centuries of Islamic architecture. Many photographs.

HILL, Derek. *Islamic architecture and its decoration, A.D. 800-1500*. A photographic survey by Derek Hill, with an introductory text by Oleg Grabar. 2nd ed. London, Faber; Chicago, University of Chicago Press, 1967

Over 500 photographs of Islamic architectural masterpieces in Soviet Central Asia, Afghanistan, Iran, and Turkey, with an informative general introduction.

HOAG, John D. *Western Islamic architecture*. New York, Braziller, 1963 C&P (The Great Ages of World Architecture series)

Covers the Islamic world from Mesopotamia to Spain, including Turkey, and Arabia. Text not always reliable but many good illustrations.

HRBAS, Miloš. *The art of Central Asia*. [By] Miloš Hrbas [and] Edgar Knobloch. London, Hamlyn, 1965

Mainly fine mediaeval Islamic architecture, much of it now falling into ruin.

MARÇAIS, Georges. *L'architecture musulmane d'Occident: Tunisie, Algérie, Maroc, Espagne, Sicilie*. Paris, Arts et Métiers graphiques, 1954

A good work.

POPE, Arthur Upham. *Persian architecture: the triumph of form and color*. New York, Braziller; London, Thames & Hudson, 1965

Architecture examined and discussed as a "fine" art. Excellent illustrations, many in colour, and good text.

RICE, David Talbot. *Constantinople, Byzantium, Istanbul.* Photographs by Wim Swaan. London, Elek; Toronto, Ryerson, 1965
A historical review of the notable architectural monuments of a wonderful city. Beautiful photographs.

RICE, David Talbot. *Constantinople, Byzance, Istanbul.* Tr. R. Latour. Paris, Albin Michel, 1966
See preceding note.

TERRASSE, Henri. *L'Espagne du Moyen âge: civilisations et arts.* Paris, Fayard, 1966
A good work, largely devoted to Muslim architecture.

ÜNSAL, Behçet. *Turkish Islamic architecture in Seljuk and Ottoman times, 1071-1923.* London, Tiranti, 1959
A brief but informative short outline of all the main types of building. Text cross-refers to the numerous illustrations.

*VOGT-GÖKNIL, Ulya. *Ottoman architecture.* Photographs by Edward Widmer. London, Oldbourne, 1966 (Living Architecture series)
A good general introduction to public architecture, with splendid illustrations. Inadequate treatment of domestic architecture.

*VOGT-GÖKNIL, Ulya. *Turquie ottomane.* Photos par Edward Widmer. [Tr. Marie-Claire Thiebaud.] Fribourg, Office du Livre, 1965 (Collection Architecture Universelle)
See preceding note.

WILBER, Donald Newton. *The architecture of Islamic Iran: the Ilkhanid period.* Princeton, Princeton University Press, 1955

4 CERAMICS, METALWORK,
AND MOSAICS

AVI-YONAH, Michael. *Israel: ancient mosaics.* Introduction by M. Avi-Yonah. Greenwich, Conn., New York Graphic Society, 1960 (Unesco World Art series)
Fine large reproductions.

AVI-YONAH, Michael. *Israël: mosaiques anciennes.* Introduction par M. Avi-Yonah. Greenwich, Conn., New York Graphic Society; Paris, Braun, 1960 (Collection Unesco de l'Art Mondial)
See preceding note.

BARRETT, Douglas. *Islamic metalwork in the British Museum.* London, British Museum, 1949 P

An excellent short introduction, with illustrations from the museum's treasures.

LANE, Arthur. *Early Islamic pottery: Mesopotamia, Egypt and Persia.* 5th ed. London, Faber, 1965
The best work of its type, well illustrated.

LANE, Arthur. *Later Islamic pottery: Persia, Syria, Egypt, Turkey.* London, Faber, 1957
An important standard work, with numerous plates.

5 CARPETS

*BODE, Wilhelm von. *Antique rugs from the Near East.* 4th ed. By W. von Bode and E. Kühnel. Tr. Charles Grant Ellis. Braunschweig, Klinkhardt & Biermann, 1958
A reliable standard work, treating each class of carpet monographically.

EDWARDS, Arthur Cecil. *The Persian carpet.* London, Duckworth, 1953 and 1960
A standard work.

*ERDMANN, Kurt. *Oriental carpets: an essay on their history.* Tr. Charles Grant Ellis. 2nd ed. New York, Universe, 1962
Basic information on the history and development of the oriental carpet, mainly Islamic. Interesting introductory chapter on the Oriental rug in western culture.

LIEBETRAU, Preben. *Oriental rugs in colour.* [Translated from the Danish by Katherine John.] New York, London, Galt, Ont., Macmillan, 1963
A useful little book describing in simple terms the basic techniques and main types, with 65 colour plates and numerous diagrams.

*ROPERS, Heinrich. *Les tapis d'Orient: manuel pour amateurs et collection-neurs.* Tr. Simone Wallon d'après la 7. éd. allemande, entièrement refondue par R. Dieke. Paris, Presses Universitaires de France, 1958
A standard work.

TURKHAN, Kudret H. *Islamic rugs.* Ed. Lynne Thornton. London, Barker, 1968 (Collectors' Handbook series)
A very handy short book, consisting of a general historical introduction and description of carpet making, followed by brief paragraphs on the main types. Well illustrated.

6 OTHER ARTS AND CRAFTS

FARMER, Henry George. *A history of Arabian music to the XIIIth century.* London, Luzac, 1929, repr. 1967; Mystic, Conn., Verry, 1967
A detailed standard work.

KHAYAT, Marie Karam. *Food from the Arab world.* By Marie Karam Khayat and Margaret Clarke Keatinge. Beirut, Khayat, 1959
A handy book for the greedy; recipes for 140 traditional dishes.

LANDAU, Jacob M. *Studies in the Arab theater and cinema.* Philadelphia, University of Pennsylvania Press, 1958
An important work, consisting of (1) historical background, including such precursors as the shadow play, (2) theatre, (3) cinema. Valuable bibliography. The 1965 French translation (below) is partially revised.

LANDAU, Jacob M. *Études sur le théâtre et le cinéma arabes.* Tr. Francine Le Cleac'h. Paris, G.-P. Maisonneuve, 1965
See preceding note.

WILBER, Donald Newton. *Persian gardens and garden pavilions.* Rutland, Vt., Tuttle, 1962
A historical survey of a characteristic and highly developed Persian cultural feature, with numerous illustrations.

7 SCIENCE AND MEDICINE

BROWNE, Edward Granville. *Arabian medicine.* Cambridge, Cambridge University Press, 1963 [repr. of 1921 ed.]
An outline history of Islamic medicine (called "Arabian" in Europe because the traditional Islamic medical literature was written in Arabic). The author was a physician turned orientalist.

BROWNE, Edward Granville. *La médecine arabe.* Édition française, mise à jour et annotée par H. P. J. Renaud. Paris, Larose, 1933
See preceding note.

ELGOOD, Cyril. *A medical history of Persia and the Eastern Caliphate.* London, New York, Cambridge University Press, 1951
Islamic medicine to the recent past.

MIELI, Aldo. *La science arabe et son rôle dans l'évolution scientifique mondiale.* Réimpression de la première édition de 1938. Augmentée d'une bibliographie par A. Mazahéri. Leiden, Brill, 1966
The best study available, though inadequate. Covers the 8th to 13th centuries.

H THE ISLAMIC WORLD IN MODERN TIMES†

1 GENERAL WORKS

ABBOUCHI, W. F. *Political systems of the Middle East in the 20th century.*
New York, Dodd Mead; Toronto, Burns and MacEachern, 1970
A dispassionate balanced country-by-country survey of the historical
background, constitutional development, ideological traditions, political
set-up, and basic social and economic factors of the following lands:
Turkey, Iran, Egypt, Iraq, Israel, Jordan, Lebanon, and Syria.

BINDER, Leonard. *The ideological revolution in the Middle East.* New York,
Wiley, 1964
An original and very penetrating study, by a political scientist, of the intel-
lectual bases of Near Eastern nationalisms, with particular emphasis on
Arab nationalism and Egypt.

FERNAU, Friedrich Wilhelm. *Le réveil du monde musulman.* Traduit de l'allemand par Guy Robert Adoue. Paris, Seuil, [1953] (Collection Esprit "Frontière Ouverte")
A balanced journalistic survey of the recent past, now slightly outdated.

HALPERN, Manfred. *The politics of social change in the Middle East and North
Africa.* Princeton, Princeton University Press; Toronto, Saunders, 1963; 1965 P
A good discussion of many aspects of modernization in the Muslim lands.

KARPAT, Kemal H. (ed.) *Political and social thought in the contemporary
Middle East.* New York, Praeger, 1968
An interesting and enlightening collection of recent writing on the area, as
seen from the inside by local writers. The greater part of the book is devoted to the Arab countries, with shorter sections on Turkey and Iran; Israel is not covered.

LENCZOWSKI, George. *The Middle East in world affairs.* 3rd ed. Ithaca, Cornell University Press, 1962
A good survey of international politics from 1914 onwards.

LERNER, Daniel. *The passing of traditional society: modernizing the Middle East.*
Toronto, Collier-Macmillan; New York, Free Press of Glencoe, 1958; 1964 P

†Those who wish to read further about the history of specific areas and periods may find
it useful to consult a "model syllabus," edited by J. Jankowski, for university courses in
Middle Eastern history since the beginning of the 19th century (*Middle East Studies
Association Bulletin,* New York, vol. 4, no. 2, May 1970, pp. 20-32). This includes a good
bibliography (pp. 26-32), consisting of books recommended for, and keyed to, the large
number of courses listed in the "model syllabus."

An excellently written valuable country-by-country sociological survey of rapid change in the region.

MEINERTZHAGEN, Richard. *Middle East diary, 1917-1956.* London, Cresset, 1959
Selections from the diary of a British soldier and civil servant, who views the political and other developments in Palestine, Israel, and elsewhere from a distinctive angle.

MONROE, Elizabeth. *Britain's moment in the Middle East, 1914-1956.* London, Chatto; Toronto, Methuen; Baltimore, Johns Hopkins Press, 1963 P
An interesting attempt to study the nature of Britain's power in the Middle East, to account for its achievements and explain away its failures.

NOLTE, Richard H. (ed.) *The modern Middle East.* New York, Atherton Press; London, Prentice-Hall, 1963
Distinguished essays on the social, political, and economic problems which have resulted from the meeting of East and West in the Middle East.

*PERETZ, Don. *The Middle East today.* New York, Toronto, London, Holt, 1963
An informative general work on "the basic political and social forces that shape its contemporary image," in general and then country by country.

RIVLIN, Benjamin (ed.) *The contemporary Middle East: tradition and innovation.* Edited with an introduction and notes by Benjamin Rivlin and Joseph S. Szyliowicz. New York, Toronto, Random House, 1965 C&P
A good, large anthology of some fifty articles on the theme of culture, social and political change, by a variety of oriental and western specialists.

RONDOT, Pierre. *Destin du Proche-Orient.* Paris, Editions du Centurion, 1959 P
A study of the basic political changes which took place in the region between 1919 and 1958, by a French soldier and administrator.

RONDOT, Pierre. *The changing patterns of the Middle East.* [Tr. Mary Dilke.] London, Chatto; New York, Praeger, 1961 P
See preceding note.

RONDOT, Pierre. *Les Chrétiens d'Orient.* Paris, Peyronnet, 1955
Valuable information about the historic Christian communities of the Middle East, most of whom have for centuries been minorities in a predominantly Muslim world.

ROUX, Jean-Paul. *L'Islam en Asie.* Paris, Payot, 1958 P (Collection Bibliothèque Historique)

An examination of Islam in the non-Arab lands of Asia, explaining its situation in the modern world. The subtitles convey the scope of the book: sa propagation; les états musulmans d'Asie; la laïcisation; la patrie musulmane; l'anticolonialisme; la tentation du communisme; l'Islam minoritaire.

SHARABI, Hisham B. *Government and politics of the Middle East in the twentieth century.* Princeton, Toronto, London, Van Nostrand, 1962 (and repr.)
A very useful summary, country by country, until about 1960.

SHILOH, Ailon (ed.) *Peoples and cultures of the Middle East.* New York, Toronto, Random House, 1969
The "behavioral processes" of the different peoples of the area are revealed in these excellently chosen extracts, mainly from standard works by well-known writers.

STEVENS, Georgiana G. (ed.) *The United States and the Middle East.* Englewood Cliffs, N.J., Prentice-Hall (for the American Assembly, Columbia University), 1964 C&P
Six helpful papers on the modern Middle East, covering: (1) background — peoples and nationalisms; (2) social and (3) economic modernization; (4) regional and international politics; (5) the Arab-Israeli conflict; (6) US policy.

TÜTSCH, Hans E. *From Ankara to Marrakesh: Turks and Arabs in a changing world.* London, Allen & Unwin, 1964
An exceptionally understanding analysis of the events of recent years by a very well-informed Swiss journalist.

ZEINE, Zeine N. *The emergence of Arab nationalism, with a background study of Arab-Turkish relations in the Near East.* [2nd ed.] Beirut, Khayat, 1966
An interesting documented account with particular reference to Turkey and Syria-Lebanon.

2 ARAB LANDS

a/General Works

ALEM, Jean-Pierre. *Le Proche-Orient arabe.* 2ᵉ éd. Paris, Presses Universitaires de France, 1964 P (Collection "Que sais-je?")
An elementary outline.

BAER, Gabriel. *Population and society in the Arab East.* Tr. Hanna Szöke. London, Routledge; New York, Praeger, 1964
A valuable study of contemporary society in the Arab world.

BENOIST-MÉCHIN, Jacques Gabriel Paul Michel, baron. *Un printemps arabe.* Paris, Albin Michel, 1959; 1963 P

The record by a sensitive and alert traveller of a journey through seven Arab lands from Egypt to Iraq and through Turkey, meeting with people from all ranks of society.

BERGER, Morroe. *The Arab world today.* New York, Doubleday; London, Weidenfeld, 1962; 1964 P

A good "sociological approach" to contemporary Arab society. Examines "how [the Arabs] live, work ... how what they do makes them what they are."

FLORY, Maurice. *Les régimes politiques des pays arabes.* Paris, Presses Universitaires de France, 1968 P (Collection Thémis, Manuels juridiques, économiques et politiques)

A sound general text, with useful historical introduction and sections on economics as well as politics.

GABRIELI, Francesco. *The Arab revival.* [Translated from the Italian by Lovett F. Edwards.] London, Thames & Hudson; Toronto, Longmans, 1961 (Great Revolutions series)

A level-headed appraisal of the recent past of the Arab world and its present problems.

MORRIS, James. *The Hashemite kings.* London, Faber; New York, Pantheon, 1959

A well-written journalistic biography of the dynasty which produced kings of Arabia, Iraq, and Jordan. Some interpretations are open to question.

THOMPSON, Jack Howell. *Modernization of the Arab world.* Ed. Jack H. Thompson and Robert D. Reischauer. Princeton, Toronto, London, Van Nostrand, 1966 P (New Perspectives in Political Science series)

Well-informed articles by 17 qualified authors on various aspects of modernization. (Reprinted from Columbia University's *Journal of International Affairs.*)

TÜTSCH, Hans E. *Facets of Arab nationalism.* Detroit, Wayne State University Press; Toronto, Ambassador, 1965 (Waynebooks)

A balanced examination for the layman.

b/Lebanon, Jordan, Iraq

ALEM, Jean-Pierre. *Le Liban.* Paris, Presses Universitaires de France, 1963 (Collection "Que sais-je?")

A compressed survey.

FERNEA, Elizabeth Warnock. *Guests of the Sheik: an ethnography of an Iraqi village.* Garden City, N.Y., Doubleday, 1965; 1969 P

The author lived among the veiled ladies of a southern Iraqi village. In this autobiography she gives an interesting (and non-technical) insight into their way of life.

HARRIS, George Lawrence. *Jordan: its people, its society, its culture.* [2nd ed.] New Haven, Human Relations Area Files, 1965 C&P
A factual but dull source of information.

LONGRIGG, Stephen Hemsley. *Iraq.* By Stephen Hemsley Longrigg and Frank Stoakes. London, Benn; New York, Praeger, 1958 (Nations of the Modern World series)
A sound, readable introduction to modern Iraq, now getting slightly out of date.

PATAI, Raphael. *The kingdom of Jordan.* Princeton, Princeton University Press, 1958
A good general book, now needing some revision.

THESIGER, Wilfred. *The marsh Arabs.* London, Longmans, 1964
Life among an unusual group of people living in the marshes at the junction of the Tigris and the Euphrates, described in detail by the veteran explorer.

VERNIER, Bernard. *L'Irak d'aujourd'hui.* Paris, Colin, 1963
The best book available in French.

c/Arabia, Yemen

DEFFARGE, Claude. *Yemen, 62-69: de la révolution "sauvage" à la trève des guerriers.* Par Claude Deffarge et Gordian Troeller. Paris, Laffont, 1969 P
Eyewitness accounts of the upheavals which have wracked this once isolated and still interesting land. Interesting on modern attitudes.

HEWINS, Ralph. *A golden dream: the miracle of Kuwait.* London, W. H. Allen, 1963
A rather sarcastic account of an oil kingdom.

HOLDEN, David. *Farewell to Arabia.* London, Faber, 1966
A readable survey of the various states of the Arabian peninsula in the last few years, by a journalist with a keen eye.

INGRAMS, Harold. *The Yemen: imams, rulers and revolutions.* London, Murray; Toronto, Macmillan, 1963; New York, Praeger, 1964
An interesting and useful account of a little-known country by a British official with long experience in the area. Much first-hand personal material on recent decades.

LITTLE, Tom. *South Arabia: arena of conflict.* London, Pall Mall; New York, Praeger, 1968
A new state on the southwest corner of Arabia, surveyed in the light of its past history by a British journalist.

THESIGER, Wilfred. *Arabian sands.* London, Longmans; New York, Dutton, 1959 (and repr.); Harmondsworth, Penguin, 1964 P
A recent "classic" travel book, by the last of the great travellers in Arabia.

TOMICHE, Fernand-J. *L'Arabie séoudite.* Paris, Presses Universitaires de France, 1962 (Collection "Que sais-je?")
A model of the compression of factual information, but already out of date in some respects.

WENNER, Manfred W. *Modern Yemen, 1918-1966.* Baltimore, Johns Hopkins Press, 1967
A good internal and external political history.

d/Egypt

AYROUT, Henry Habib. *The Egyptian peasant.* Translated from the French by John Alden Williams. Boston, Beacon; Toronto, Saunders, 1963; 1968 P
A readable study of the *fellāhīn,* the real backbone of the populations of the Middle East, by a genuine expert. (A revised English version of the original, *Moeurs et coutumes des Fellahs.* Paris, 1938.)

COLOMBE, Marcel. *L'évolution de l'Egypte, 1924-1950.* Paris, G.-P. Maisonneuve, 1951
A good book.

HARRIS, Christina Phelps. *Nationalism and revolution in Egypt: the role of the Muslim Brotherhood.* The Hague, Mouton (for the Hoover Institution on War, Revolution and Peace), 1964
An important examination of the relationship between Egyptian nationalism and Islamic radicalism.

HOPKINS, Harry S. *Egypt the crucible: the unfinished revolution of the Arab world.* London, Secker, 1969
A well-informed account of the new Egypt and an exposition of the author's views about its key role in the Arab world.

LACOUTURE, Jean. *L'Egypte en mouvement.* Par Jean et Simonne Lacouture. [2ᵉ éd.] Paris, Seuil, 1962
A good account of Egyptian social and political life since Napoleon, with the main emphasis on the period following 1952.

LACOUTURE, Jean. *Egypt in transition.* By Jean and Simonne Lacouture.
[Tr. Francis Scarfe.] London, Methuen, 1958
See preceding note.

LITTLE, Tom. *Modern Egypt.* London, Benn; New York, Praeger, 1967
An examination of Egyptian history and politics, particularly since World
War II and up to the Six Day War (June 1967) between the Arab States
and Israel. The author, a journalist with long experience in the area, treats
his subject from a viewpoint broadly sympathetic to the expressed aspira-
tions of Nasser's Egypt.

MAHFŪẒ, Najīb. *The life of an Egyptian doctor.* By Naguib Mahfouz. London,
Livingstone, 1966
A non-political autobiography which throws much light on Egyptian social
conditions.

TOMICHE, Nada. *L'Égypte moderne.* Paris, Presses Universitaires de France,
1966 P (Collection "Que sais-je?")
A short, handy survey covering 1798 to 1966; good on economic and social history.

e/North Africa

i/General Works

*BARBOUR, Nevill (ed.) *A survey of North West Africa (the Maghrib).* 2nd ed.
London, Toronto, New York, Oxford University Press (for Royal Institute of
International Affairs), 1962
A valuable, essentially factual survey of Morocco, Algeria, Tunisia, and
Libya. Mostly still relevant.

BROWN, Leon Carl (ed.) *State and society in independent North Africa.* Washington, D.C., The Middle East Institute, 1966 (The James Terry Duce Memorial series)
Fifteen papers of varying value (several very good) discussing North Africa
in its present transitional state.

JULIEN, Charles André. *L'Afrique du nord en marche: nationalismes musulmans et souveraineté française.* Paris, Julliard, 1952
Detailed coverage of political development.

LE TOURNEAU, Roger. *Evolution politique de l'Afrique du Nord musulmane,
1920-1961.* Paris, Colin, 1962 P
A sound political history, preceded by a summary of the period before
1920. Useful annotated bibliography.

ii/Libya, Tunisia

BASSET, A. *Initiation à la Tunisie.* Paris, A.-Maisonneuve, 1950
Useful, though becoming dated.

EVANS-PRITCHARD, Edward Evan. *The Sanusi of Cyrenaica.* Oxford, Clarendon; Toronto, New York, Oxford University Press, 1949
A study by a distinguished anthropologist.

KHADDURI, Majid. *Modern Libya: a study in political development.* Baltimore, Johns Hopkins Press, 1963
A competent work.

KNAPP, Wilfrid. *Tunisia.* London, Thames & Hudson; New York, Walker, 1966
(New Nations and Peoples series)
A competent simplified outline of modern Tunisia's development and problems, told in the context of its history.

LING, Dwight L. *Tunisia: from protectorate to republic.* Bloomington, London, Indiana University Press, 1967 (Indiana University International Studies)
A history, mainly political, from the establishment of French rule to 1959; from an "anti-colonialist" viewpoint.

RAYMOND, André. *La Tunisie.* Paris, Presses Universitaires de France, 1961
(Collection "Que sais-je?")
A very brief general outline, mostly dealing with the last half century.

ZÉRAFFA, Michel. *Tunisie.* [2ᵉ éd.] Paris, Seuil, 1963 P (Collection Petite Planète)
An impressionistic picture, short text, effective photographs.

ZÉRAFFA, Michel. *Tunisia.* Tr. R. A. Dean. London, Studio Vista; New York, Viking, 1965 P
See preceding note.

iii/Algeria, Morocco

ALAZARD, Jean. *Initiation à l'Algérie.* Par Jean Alazard [et al.] Paris, A.-Maisonneuve, 1957
Useful, but getting out of date.

BARBOUR, Nevill. *Morocco.* London, Thames & Hudson; New York, Walker, 1965 C&P (New Nations and Peoples series)
An introduction to Morocco's past and present, particularly suitable for non-specialists.

COHEN, Mark I. *Morocco: old land, new nation*. By Mark I. Cohen and Lorna Hahn. New York, Praeger, 1966
A serious work on modern Morocco, largely political and economic, but with some attention to social affairs.

LACOUTURE, Simonne. *Le Maroc à l'épreuve*. Par Simonne et Jean Lacouture. Paris, Seuil, 1958
A good sympathetic account of modern Morocco.

LANDAU, Rom. *Morocco independent under Mohammed the Fifth*. London, Allen & Unwin, 1961
A rather enthusiastic account of Morocco since the departure of the French, by an experienced observer of that country.

MONTEIL, Vincent. *Maroc*. Paris, Seuil, 1962 P (Collection Petite Planète)
A good impressionistic look at Morocco in words and pictures.

MONTEIL, Vincent. *Morocco*. Tr. V. Hull. London, Studio Vista; New York, Viking, 1964 P
See preceding note.

3 PERSIA (IRAN), THE KURDS

*AVERY, Peter. *Modern Iran*. London, Benn; New York, Praeger, 1965; 1967 P (Nations of the Modern World series)
The most comprehensive work of its kind at present available. Detailed historical account of the 19th and 20th centuries, written with insight.

BANANI, Amin. *The modernization of Iran, 1921-1941*. Stanford, Stanford University Press, 1961
A useful study, marred by inadequate historical and political perspective.

*BINDER, Leonard. *Iran: political development in a changing society*. Berkeley. University of California Press; London, Cambridge University Press, 1962
An excellent political analysis.

BLAU, Joyce. *Le problème kurde: essai sociologique et historique*. Bruxelles, Centre pour l'Etude des Problèmes du Monde Musulman Contemporain, 1963 P (Collection Le Monde Musulman Contemporain: Initiations)
A good short survey concentrating on sociology and politics in the 20th century.

BOIS, Thomas. *Connaissance des Kurdes*. Beyrouth, Khayat, 1965
A useful general account covering all aspects of this people, who are divided between Turkey, Iraq, and Iran.

BOIS, Thomas. *The Kurds.* Tr. M. W. Welland. Beyrouth, Khayat, 1966
See preceding note.

COTTAM, Richard W. *Nationalism in Iran.* Pittsburgh, University of Pittsburgh Press, 1964
A comprehensive study.

MARLOWE, John. *Iran: a short political guide.* London, Pall Mall; New York, Praeger, 1963
A perceptive analysis of the Iranian political scene since World War I.

MEHDEVI, Anne Sinclair. *Persia revisited.* New York, Knopf; Toronto, Random House, 1965
This pleasantly written autobiography of the American wife of a Persian describes the patriarchal life of her husband's family of 90 relatives, and the gradual change coming over the country.

MONTEIL, Vincent. *Iran.* Paris, Seuil, 1959 P (Collection Microcosme Petite Planète)
A brief impressionistic look in words and photographs at Iran's picturesque past and its present situation.

MONTEIL, Vincent. *Iran.* Tr. A. Jaffa. London, Studio Vista; New York, Viking, 1965 C&P
See preceding note.

NAJAFI, Najmeh. *A wall and three willows.* By Najmeh Najafi and Helen Hinckley. New York, Harper, 1967
A young Iranian woman describes her attempts to bring modern life to traditional conservative villages.

PALOU, Christiane. *La Perse antique.* Par Christiane et J. Palou. Paris, Presses Universitaires de France, 1962 (Collection "Que sais-je?")
A short general outline of pre-Islamic Persia.

SAHEBJAM, Freidoune. *L'Iran des Pahlavis.* Paris, Berger-Levrault, 1966
A description of Iran's recent history, politics, economics, and social system from the official government viewpoint.

UPTON, Joseph M. *The history of modern Iran: an interpretation.* Cambridge, Mass., Harvard University Press, 1960 (and repr.) (Harvard Middle Eastern Monographs)
Not a history as such, but rather a study of the effects of traditional Persian popular attitudes and characteristics on the modern history of Iran.

WILBER, Donald Newton. *Contemporary Iran.* New York, Praeger, 1963
An examination of the problems facing Iran and the attempts being made
to solve them.

4 TURKEY

BENOIST-MÉCHIN, Jacques. *Mustapha Kémal: ou, la mort d'un empire.* Paris,
Albin Michel, [1960] P
A popular biography, not always reliable.

BISBEE, Eleanor. *The new Turks: pioneers of the Republic, 1920-1950.* Philadelphia, University of Pennsylvania Press, 1951
A sympathetic account by an American professor long resident in Turkey.

EREN, Nuri. *Turkey today – and tomorrow: an experiment in westernization.*
New York, Praeger; London, Pall Mall, 1963
A Turkish diplomat's detached account of the recent present, well explained
in its historical perspective. Useful chapters on political parties, economics,
social problems, education, and literature.

*LEWIS, Geoffrey L. *Turkey.* 3rd ed. London, Benn; New York, Praeger, 1965
C&P (Nations of the Modern World series)
One of the best succinct accounts of modern Turkey. Somewhat over-simplified because of its brevity. Useful historical introduction on the Ottoman Empire.

*LEWIS, Geoffrey L. *La Turquie.* Verviers (Belgique), Gérard; Québec, Kasan;
Paris, Inter, 1968 P (Collection Marabout Université)
See preceding note.

*MANGO, Andrew. *Turkey.* London, Thames & Hudson; New York, Walker,
1968 (New Nations and Peoples series)
An excellent short introduction to Turkey since the establishment of the
republic after World War I, especially the past decade. Adequate general-
ized treatment of social and economic matters.

MAYNE, Peter. *Istanbul.* London, Phoenix House (Dent); New York, A. S.
Barnes, 1967 (Cities of the World series)
An enjoyably written "non-guide book." "It is a personal view of the City
against the visible background of its past" (Author). Gives a good perspective, in spite of errors.

ORGA, Irfan. *Portrait of a Turkish family.* London, Gollancz, 1950; New York,
Macmillan, 1957

A readable autobiography of a generation, showing how the transition from the Ottoman Empire to the Turkish Republic affected the lives of individuals.

ROBINSON, Richard D. *The first Turkish republic: a case study in national development.* Cambridge, Mass., Harvard University Press, 1963 (and repr.) (Harvard Middle Eastern Studies)
> The economic aspects of the development of a country under a western-oriented leadership; a study of the period 1923-60.

*ROUX, Jean-Paul. *La Turquie: géographie, économie, histoire, civilisation et culture.* Paris, Payot, 1953 P (Collection Bibliothèque Historique)
> One of the most useful general introductions to modern Turkey available in French. Enough information is given about its Islamic and Ottoman past to make the modern state intelligible.

STIRLING, Paul. *Turkish village.* London, Weidenfeld, 1965; New York, Wiley. 1966 P
> The vast majority of Turks live in villages. An anthropologist and his wife describe their two years' stay in two remote villages.

YALMAN, Ahmet Emin. *Turkey in my time.* Norman, University of Oklahoma Press, 1956
> Autobiography of an outstanding Turkish journalist, born in 1888, who had an inside knowledge of marv unknown aspects of recent Turkish history and politics.

YAN, pseud. *Trésors de la Turquie.* Texte M. de St.-Pierre, notes et commentaires de Robert Mantran. Photographies de Yan. Paris, Arthaud, 1959
> One of the best "picture books" of Turkey. Excellent and evocative photographs with good commentary.

YAN, pseud. *Turkey.* Introduced by Lord Kinross, photographed by Yan; descriptive commentaries and notes by Robert Mantran. Tr. Daphne Woodward. London, Thames & Hudson, 1959
> See preceding note.

5 PAKISTAN

ABBOTT, Freeland. *Islam and Pakistan.* Ithaca, Cornell University Press, 1968
> A generally perceptive examination of the search for the form and nature of Islam's place in the modern state, and an attempt to understand the various gradations between Islamic "traditionalist" and "modernist" positions.

BINDER, Leonard. *Religion and politics in Pakistan.* Berkeley, University of
California Press, 1963
> An important investigation into the position of Islam in political life.

EGLAR, Zekiye Süleyman. *A Punjabi village in Pakistan.* New York, Columbia
University Press; London, Oxford University Press, 1960
> An interesting account of life in a Muslim village by a woman anthropolo-
> gist who lived there and participated in the village activities for several years.

*STEPHENS, Ian. *Pakistan: old country, new nation.* Harmondsworth, Baltimore, Penguin, 1964 P; [2nd ed.] London, Benn; New York, Praeger, 1968
(Nations of the Modern World series)
> Pakistan's history and problems surveyed by the British former editor of
> the Indian newspaper *The Statesman,* who had first-hand knowledge of
> many of the principals and events.

TAYYEB, Ali. *Pakistan: a political geography.* London, Toronto, New York,
Oxford University Press, 1966
> The geographical, political, and social and economic problems posed by
> Pakistan's duality and history.

TESTA, François de. *Le Pakistan.* Paris, Presses Universitaires de France, 1962
(Collection "Que sais-je?")
> A very generalized introduction.

WILBER, Donald Newton. *Pakistan: its people, its society, its culture.* New
Haven, Human Relations Area Files, 1964 (Survey of World Cultures series)
> Packed with valuable information, but rather dry reading.

WILBER, Donald Newton. *Pakistan yesterday and today.* New York, Holt,
1964 P (Contemporary Civilizations series)
> A useful if rather elementary introduction, containing many sweeping over-
> simplifications.

WILLIAMS, Laurence Frederick Rushbrook. *The state of Pakistan.* [2nd ed.]
London, Faber, 1966
> An informative work addressed to the general reader.

6 ISRAEL, PALESTINE

BAR-ZOHAR, Michel. *Ben-Gourion: le prophète armé.* Paris, Fayard, 1966
(Collection des Études Contemporaines)
> An admiring though not servile biography by a journalist who spent 18
> months in the constant company of Ben Gurion and had access to his pri-

vate papers. Very valuable in filling in the background to Israel's political development during the past half century.

BAR-ZOHAR, Michel. *The armed prophet: a biography of Ben Gurion.* Tr. Len Ortzen. London, Barker, 1967
See preceding note.

BEN GURION, David. *Ben Gurion looks back, in talks with Moshe Pearlman.* New York, Simon & Schuster, 1965
Reminiscences of the Israeli statesman.

BENTWICH, Norman. *Israel resurgent.* London, Benn, 1960 (Nations of the Modern World series)
A sound basic outline, now slightly dated, with emphasis on foreign relations.

CHOURAQUI, André. *L'État d'Israël.* 5ᵉ éd. Paris, Presses Universitaires de France, 1967 P (Collection "Que sais-je?")
A brief historical sketch, and a survey of the state, its politics, economics, and society.

CHOURAQUI, André. *Lettre à un ami arabe.* Paris, Mame, 1969
An interesting "apologia" for the existence of Israel and a plea for its acceptance by the Arabs. The Algerian-born author was advisor on Arab affairs to Israeli premier David Ben Gurion.

DARIN-DRABKIN, Haim. *The other society.* London, Gollancz; Toronto, Doubleday, 1962; New York, Harcourt, 1963
A history and study of the kibbutz (Jewish communal settlement) in Israel.

DIQS, Isaak. *A Bedouin boyhood.* London, Allen & Unwin, 1967; New York, Praeger, 1969
An interesting non-political autobiography of a Palestinian Bedouin who now lives and works in Saudi Arabia.

DODD, Clement H. *Israel and the Arab world.* By C. H. Dodd and M. E. Sales. London, Routledge, 1970
A well-selected collection of material intended to tell the story of Arab-Israeli relations; includes basic documents, interviews, articles, and maps stating differing viewpoints. The compilers supply intelligent occasional commentary and links.

DOUGLAS-HOME, Charles. *The Arabs and Israel.* London, Toronto, Bodley Head, 1968 (Background Books series)
A somewhat elementary but reasonably balanced view of the problem since 1948, by an alert journalist.

EDELMAN, Maurice. *Ben Gurion: a political biography*. London, Holder, 1964. Published in the United States as: *David: the story of Ben Gurion*. New York, Putnam, 1965
> A sympathetic though critical biography which throws light on the emergence of Israel.

EDELMAN, Maurice. *Ben Gourion*. Tr. R. Jouan. Paris, Presses de la Cité, 1965
> See preceding note.

ELSTON, D. R. *Israel: the making of a nation*. London, Toronto, New York, Oxford University Press, 1963
> A fair introduction to the state, its institutions and peoples.

EMANUEL, Muriel (ed.) *Israel: a survey and a bibliography*. London, Chicago, St. James Press, 1971
> Twenty-five useful essays by informed writers (mostly Israelis) on various major aspects of life in Israel — historical, religious, cultural, and political and economic. Many of the essays are of general interest but some are rather specialized. Each one is followed by a selective reading list of books in English, French, and German.

HELLER, Abraham Mayer. *Israel's odyssey: a survey of Israel's renaissance, achievements and problems*. New York, Farrar, 1959
> A good review.

JANOWSKY, Oscar Isaiah. *Foundations of Israel: emergence of a welfare state*. Princeton, Toronto, Van Nostrand, 1959 P (Anvil Books)
> A helpful short description of the origins of Israel and its political, economic, and social organization, followed by illustrative readings.

KHOURI, Fred John. *The Arab-Israeli dilemma*. Syracuse, N.Y., Syracuse University Press, 1968 C&P
> The origins and history of the conflict, since the beginning of the British Mandate. Rather heavy on "official" documentation and less lively than Dodd (above). "Throughout the book staunch support is given to the United Nations" (Author's Foreword).

KIMCHE, Jon. *Both sides of the hill: Britain and the Palestine war*. London, Secker, 1960
> A well-written study of the "Israel War of Independence, 1948."

KISHON, Ephraim. *Noah's Ark, tourist class*. Tr. Y. Goldman. New York, Atheneum, 1961; London, Deutsch, 1963; New York, T. Langman, 1962
> Sharp humour by Israel's leading satirist of the state, its people and institutions. Excellent idiomatic translation.

LANDAU, Jacob. *The Arabs in Israel: a political study.* London, New York, Toronto, Oxford University Press (for Royal Institute of International Affairs), 1969
Solid and rather detailed.

LAQUEUR, Walter (ed.) *The Israel-Arab reader: a documentary history of the Middle East conflict.* New York, Citadel; London, Weidenfeld, 1969
Forty-two well-selected documents, from the Bilu (Zionist) Manifesto of 1881 and the conflicting "Program of the League of the Arab Fatherland" of 1905, to speeches by Gamal Abd al-Nasir (Nasser) in 1967. The last third of the book consists of interesting articles on the conflict from various viewpoints.

LEON, Dan. *The kibbutz: a new way of life.* London, New York, Toronto, Oxford University Press, 1969 C&P (The Commonwealth and International Library series)
What it is like to be a kibbutznik, described by a member of a left-wing kibbutz.

MIKES, George. *Milk and honey: Israel explored.* London, Deutsch; New York, Wingate, 1950 (and repr.)
A good-humoured satirical look at Israel and the Israelis.

NUSSBAUM, Elizabeth. *Israel.* London, Toronto, New York, Oxford University Press, 1968 P (The Modern World series)
A helpful, though over-simplified, short introduction to the complex problems of modern Israel.

PARAF, Pierre. *L'État d'Israël dans le monde.* Paris, Payot, 1958 P (Collection Bibliothèque Historique)
A brief outline of Israel's history and present political, social, economic, and cultural structure.

PATAI, Raphael. *Israel, between East and West.* 2nd ed. Westport, Conn., Greenwood Press, 1970
Describes the differences between the various Jewish immigrant groups to Israel, as well as the non-Jewish minorities, the economic, social, and political problems thus created, and the attempts at resolving them. Originally published 1950 and still useful.

PAYNE, Robert. *The splendor of Israel.* New York, Harper; London, Hale, 1963
An impressionistic account of the land and people of modern Israel in relation to the historic Jewish and Christian background of the land.

PRITTIE, Terence. *Eshkol: the man and the nation.* New York, Toronto, Pitman; London, Museum Press, 1969

The life of an Israeli prime minister (d. 1969) which can also serve incidentally as a partial "biography" of the state of Israel. Levi Eshkol was a Zionist pioneer settler early in the 20th century.

PRITTIE, Terence. *Israel: miracle in the desert.* [2nd ed.] New York, London, Praeger; Baltimore, Penguin, 1968 P
   A readable and up-to-date survey, by an English journalist, marred by some factual errors.

RENGLET, Claude. *Israël, an 20.* Verviers (Belgique), Gérard; Québec, Kasan; Paris, Inter, 1967 P (Collection Marabout Université)
   A fair general introduction to the modern state and its historical background.

ROUSSAN, Jacques de. *Israël, terre de promesses.* Montréal, Cercle du Livre de France, 1964
   A travelogue by a Canadian; sympathetic but not always accurate.

*SAFRAN, Nadav. *The United States and Israel.* Cambridge, Mass., Harvard University Press; London, Oxford University Press, 1963 (American Foreign Policy Library)
   A well-written and balanced review of the origins, character, and institutions (political, economic, social, and religious) of Israel, from a secularist viewpoint. Its scope is much wider than its title indicates; in fact only a small proportion is concerned with US-Israel relations. Very useful appendices include selected statistics and a 14-page essay evaluating helpful "suggested reading."

SAMUEL, Edwin. *The structure of society in Israel.* London, Peter Smith; New York, Toronto, Random House, 1969 P (Studies in Modern Societies series)
   A useful simple sociological work.

SAMUEL, Maurice. *Light on Israel.* New York, Knopf, 1968
   A "popular" presentation of Zionism and Israel up to the Six Day War of June 1967.

WARBURG, James Paul. *Crosscurrents in the Middle East.* A primer for the general reader, including a history of the region, a survey of recent developments, an appraisal of western responsibility and the prospects for peace. New York, Atheneum, 1968; London, Gollancz, 1969
   A fairly objective book for the layman. Devoted mainly to the Palestine/Israel and Arab-Jewish problems since the beginning of the 19th century, explaining simply but effectively the complex international political background and currents.

WEINGROD, Alex. *Israel: group relations in a new society.* London, Pall Mall; New York, Praeger, 1965 (Institute of Race Relations Publications)

A short but interesting analysis of some of the major problems of cultural relationships in a largely immigrant, multi-ethnic society – between Jews from many different parts of the world, and between Arabs and Jews. The important religious factor (secular Jews versus religious Jews) is not discussed adequately.

WILLIAMS, Laurence Frederick Rushbrook. *The state of Israel.* London, Faber, 1957
    A balanced factual informative description, now needing some updating.

7 CENTRAL ASIA, AFGHANISTAN

BENNIGSEN, Alexandre. *Les mouvements nationaux chez les Musulmans de Russie.* Par Alexandre Bennigsen and Chantal Lemercier. 2 vols. Paris, La Haye, Mouton, 1960-64
    A documented account by experts.

BENNIGSEN, Alexandre. *L'Islam en Union soviétique.* [Par] A. Bennigsen et C. Lemercier Quelquejay. Paris, Payot, 1968 P (Collection Bibliothèque Historique)
    A documented account by experts.

BENNIGSEN, Alexandre. *Islam in the Soviet Union.* By Alexandre Bennigsen and Chantal Lemercier-Quelquejay. Tr. Geoffrey E. Wheeler and Hubert Evans. London, Pall Mall; New York, Praeger, 1967
    See preceding note.

GRIFFITHS, John C. *Afghanistan.* With a historical note by Sir Olaf Caroe. London, Pall Mall; New York, Praeger, 1967 C&P
    A balanced survey of contemporary Afghanistan.

LEVIN, Maksim Grigor'evich (ed.) *The peoples of Siberia.* Ed. M. G. Levin and L. P. Potapov. [Translation edited by Stephen P. Dunn.] Chicago, London, University of Chicago Press, 1964
    The standard Russian work on 30 native Siberian peoples.

RYWKIN, Michael. *Russia in Central Asia.* New York, Collier; Galt, Ont., Collier-Macmillan, 1963 P
    A good non-technical study of Central Asia under Soviet rule, with particular reference to Uzbekistan.

SPAIN, James William. *The Pathan borderland.* The Hague, Mouton, 1963 (Publications in Near and Middle East Studies, Columbia University)
    A thorough study of the Pathans of Afghanistan and Pakistan.

SPAIN, James William. *People of the Khyber: the Pathans of Pakistan.* London, New York, Praeger, 1963
    A readable traveloguish account, containing some useful material.

WATKINS, Mary Bradley. *Afghanistan: land in transition.* Princeton, Toronto, London, Van Nostrand, 1963 (Asia Library series)
    An elementary introduction, useful for the real beginner, but containing many mistakes.

WHEELER, Geoffrey. *The peoples of Soviet Central Asia.* London, Bodley Head, 1966 (Background Books series)
    A very brief readable outline; a short history precedes a survey of the present political, economic and cultural situation.

*WILBER, Donald N. *Afghanistan: its people, its society, its culture.* New Haven, Human Relations Area Files, 1962 (Survey of World Cultures series)
    A sound book, containing much very useful and otherwise inaccessible information.

III India, South and Southeast Asia

*General and Indian Buddhism only. Books on Buddhist developments in other individual countries are listed under those countries in part III, section D, and part IV, sections B (subsection 6b) and C (subsection 6).
†Excluding Islam, which is covered in part II (subsections C5, D5, E5, and H5).

INTRODUCTION

Indian civilization dominates South and Southeast Asia. Its heartland is the Indian subcontinent, which is comparable in size to Western Europe and equal to it in ethnic diversity but 25 per cent larger in population. Until a couple of centuries ago (when the British period began), there had been no tradition of political unity, yet for perhaps 3000 years the area has formed what is fundamentally a single cultural unit, one bound together by a religious civilization, by beliefs and practices which transcend the numerous differences of its peoples. Indian religion is not just a system of beliefs but a total way of life, governing even such non-theological activities as what one may eat and with whom, what work one does, whom one may marry, and what one may touch. Every aspect of daily living, even things regarded as totally secular in the West, is minutely regulated.

The distinctive features of Indian civilization began to emerge perhaps 3500 years ago with the invasion of the subcontinent by Aryan people from the northwest. With them they brought their religious literature, called the Vedas. The oldest surviving portions, dating back some 3000 years, are the group of hymns known as the Rigveda, and auxiliary to them are priestly ritual texts (Brāhmanas). About the middle of the first millennium before the Christian era the basic philosophical works called the Upanishads were composed. These sacred writings together set out the group of concepts which have ever since dominated Indian thought: rebirth, governed by the law of moral causality (*karma*), and the ultimate aim of freedom from rebirth. A man's deeds in previous lives were considered to be responsible for the caste status into which he was born, and this had to be accepted with resignation. On the practical level this has meant the persistence of the caste system and the ideal of "withdrawal" from the present life in order to achieve sanctity. Most expressions of Indian civilization are governed by these factors, including even Buddhism, which may in some respects be considered to have been a partial revolt, arising from the intellectual and social ferment of the sixth century B.C.E. Buddhism died out in its homeland, but developed and still continues to flourish in one form or another in many of the neighbouring countries.

The mainstream of Indian religion continued in Hinduism. This could perhaps be more accurately be considered as a group of religions, since it runs the whole gamut from simple animism at one extreme, through any number of stages and variations of polytheism and idolatry, to monotheism, pantheism, mysticism, and complicated forms of philosophical monism at the other.

Hinduism's acceptance of inequalities — social, economic, and political — as expressed in such linked concepts as rebirth and the caste system, have given rise to various reform movements, which are naturally expressed also in religious terms. In recent times contact with European political ideas, and some of the social values associated with the Judaeo-Christian tradition, have had some influence on reform movements and political currents alike.

Traditional forms of aesthetic expression have equally naturally been religious. Until quite recently "literature" meant principally the Hindu scriptures and associated works. Knowledge of the Vedas at first hand was largely confined to trained Brahman priests. Other people got to know the basic Vedic religious ideas and attitudes mainly from two great epics of varied contents, composed in Sanskrit (the classical Indian literary language) about 2000 years ago, and later translated into many of the Indian vernaculars. These epics are the Ramāyana and the Mahābhārata; the latter includes a self-contained remarkable long ethical religious poem called the Bhagavad Gītā which has been a particular source of inspiration to modern Hindus, including Gandhi. In later times, the large amount of devotional poetry should be mentioned.

The aesthetic tradition of Indian architecture and art was also conveyed mainly in religious terms, particularly in the form of temples, and the mass of sculpture which adorned them — sculpture which was a combination of sensuous naturalism and symbolism. Music and dancing too were modes of religious expression, while the classical drama found its subject matter mainly in religious themes. (It is only in the 20th century that really secular literature has become important. The Indian novels and short stories which abound today owe their form and content mainly to English and other European models of the 19th and 20th centuries.) The classification of the traditional expressions of Indian civilization under headings in this reading guide is often difficult, since so much might be entered under "religion," used in a broad sense. The overlaps between such classes as "literature," "history," "religion," and "art" are bound to be frequent, and the division has of necessity been somewhat arbitrary.

Indian society is, and always has been, mainly agricultural. With the vast majority of the population inhabiting 700,000 villages, the basic social framework is still provided by kinship, village organization, and above all by caste. Caste remains the major reality, at one and the same time the principal unifying factor and the chief divisive factor, despite the efforts of reformers to mitigate its less desirable consequences. Modern India is a secular state, in which caste has no official standing, and Untouchability, the status of some 10 per cent of its population, has been outlawed by the Indian Constitution. Yet these millennial traditions are very persistent and reign supreme all over India. Only in the rapidly growing towns is the social order changing visibly, with the emergence of an urban middle class and a mass influx of villagers into towns.

Men of non-Indian religions exercised political control over much of the subcontinent for many centuries. The first Muslim conquests took place in Sind (the lower Indus valley) in 712, although real control of the Hindu heartland may be considered to begin with the establishment of the Muslim Sultanate of Delhi in 1206. Among the many Muslim states existing at various times in India in the following five centuries, the most important was certainly the Mughal Empire (1526-1707), founded by Babur, who, like most of the other Muslim rulers, was of Central Asian Turkish stock. Islam became a permanent part of the Indian scene but was never fully assimilated into it.

The British have been the major European influence since the 18th century, at first "unofficially" in the form of the East India Company, and then officially, from 1858 to 1947, as the rulers. For the first time in history they linked up the disparate elements of India in several ways: administratively and physically by a good communications system of roads, railways, posts, and telegraph; and linguistically to the extent that English, and a western educational system using that tongue, gave Indians from all parts of the subcontinent a common language. Through it they learned of European ideas and values, including words like political democracy and independence. The western-educated élite demanded the westernization and modernization of Indian political institutions. Their main instrument was the Indian National Congress, founded in 1885. As political democracy began to appear as a possibility, the Muslim minority in India started to fear for its survival if India were to be dominated politically by a Hindu majority, and so the All-India Muslim League was established in 1906. From this grew the movement which was to lead to partition of the subcontinent in 1947. Its Indian pupils having made it clear to Britain that they felt their political education was complete, the British divided the country into a new India with a Hindu majority, and Pakistan with a Muslim majority, and withdrew.

After rather bloody beginnings, the two successor states seem to have found a more or less peaceful though sullen modus vivendi; each is preoccupied with its colossal, almost insoluble, economic and social problems. The population continues to grow ever more rapidly. Agricultural methods are improving only slowly; the overwhelming majority of the labour force is still engaged in subsistence agriculture. Hunger and undernourishment are widespread, even though actual starvation to death is much reduced. Industry remains extremely underdeveloped in spite of Five Year Plans, foreign technical assistance, and the like. As if these problems were not enough, other divisive factors threaten India's unity. For reasons of nationalist pride, English is being phased out as the official federal administrative language in favour of Hindi. Non-Hindi-speaking areas now fear domination by northern Hindi-speaking officials. This is especially so in South India, where a fifth of India's population lives and speaks Dravidian languages. Of the large number of languages spoken in India, 14 are recognized as major, and in many areas of the country there are strong movements demanding the establishment of language-based states. As English loses ground, young Indians are being cut off from access to the modern western world and its skills, just when their country needs them most. In the past, India's distinctive contribution to world civilization has been in matters of religion and thought. Some modern Indians have asserted that their ancestors' propensity for abstract speculation, and their ideal of withdrawal from the world's affairs while concentrating on the individual's own spiritual advancement, have for centuries held India back from taking her rightful place in the world. However that may be, the welfare of its masses is now India's declared major preoccupation.

Among her neighbours to the east and southeast, her daughter "religion," Buddhism, is even now not only a major intellectual influence but an activist political force, riven though these countries are by nationalist and communist civil wars and the effects of Great Power rivalries. Subsections listing books on each of these countries are to be found after the subsections devoted to India itself. As for countries where Islam is dominant, works on Pakistan and Islam in India will be found in part II, particularly subsections C5, D5, E5, and H5, and books on the two other mainly Muslim lands in the area are listed below, Malaysia in subsection D8 and Indonesia in D9.

A REFERENCE WORKS

*BROWN, William Norman (ed.) *India, Pakistan, Ceylon.* [2nd ed.] Philadelphia, University of Pennsylvania Press; London, Oxford University Press, 1964
This collection of articles, originally written for the *Encyclopedia Americana*, forms a handy short reference book.

*MAHAR, J. Michael. *India: a critical bibliography.* Tucson, University of Arizona Press, 1964 P
A very valuable bibliography (mainly of works in English), divided by topic, on facets of India's past and present. 2000 entries. Helpful annotations to each entry and introductory orientation to each main section or subsection. Particularly good on history.

PATTERSON, Maureen L. P. *South Asia: an introductory bibliography.* By Maureen L. P. Patterson and Ronald B. Inden. Chicago, University of Chicago Bookstore, 1962 P
A useful reference book containing entries for almost 4000 books and articles on many aspects of Indian culture.

*RENOU, Louis. *L'Inde classique: manuel des études indiennes.* Par Louis Renou et Jean Filliozat. 2 vols. Paris, 1947-53. Tome 1: Paris, Payot, 1947; Tome 2: Paris, Imprimerie Nationale, 1953
An absolutely basic reference work on all aspects of traditional India.

B GENERAL WORKS

*BURLING, Robbins. *Hill farms and padi fields: life in mainland South East Asia.* Englewood Cliffs, N.J., Prentice-Hall, 1965 C&P (Spectrum Books)
A good, simple comparative introduction to present-day rural life in a vast region.

DOBBY, Ernest Henry George. *Monsoon Asia.* 2nd ed. London, University of London Press; Toronto, Clarke Irwin; Chicago, Quadrangle, 1962 (Systematic Regional Geography series)
A sound geographical analysis covering East, Southeast, and South Asia.

DUMONT, Louis. *La civilisation indienne et nous. Esquisse de sociologie comparée.* Paris, Colin, 1964 P (Collection Cahiers des Annales)
Three good lectures: (1) Society, religion and thought; (2) The problem of history; (3) Contemporary change.

FERSH, Seymour. *India and South Asia.* New York, London, Macmillan, 1965 P
A 150-page general introduction which picks out the main features and explains them readably.

*FILLIOZAT, Jean. *Inde: nation et tradition.* Paris, Horizons de France, 1961
An excellent introduction to India's past and present, written for laymen by a leading scholar; handsomely illustrated.

*FILLIOZAT, Jean. *India: the country and its traditions.* Tr. M. Ledésert. London, Toronto, Harrap, 1962
See preceding note.

*GARRATT, Geoffrey Theodore (ed.) *The legacy of India.* Oxford, Clarendon Press; Toronto, New York, Oxford University Press, 1937 (and repr.)
A valuable collection of articles outlining major aspects of Indian civilization. A fine introduction for the non-specialist.

KABIR, Humayun. *The Indian heritage.* 3rd ed. Bombay, London, New York, Asia Publishing House, 1955 (and repr.)
A useful and readable description of Indian culture and religion.

MACDONELL, Anthony Arthur. *India's past: a survey of her literatures, religions, languages and antiquities.* Oxford, Clarendon Press, 1927; repr. Delhi, Banarsidass, 1956
Still a useful general work, though partly outdated.

MAUDE, Angus. *South Asia.* London, Bodley Head, 1966; New York, Putnam, 1967 P
   A short lucid piece of journalism that seeks to explain the present problems of South and Southeast Asia in the perspective of its past.

RENOU, Louis. *Sanskrit et culture: l'apport de l'Inde à la civilisation humaine.* Paris, Payot, 1950 P (Collection Bibliothèque Historique)
   The author is one of the most important French scholars in this field.

TINKER, Hugh. *Re-orientations: studies on Asia in transition.* London, Pall Mall; New York, Praeger, 1965
   Thoughtful essays, mainly on South and Southeast Asia.

TOUSSAINT, Auguste. *Histoire de l'océan indien.* Paris, Presses Universitaires de France, 1961 P (Collection Pays d'Outre-mer. 6ᵉ série: Peuples et Civilisations d'Outre-mer)
   A fascinating history of navigation since early times in the Indian Ocean and of the lands around it from Arabia and Africa to Indonesia.

TOUSSAINT, Auguste. *History of the Indian Ocean.* Tr. June Guicharnaud. London, Routledge; Chicago, University of Chicago Press, 1966
   See preceding note.

*WALPOLE, Norman C. *U.S. Army area handbook for India.* By Norman C. Walpole and Sharon Arkin [and others]. Washington, Govt. Printing Office, 1964
   A useful general work on all aspects of modern India. Also contains statistics of all kinds not available in similar works. An excellent 800-page work of reference value at a very low price.

WARD, Barbara E. (ed.) *Women in the new Asia: the changing social roles of men and women in South and Southeast Asia.* Amsterdam, Unesco, 1965
   A collection of 19 uneven articles on the place of women in various countries. Excellent 74-page introductory essay by the editor.

C INDIA

1 HISTORY, SOCIAL SCIENCES, AND LAW

ALLCHIN, Bridget. *The birth of Indian civilization: India and Pakistan before 500 B.C.* By Bridget and Raymond Allchin. Harmondsworth, Baltimore, Penguin, 1968 P
A good up-to-date survey and interpretation of the findings of archaeology about the ancient period.

ALTEKAR, Anant Sadashiv. *State and government in Ancient India.* 3rd ed. Benares, Banarsidass, 1958
A good introductory survey, to about 1000 A.D.

AUBOYER, Jeannine. *La vie quotidienne dans l'Inde ancienne.* Paris, Hachette, 1961
An excellent description, providing a background to understanding traditional India.

AUBOYER, Jeannine. *Daily life in ancient India, from approximately 200 B.C. to 700 A.D.* Tr. Simon Watson Taylor. London, Weidenfeld; New York, Macmillan, 1965
See preceding note.

*BASHAM, Arthur Llewellyn. *The wonder that was India: a study of the history and culture of the Indian sub-continent before the coming of the Muslims.* [2nd ed.] London, Sidgwick; New York, Hawthorn, 1963. Also available: an inexpensive reprint of 1st ed., New York, Grove, 1959 P (Evergreen Books)
An outstanding review of classical Indian civilization addressed to westerners without previous knowledge. Well illustrated.

BEALS, Alan R. *Gopalpur: a south Indian village.* New York, Holt, 1962 P (Case Studies in Cultural Anthropology series)
Life in a village in Mysore state, simply described for students; contains a very good examination of interpersonal relationships.

Cambridge history of India. 5 vols. (all published). Repr. Delhi, Chand, 1957-64
Reprint of Cambridge University Press edition of 1922-37, with supplement by an Indian historian for the years 1919-47. Detailed but important. Vol. 1: *Ancient India*, ed. E. J. Rapson. Vol. 2: Not published. Vol. 3: *Turks and Afghans*, ed. T. W. Haig. Vol. 4: *Mughal Period*, ed. R. Burn. Vol. 5: *British India, 1497-1858*, ed. H. H. Dodwell. Vol. 6: *The Indian Empire, 1858-1918*, ed. H. H. Dodwell, with additional chapters on The Last Phase, 1919-1947, by R. R. Sethi.

Cambridge shorter history of India. Ed. John Allen, T. W. Haig, Henry Herbert Dodwell and R. R. Sethi. London, Cambridge University Press; New York, Macmillan, 1934; repr. [with additional chapters] Delhi, Chand, 1958
A standard work.

CHAVARRIA-AGUILAR, Oscar Luis. *Traditional India.* Englewood Cliffs, N.J., Prentice-Hall, 1964 C&P (Spectrum Books)
Extracts from writings by experts on traditional Indian religion and culture; suitable as introductory reading.

COMMISSARIAT, M. Sorabshah. *A history of Gujarat.* 3 vols. Bombay, Orient Longmans, 1938-57
A good regional history of the Muslim period, covering 1297-1758.

CORBETT, James Edward. *My India.* London, Toronto, New York, Oxford University Press, 1952.
A good evocation of the world of India's peasants.

CRANE, Robert I. *The history of India: its study and interpretation.* Washington, Service Center for Teachers of History (American Historical Association); [New York, Macmillan], 1958 P
A very helpful pamphlet describing the problems of Indian history and discussing books in English suitable for consultation by teachers giving history courses in schools and colleges. The books relating to each chronological period are evaluated. Unfortunately many are now out of print.

DAVIES, Cuthbert Collin. *An historical atlas of the Indian peninsula.* 2nd ed. Madras, Toronto, London, New York, Oxford University Press, 1959 (and repr.)
Forty-seven maps with brief notes; a useful aid in reading any of the standard histories.

DUPUIS, Jacques. *Histoire de l'Inde et de la civilisation indienne.* Paris, Payot, 1963 P (Collection Petit Bibliothèque Payot)
A culturally oriented introductory history.

EDWARDES, Michael. *Bound to exile: the Victorians in India.* London, Sidgwick, 1969; New York, Praeger, 1970
The social life of the Englishmen and their families; amusingly described with copious quotations from contemporary letters, memoirs, newspapers, and travellers' accounts.

EDWARDES, Michael. *British India, 1772-1947: a survey of the nature and effects of alien rule.* London, Sidgwick, 1967; New York, Taplinger, 1968
An unusual broad approach, which includes a particularly good analysis of "the nature of British rule."

EDWARDES, Michael. *Everyday life in early India.* London, Batsford; New
York, Putnam, 1969
A readable well-illustrated description of life in India to about the 8th cen-
tury, under such chapter headings as Strife, the Daily round, War, Arts and
Sciences. Less detailed than Auboyer's excellent book (above).

EDWARDES, Michael. *A history of India from the earliest times to the present
day.* London, Thames & Hudson; New York, Farrar, 1961
A well-written outline; the emphasis is social and cultural rather than political.

FERGUSON, James P. *Kashmir: an historical introduction.* London, Centaur
Press, 1961
A somewhat bland description of the historical heritage of a disputed land,
held by India and claimed by Pakistan. Contains a special chapter on early
travellers, Chinese, Mughal, and European.

GOKHALE, Balkrishna Govind. *Asoka Maurya.* New York, Twayne, 1966
The life and times of the great Buddhist emperor (died 232 B.C.) who
reigned for 40 years and left inscriptions containing moral edicts in various
parts of India.

GOPAL, Ram. *British rule in India: an assessment.* Bombay, London, New
York, Asia Publishing House, 1963
A well-documented attempt at an objective presentation.

GRIFFITHS, Percival Joseph. *The British impact on India.* London, Cass, 1965
(repr. of 1952 ed.)
A study of the administrative, political, and economic aspects by a former
(British) Indian civil servant. Compare with the preceding title, which is an
Indian's appraisal.

HEIMSATH, Charles Herman. *Indian nationalism and Hindu social reform.*
Princeton, Princeton University Press, 1964
A pioneer work, limiting itself to the 19th century.

HUTTON, John Henry. *Caste in India: its nature, function and origins.* 4th ed.
Bombay, Toronto, London, Oxford University Press, 1963 P
A standard work on this important feature of Indian social life and history.

KAPADIA, Kanailal Motilal. *Marriage and family in India.* 2nd ed. Bombay,
Toronto, New York, London, Oxford University Press, 1958
Useful descriptions of family life by a sociologist.

*KOSAMBI, Damodar Dharmanand. *The culture and civilization of ancient In-
dia in historical outline.* London, Routledge, 1965. American edition entitled

Ancient India: a history of its culture and civilization. New York, Pantheon; Toronto, Random House, 1966
An original and valuable attempt to reconstruct the "main currents" of the history and culture of ancient India; less specialized than the work below.

KOSAMBI, Damodar Dharmanand. *An introduction to the study of Indian history.* Bombay, Popular Book Depot, 1956
"A seminal work by the foremost exponent of Marxistic economically oriented history of ancient India." Partly technical.

LACH, Donald Frederick. *India in the eyes of Europe: the 16th century.* Chicago, University of Chicago Press, 1968 P (Phoenix Books)
The impact of the increasing knowledge of India on the western world four centuries ago.

LAMB, Harold. *Babur the tiger: first of the Great Moguls.* Garden City, N.Y., Doubleday, 1961; Toronto, New York, Bantam, 1964 P (and repr.)
A dramatized historical biography, giving a vivid picture of the life of the Turkish conqueror of India (1483-1530) who established the Mughal dynasty.

LEWIS, Oscar. *Village life in northern India. Studies in a Delhi village.* New York, Toronto, Random House, 1965 P
An informative study of the life of peasants, who still constitute the vast majority of India's population.

MAJUMDAR, Ramesh Chandra. *An advanced history of India.* By R. C. Majumdar, H. C. Rayachaudhuri [and] Kalikinkar Datta. 2nd ed. London, Toronto, Macmillan; New York, St. Martin's, 1950 (and repr.)
A standard textbook for university students in India from a rather different viewpoint than books by the British school of historians of India.

MASANI, Rustom Pestonji. *Britain in India: an account of British rule in the Indian subcontinent.* Bombay, Toronto, London, New York, Oxford University Press, 1960 (and repr.)
An Indian's evaluation, to be compared with works on the same theme by such British writers as P. J. Griffiths (above) and P. Spear (below).

MAZUMDAR, Bhakat Prasad. *Socio-economic history of northern India.* Calcutta, Mukhopadhyay, 1960
The daily life and the rise of "feudalism" in the 11th and 12th centuries.

MEILE, Pierre. *Histoire de l'Inde.* 2e éd., mise à jour par Jean-Luc Chambard, avec le concours d'André Guimbretière pour le Pakistan. Paris, Presses Universitaires de France, 1965 (Collection "Que sais-je?")
A brief outline from ancient times to the mid-sixties.

MISRA, Bankey Bihari. *The Indian middle classes: their growth in modern times.* London, Toronto, New York, Oxford University Press (for Royal Institute of International Affairs), 1961
    The social consequences of British influence in India.

MORELAND, William Harrison. *A short history of India.* By W. H. Moreland and Atul Chandra Chatterjee. 4th ed. London, Longmans, 1957; New York, McKay, 1965
    A lucid and balanced introductory text, especially good on economic and administrative history.

MURTY, K. Satchidananda. *Readings in Indian history, politics and philosophy.* Bombay, Allied; London, Allen & Unwin, 1967
    An interesting wide-ranging selection, giving interpretations by modern Indians of their past and present.

NAIDIS, Mark. *India: a short introductory history.* New York, Macmillan; Toronto, London, Collier-Macmillan, 1966
    A good very elementary account, with useful annotated bibliography for further reading.

NEHRU, Jawaharlal. *The discovery of India.* Edited, with comments, by Robert I. Crane. Garden City, N.Y., Doubleday, 1960 P
    Indian history as seen through the eyes of Nehru, when a political prisoner in 1944. Throws more light on Nehru and his generation of Indians than on history.

NILAKANTA SASTRI, K. A. *The culture and history of the Tamils.* Calcutta, Mukhopadhyay, 1964
    A short and rather simplified cultural history of this people of South India and Ceylon.

NILAKANTA SASTRI, K. A. *A history of South India from prehistoric times to the fall of the Vijayanagar.* 3rd ed. Madras, Toronto, London, New York, Oxford University Press, 1966
    Political, social, and cultural history to the 17th century. South India is neglected in most of the standard histories of India.

PHILIPS, Cyril Henry (ed.) *The evolution of India and Pakistan, 1858-1947.* London, Toronto, New York, Oxford University Press, 1962
    A collection of source material to document political, economic, and social developments.

PHILIPS, Cyril Henry (ed.) *Historians of India, Pakistan and Ceylon.* London, Toronto, New York, Oxford University Press, 1961 (School of Oriental and African Studies, University of London: Historical Writing on the Peoples of Asia series)

A series of important papers by many notable scholars, dealing with: (1) ideas of history in the early Indian empires; (2) European writings on India; (3) historical work in Indian languages.

PHILIPS, Cyril Henry (ed.) *Politics and society in India.* New York, Praeger, 1962; London, Allen & Unwin, 1963 (Studies of Modern Asia and Africa series)
   Interesting essays by several scholars on India's political past and the trends since independence.

PRASAD, Ishwari. *The life and times of Humayun.* [Rev. ed.] Calcutta, Orient Longmans; Toronto, New York, Longmans, 1956
   A scholarly biography of Humayun, a 16th century emperor of India.

PRASAD, Ishwari. *History of mediaeval India.* 3rd ed. Allahabad, Indian Press, 1966
   This standard textbook used in Indian universities gives an Indian viewpoint.

PRAWDIN, Michael. *The builders of the Mogul Empire.* London, Allen & Unwin, 1963
   A readable account, for the general reader, of the conquests and accomplishments of the emperors Babur, Humayan, and Akbar, covering Indian history throughout the 16th century.

RAGHUVANSHI, V. P. S. *Indian society in the eighteenth century.* New Delhi, Associated, 1969
   An interesting thesis, based mainly on the author's evaluation of contemporary accounts by Europeans, travellers, administrators, missionaries, and scholars.

RAWLINSON, Hugh George. *India: a short cultural history.* 4th ed. London, Cresset; New York, Praeger, 1952 (and repr.); 1965 P
   A well-written religious, intellectual, and aesthetic history; contains little material on the last two centuries and is becoming a bit dated.

RENOU, Louis. *La civilisation de l'Inde ancienne, d'après les textes sanskrits.* Paris, Flammarion, 1950 P
   A short but expert survey, to the 7th century.

RENOU, Louis. *The civilization of ancient India.* Tr. Philip Spratt. 2nd ed. Calcutta, Susil Gupta, 1959
   See preceding note.

SINGH, Harbans. *The heritage of the Sikhs.* Bombay, London, New York, Asia Publishing House, 1965
   A study of Sikh history.

SINGH, Khushwant. *A history of the Sikhs.* 2 vols. Princeton, Princeton University Press; London, Oxford University Press, 1963-66
> A detailed history of this people and religion of the Punjab, since the beginning of Sikhism in the 15th century.

*SMITH, Vincent Arthur. *The Oxford history of India.* 3rd ed. Ed. Percival Spear. Oxford, Clarendon Press; Toronto, New York, Oxford University Press, 1958 (and repr.) C&P
> Often considered the best standard one-volume history of India from the western point of view.

*SPEAR, Percival. *India: a modern history.* Ann Arbor, University of Michigan Press, 1961 (History of the Modern World series)
> A balanced general history, emphasizing historical trends. Particularly good on the social and intellectual background to the development of nationalism and modernization.

SPEAR, Percival. *A history of India.* Vol. 2: *From the Mughals to 1960.* Harmondsworth, Baltimore, Penguin, 1965 P (Pelican Books)
> Adequate only as a sketch; more details are given in the author's other works. Vol. 1, to 1526, is by Romila Thapar (see below).

SPEAR, Percival. *India, Pakistan and the West.* 4th ed. London, Toronto, New York, Oxford University Press, 1967 P (Galaxy Books)
> An excellent analysis of the confrontation between Indian tradition and western ideas in 19th century India, and developments since that time, which make the history of modern India and Pakistan intelligible.

*SPEAR, Percival. *The Oxford history of modern India, 1740-1947.* Oxford, Clarendon Press; Toronto, New York, Oxford University Press, 1965
> A thoroughly competent general history of the British period, being a reprint of part III of Vincent Smith's *Oxford history of India.* (This 400-page section was entirely rewritten by Spear.)

STAMP, Lawrence Dudley. *India, Pakistan, Ceylon and Burma.* London, Methuen, 1958, repr. 1960
> A sound short geographical introduction adapted from the same author's standard work, *Asia: a regional and economic geography.*

THAPAR, Romila. *Asoka and the decline of the Mauryas.* Oxford, Clarendon Press; Toronto, New York, Oxford University Press, 1961
> A scholarly reconstruction and assessment of the life and times of the great emperor (3rd century B.C.).

THAPAR, Romila. *A history of India.* Vol. 1. Harmondsworth, Baltimore, Penguin, 1966 P (Pelican Books)
> Vol. 1, to 1526, is a useful outline, with "modern" historians' emphasis on economic rather than religious factors. Vol. 2, 1500-1960, is by Percival Spear (see above).

*TINKER, Hugh. *South Asia: a short history.* London, Pall Mall; New York, Praeger, 1967
> Excellent coverage in a small compass, especially economic and political.

WALLBANK, Thomas Walter. *A short history of India and Pakistan.* New York, Toronto, New American Library; London, New English Library, 1965 P
> Concentrates on the period since the middle of the 19th century, especially on the nationalist movement and subsequent political developments. Useful, though not outstanding. (Revised printing of 1958 ed., recording events to 1964.)

WISER, William H. *Behind mud walls, 1930-1960.* By William H. Wiser and Charlotte Viall Wiser. 2nd ed. Berkeley, University of California Press; London, Cambridge University Press, 1963 C&P
> Indian village life near Agra, well observed from 1925 to 1930, and then revisited 30 years later.

WOLPERT, Stanley. *India.* Englewood Cliffs, N.J., Prentice-Hall, 1965 P
> A short, clear history crammed with detail, and preceded by a look at present-day India.

WOLPERT, Stanley. *Tilak and Gokhale: revolution and reform in the making of modern India.* Berkeley, University of California Press, 1962
> Biographies of two early nationalist leaders and reformers of differing and sometimes opposing views.

2 HISTORY OF INDIAN LITERATURES

BANERJEE, Sunil Kumar. *Bankim Chandra: a study of his craft.* Calcutta, Mukhopadhyay, 1968
> A detailed critical study of the work of the first modern novelist in Bengali, who started publishing in 1865.

BARUA, Birinchi Kumar. *History of Assamese literature.* New Delhi, Sahitya Akademi, 1964; Honolulu, East-West Center Press, 1965
> An uncritical account of the literature written in the Assamese language of northeast India, which treats its subject in a vacuum, giving little indication

of its relationship to Indic literature in general, or of the limited area in which it showed originality. Cited here for lack of alternative works.

CHAITANYA, Krishna. *A new history of Sanskrit literature.* Bombay, London, New York, Asia Publishing House, 1962
An attempt at a balanced "literary," rather than religious or philosophical, evaluation of the whole range of Sanskrit literature.

CHANDRASEKHARAN, K. *Sanskrit literature.* By K. Chandrasekharan and Brahmasri V. H. Subrahmanya Sastri. Bombay, International Book House (for P.E.N. All-India Centre), 1951
A general survey.

Contemporary Indian literature. New Delhi, Sahitya Akademi (National Academy of Letters), 1959
Contributions to a symposium by leading Indian scholars and writers. Uneven, but generally interesting.

*DASGUPTA, Surendra Nath. *A history of Sanskrit literature.* 1: *Classical period.* By S. N. Dasgupta and S. K. De. Calcutta, Calcutta University Press, 1947 (and repr.)
A detailed standard reference.

DWIVEDI, Ram Awadh. *A critical survey of Hindi literature.* Varanasi, Banarsidass, 1966
A helpful broad general survey from the 8th century to the present, indicating the changing contents and concerns. Unsympathetic to the "frankness" of recent novelists.

GHOSH, Jyotish Changra. *Bengali literature.* London, Toronto, New York, Oxford University Press, 1948
A history of the literature to the end of the 19th century, with an additional essay on its leading recent writer, Tagore.

*GLASENAPP, Helmuth von. *Les littératures de l'Inde, des origines à l'époque contemporaine.* Tr. Robert Sailley. Paris, Payot, 1963 P (Collection Bibliothèque Historique)
A very useful survey, covering ancient, classical, mediaeval, and modern literatures in the main indigenous languages.

GOPAL, Madan. *Munshi Premchand: a literary biography.* Bombay, London, New York, Asia Publishing House, 1964

A detailed study of Premchand (1880-1936), an outstanding Hindi novelist and short-story writer with a social conscience, whose favourite themes are the Indian masses and the conflict between village and town. The biography is not too well organized. Contains summaries of all Premchand's main works.

KABIR, Humayun. *The Bengali novel.* Calcutta, Mukhopadhyay, 1968 (Rabindranath Tagore Centennial Lectures at the University of Wisconsin)
Four illuminating lectures trace the development, starting with the pioneer Bankimchandra in the mid-19th century, and continuing to the 1960s. Contains a list of English translations of Bengali novels and short stories.

KEAY, Frank Ernest. *A history of Hindi literature.* 3rd ed. Calcutta, Y.M.C.A. Publishing House, 1960
A short survey.

KEITH, Arthur Berriedale. *A history of Sanskrit literature.* Oxford, Clarendon Press; Toronto, New York, Oxford University Press, 1928, repr. 1961
Less a balanced history than a collection of the author's reading notes.

KRIPALANI, Krishna. *Rabindranath Tagore: a biography.* London, Toronto, New York, Oxford University Press, 1962
A distinguished biography of the great Bengali poet.

MANSINHA, Mayadhar. *History of Oriya literature.* New Delhi, Sahitya Akademi (National Academy of Letters), 1962

Modernity in contemporary Indian literature. Proceedings of a seminar [1966]. Simla, Indian Institute of Advanced Study, 1968
A series of papers of unequal value. The section "Modernity in Indian languages" contains reviews of developments in the various regional languages.

RAY, Nihar-ranjan. *An artist in life.* Trivandrum, University of Kerala, 1967
An excellent and thorough biographical and critical study of Tagore in the context of his cultural tradition. A final section contains quotations on such topics as religion, education, history, and society.

RENOU, Louis. *Les littératures de l'Inde.* 2ᵉ éd. Paris, Presses Universitaires de France, 1966 P (Collection "Que sais-je?")
A brief authoritative outline of Indian literatures from ancient times to the present. Appendix on "Indian literature and the West."

RENOU, Louis. *Indian literature.* Tr. Patrick Evans. New York, Walker; Toronto, McLeod, 1964 C&P (Walker Sun Books)
See preceding note.

SEN, Sukumar. *History of Bengali literature.* New Delhi, Sahitya Akademi (National Academy of Letters), 1960
A reliable and readable standard work.

3 INDIAN LITERATURE IN TRANSLATION, AND ORIGINAL INDIAN LITERATURE WRITTEN IN ENGLISH

a/Classical†

i/Vedas and Epics

BRĀHMANA. *Mythes et légendes extraits des Brâhmanas.* Traduits du sanscrit et annotés par Jean Varenne. Paris, Gallimard, 1967 (Collection Connaissance de l'Orient) (Collection Unesco d'Oeuvres Représentatives – Série Indienne)
Brāhmanas form the second of the four divisions of Vedic literature, interpreting imaginatively the ancient Indian religious tradition, often in the form of allegories.

BROUGH, John (comp.) *Selections from classical Sanskrit literature, with English translation and notes.* London, Luzac, 1951
A good selection, excellently translated.

*EDGERTON, Franklin (ed. & tr.) *The beginnings of Indian philosophy: selections from the Rig Veda, Atharva Veda, Upanisads, and Mahābhārata.* Translated from the Sanskrit, with an introduction. London, Allen & Unwin; Cambridge, Mass., Harvard University Press, 1965 (Unesco Collection of Representative Works – Indian Series)
Texts which show the early development of Indian philosophy, selected and translated by a renowned scholar. For another selection and translation from these texts, see R. C. Zaehner (below).

GHOSH, Oroon (tr.) *The dance of Shiva and other tales from India.* Toronto, New York, New American Library, 1965 P (Signet Classics series)
A pleasant selection from a wide range of sources, mostly dating from 1800 B.C. to 1200 A.D.

*MAHĀBHĀRATA. *The Mahābhārata.* An English version based on selected verses. By Chakravarthi V. Narasimhan. New York, London, Columbia Univer-

†More advanced readers will find many important complete individual religious texts accessible in such series as the Translation Series of the Pali Text Society (London) and the Sacred Books of the East (50 vols., Oxford, Clarendon Press, 1879-1910). Many of these translations are now rather dated, but only a minority have since been retranslated elsewhere. The SBE series has been reprinted recently by the firm of Motilal Banarsidass in Delhi. Some volumes have also been reprinted by Dover Publications, New York.

sity Press, 1965 (Columbia College Program of Translations from the Oriental Classics series)

A good translation. The Mahābhārata, "the Great [War] of the Bhāratas," which received something like its present form over 2000 years ago, is a great epic poem about the rivalry between two noble families. In addition to the adventure parts it contains many digressions on morals, philosophy, law, and love. One such section, expounding Hinduism's truths and ethics, is the Bhagavad Gītā, which has been a major influence on Hindus since antiquity.

*MAHĀBHĀRATA, Bhagavad Gītā. *The Bhagavad Gītā.* Translated and interpreted by Franklin Edgerton. New York, Harper, 1964 P (Harper Torchbooks series)

The scholarly translation of "India's favourite Bible," followed by an important "interpretation" of its teachings and its place in Hindu thought.

MAHĀBHĀRATA, Bhagavad Gītā. *The Bhagavadgita: an English translation and commentary* by W. Douglas P. Hill. 2nd [abridged] ed. London, Toronto, New York, Oxford University Press, 1953 P (and repr.)

A good accurate version for the general reader, with a long introduction.

MAHĀBHĀRATA, Bhagavad Gītā. *The Song of the Lord: Bhagavadgita.* Tr. Edward J. Thomas. London, Murray; New York, Paragon, 1931, repr. 1959 (Wisdom of the East series)

A rather literal translation, with a very few short notes.

MAHĀBHĀRATA, Bhagavad Gitā. *The Bhagavad-Gītā,* with a commentary based on the original sources by R. C. Zaehner. Oxford, Clarendon Press; New York, Toronto, Oxford University Press, 1969

A modern translation, followed by a detailed learned discussion.

RAGHAVAN, V. (tr. & comp.) *The Indian heritage: an anthology of Sanskrit literature.* 2nd ed. Bangalore, Indian Institute of Culture, 1958 (Unesco Collection of Representative Works – Indian Series)

Consists largely of translations from ancient religious and philosophical texts and the great epics. Many of the non-epic texts are hardly represented in other anthologies.

*UPANISHADS. *The thirteen principal Upanishads.* Translated from Sanskrit, with an outline of the philosophy of the Upanishads, by Robert Ernest Hume. 2nd ed. London, Bombay, Toronto, New York, Oxford University Press, 1931 (and repr.)

Perhaps the most readable good translation of these ancient Indian texts with an excellent introductory essay.

UPANISHADS. *The principal Upanishads.* Edited with introduction, text, translation, and notes by S. Radhakrishnan. London, Allen & Unwin; New York, Harper, 1953
  Another translation of 18 Upanishads, with an interpretative introduction by a notable scholar.

VĀLMĪKI. *The Ramayana.* Tr. Hari Prasad Shastri. 3 vols. London, Shanti Sadan, 1952-59
  The standard complete prose translation of one of the most famous Indian epics, written about 2000 years ago and attributed to a robber turned sage. About a war between the forces of good and evil.

VEDA. *Hymnes spéculatifs du Véda,* traduits du sanskrit et annotés par Louis Renou. 4ᵉ éd. Paris, Gallimard, 1956 P (Collection Unesco d'Oeuvres Représentatives — Série Indienne) (Collection Connaissance de l'Orient)
  Excellent translation for the layman of excerpts from the Rigveda and the Atharvaveda.

Le Véda, premier livre sacré de l'Inde. Textes réunis et presentés par Jean Varenne. 2 vols. Verviers (Belgique), Gérard; Québec, Kasan; Paris, Planète, 1967 P (Collection Marabout Université) (Trésors Spirituels de l'Humanité)
  A good selection of texts, accompanied by helpful introductions and comments.

ZAEHNER, R. C. (ed. & tr.) *Hindu scriptures.* Selected, translated and introduced by R. C. Zaehner. London, Dent; New York, Dutton, 1966 (Everyman's Library series)
  Representative selections from four basic scriptures: Rigveda, Atharvaveda, Upanishads, and Bhagavad Gītā. The author's aim is to be "faithful" without being "literalistic."

ii/Belles Lettres

BHARTRIHARI. *Poems.* Tr. Barbara Stoler Miller. New York, London, Columbia University Press, 1967 C&P (Translations from the Oriental Classics series) (Unesco Collection of Representative Works — Indian Series)
  One of the best examples of secular Indian love poetry, well translated. The combination of attraction to the sensual and attempted renunciation of it for the spiritual has produced a creative tension.

BUITENEN, Johannes Adrianus Bernardus van (ed. & tr.) *Tales of ancient India.* Translated from the Sanskrit. Chicago, University of Chicago Press, 1959; New York, Bantam, 1961 P
  A fine anthology of narrative literature depicting Indian life in its golden age; the translation is graceful yet accurate.

*BUITENEN, Johannes Adrianus Bernardus van (ed. & tr.). *Two plays of ancient India: the Little clay cart [and] the Minister's seal.* Translated from the Sanskrit with an introduction. New York, London, Columbia University Press, 1968 (Translations from the Oriental Classics series)
   A fine initiation into the dramatic tradition of India. Valuable introduction.

KĀLIDĀSA. *The cloud messenger.* Translated from the Sanskrit *Meghaduta* by Franklin and Eleanor Edgerton. Ann Arbor, University of Michigan Press; Toronto, Ambassador, 1964 P (Ann Arbor Paperbacks series)
   Delicate love poetry by the greatest lyric poet of ancient India (ca. 4th century B.C.).

KĀLIDĀSA. *Meghaduta (le Nuage messager), poème elegiaque.* Traduit et annoté par R. H. Assier de Pompignan ... En appendice: *Ṛtusaṃhāra (Les Saisons),* poéme descriptif attribué a Kālidāsa. Texte et tr. Paris, Les Belles Lettres, 1967 (Collection Emile Senart)
   See preceding note.

KĀLIDĀSA. *La naissance de Kumara.* Poême traduit du sanscrit et précedé d'une étude intitulée *Les Devoirs des dieux et des hommes* par Bernardette Tubini. Paris, Gallimard, 1958 (Collection Unesco d'Oeuvres Représentatives – Série Indienne) (Collection Connaissance de l'Orient)
   One of the finest Sanskrit poems, describing the events preceding the birth of Shiva's son – a religious-erotic epic.

KĀLIDĀSA. *Shakuntala, and other writings.* Translated with an introduction by Arthur W. Ryder. New York, Dutton, 1959 P
   One of the finest Sanskrit plays, enjoyably rendered into the English style typical of 1912, when it was first published. The book has an informative introduction, which includes summaries of two other plays of the same author.

PAÑCHATANTRA. *The Panchatantra.* Translated from the Sanskrit by Franklin Edgerton. London, Allen & Unwin, 1965; South Brunswick, N.J., A. S. Barnes, 1966 (Unesco Collection of Representative Works – Indian Series)
   A popular Sanskrit book of worldly wisdom, set in the form of animal fables, mingling narrative and verse. This work ultimately shares a common ancient Indian ancestor with similar collections in other languages such as the Arabic and Persian *Kalīlah and Dimnah* fables. Both the Edgerton and Ryder (below) translations are good.

PAÑCHATANTRA. *The Panchatantra.* Translated from the Sanskrit by Arthur W. Ryder. Chicago, University of Chicago Press, 1956 (and repr.); 1964 P
   See preceding note.

PAÑCHATANTRA. *Pañcatantra*. Traduit du sanscrit et annoté par Edouard Lancereau. Paris, Gallimard, 1965 (Collection Connaissance de l'Orient) (Collection Unesco d'Oeuvres Représentatives – Série Indienne)
See preceding note.

VIDYĀKARA. *An anthology of Sanskrit court poetry: Vidyākara's "Subhāṣitaratnakosa."* Tr. Daniel H. H. Ingalls. Cambridge, Mass., Harvard University Press, 1965 (Harvard Oriental series) (Unesco Collection of Representative Works – Indian Series)
A very successful translation of an 11th century anthology.

WELLS, Henry W. (ed.) *Sanskrit plays in English translation.* New York, Asia Publishing House, 1963
Classical plays rendered by various translators.

iii/Mixed and Others

DHAMMAPADA. *The Dhammapada.* With introductory essays, Pali text, English translation and notes. By Sarvepalli Radhakrishnan. London, Toronto, New York, Oxford University Press, 1950
The title of this famous ancient collection of Buddhist verse means "Verses on virtue."

HERTSENS, Marcel. *Trésors mystiques de l'Inde: les grands textes de l'hindouisme et du bouddhisme.* [Paris], Editions du Centurion, 1968
An attractively produced selection of extracts, some of them translated by acknowledged scholars. Good annotated bibliography of works in French for further reading.

JĀTAKA. *Choix de Jātaka, extraits des Vies antérieures du Bouddha.* Traduit du pâli par Ginette Terral. Paris, Gallimard, 1958 P (Collection Connaissance de l'Orient) (Collection Unesco d'Oeuvres Représentatives – Série Indienne)
Buddhist ethical teachings contained in popular traditional stories.

*LIN, Yutang (comp.) *The wisdom of India.* London, New English Library, 1964 P
One of the best selections of texts covering a broad spectrum of Indian thought; translated by various hands.

*RENOU, Louis. *Anthologie sanskrite: textes littéraires, historiques, techniques, philosophiques et religieux.* 2ᵉ éd. Paris, Payot, 1961 P (Collection Bibliothèque Historique)
A sound selection by a renowned expert.

b/Regional and Non-classical (Pre-modern)

BHATTACHARYA, Deben (ed. & tr.) *The mirror of the sky: songs of the Bāuls from Bengal.* London, Allen & Unwin, 1969; American ed. under title: *Songs of*

the bards of Bengal. New York, Grove, 1970 (Unesco Collection of Representative Works — Indian Series)
Spiritual songs of illiterate wandering minstrels in Bengal, providing for the religious needs of the peasantry.

BOWEN, John Charles Edward (tr.) *The golden pomegranate: a selection from the poetry of the Moghul Empire in India, 1526-1858, rendered into English verse.* London, Baker; Chester Springs, Pa., Dufour, 1966
A little book of engaging verse translations from originals in Persian, Urdu, Hindi, and Pashtu.

CAṆḌIDĀSA. *Love songs of Chandidās, the rebel poet-priest of Bengal.* Translated from the Bengali with introduction and notes by Deben Bhattacharya. London, Allen & Unwin, 1967; New York, Grove, 1970 P (Unesco Collection of Representative Works — Indian Series)
Somewhat free renderings of songs by a 15th century poet who greatly influenced later Bengali poets, including Tagore.

DIMOCK, Edward Cameron (ed. & tr.) *The thief of love: Bengali tales from court and village.* Chicago, University of Chicago Press, 1963
Well-translated selections from pre-modern Bengali literature, preceded by informative introductions.

IḶAṄGŌVAṬIKAḶ. *Shilappadikaram: "The ankle bracelet."* By Prince Ilangô Adigal. Tr. Alain Daniélou. New York, New Directions; Toronto, McClelland & Stewart, 1965 P; London, Allen & Unwin, 1967
An ancient Tamil tragic epic, attributed to a prince.

IḶAṄGŌVAṬIKAḶ. *Le Roman de l'anneau.* Par Ilaṅgovaḍigaḷ. Traduit du tamoul par Alain Danielou et R.-S. Desikan. Paris, Gallimard, 1961 (Collection Unesco d'Oeuvres Représentatives — Série Indienne) (Collection Connaissance de l'Orient)
See preceding note.

KABĪR. *Au cabaret de l'amour.* Traduit du Hindi par Charlotte Vaudeville. Paris, Gallimard, 1960 (Collection Unesco d'Oeuvres Représentatives — Série Indienne) (Collection Connaissance de l'Orient)
Lofty mystical poetry in Hindi attributed to the famous 15th century religious reformer who combined Muslim and Hindu elements into a new synthesis.

KABĪR. *One hundred poems of Kabir.* Translated by Rabindranath Tagore, assisted by Evelyn Underhill. London, Toronto, New York, Macmillan, 1915, repr. 1961 (Unesco Collection of Representative Works — Indian Series)
The translations often seem to bear the marks of Tagore's own genius rather than the author's meaning.

KAMBAN. *The Ayodha canto of the Ramayana*, as told by Kamban. Tr. C. Rajagopalachari. London, Allen & Unwin, 1961; New Delhi, Sahitya Akademi, 1970 (Unesco Collection of Representative Works – Indian Series)
A 9th century Tamil poet's retelling of an episode from the great Sanskrit epic.

KURUNTOKAI. *The interior landscape: love poems from a classical Tamil anthology*. Tr. A. K. Ramanujan. Bloomington, Indiana University Press, 1967; London, Peter Owen, 1970 (Unesco Collection of Representative Works – Indian Series) (Asian Literature Program of the Asia Society)
Effective translations of short passages originally written in Tamil, the second great classical language of India. This collection is ascribed to the early centuries of the Christian era. The translator has written an informative "afterword" explaining the literary conventions of Tamil poetry.

TUKĀRĀM. *Psaumes de pèlerin*. [Par] Toukaram. Traduction du marathe ... par G.-A. Deleury. 4ᵉ éd. Paris, Gallimard, 1956 (Collection Unesco d'Oeuvres Représentatives – Série Indienne) (Collection Connaissance de l'Orient)
Poems of a 17th century Marathi mystic.

TULASĪDĀSA. *L'Ayodhyakanda du Rāmāyana: "Le Lac spirituel."* Tr. Charlotte Vaudeville. Paris, A.-Maisonneuve, 1955

TULASĪDĀSA. *The petition to Rām.* [By] Tulsī Dās. Hindu devotional hymns of the seventeenth century. A translation of the Vinaya-patrika ... by F. R. Allchin. London, Allen & Unwin; New York, A. S. Barnes, 1966 (Unesco Collection of Representative Works – Indian Series)
Famous "self-communing" religious poetry.

VIDYĀPATI ṬHAKUR. *Love songs of Vidyāpati.* Tr. Deben Bhattacharya. Edited with an introduction, notes and comments by W. G. Archer. London, Allen & Unwin, 1963; New York, Grove, 1970 P (Unesco Collection of Representative Works – Indian Series)
Somewhat free translations which strive to retain the "essence" of the original poetry, composed about 1380-1406, by an author in eastern India. Archer's introductory essay places the work in historical and literary context.

c/Modern

BANDOPADHYAYA, Manik. *The puppet's tale.* Translated from the Bengali by Sachindralal Ghosh. Ed. Arthur Isenberg. New Delhi, Sahitya Akademi, 1968 (Unesco Collection of Representative Works – Indian Series)
A pioneer angry "realist-objective" novel, about the break-up of the personality of an educated man who wishes to return to village life. Implicit social criticism of life in rural India.

BANERJEE, Tarasankar. *Ganadevata (The temple pavilion)*. Tr. Lila Ray. Bombay, Pearl, 1969
A prize-winning realistic novel of Bengal village life in the author's native region, by one of Bengal's major living writers.

BANERJI, Bibhutibhushan. *Pather Panchali: Song of the road*. Tr. T. W. Clark and Tarapada Mukherji. London, Allen & Unwin; Bloomington, University of Indiana Press, 1968 (Unesco Collection of Representative Works — Indian Series)
This well-known Bengali novel depicts the life of a Brahmin family as seen through children's eyes. The film version was widely acclaimed in the West.

BANERJI, Bibhutibhushan. *La complainte du sentier*. Traduction du bengali par F. Bhattacharya. Paris, Gallimard, 1969 P (Collection Unesco d'Oeuvres Représentatives — Série Indienne)
See preceding note.

BHADURI, Satinath. *The vigil*. Translated from the Bengali by Lila Ray. Bombay, London, New York, Asia Publishing House, 1965 (Unesco Collection of Representative Works — Indian Series)
This prize-winning novel, set in the Indian struggle against British colonial rule in 1942, gives an insight into the psychology of Indian nationalism.

CHATTERJEE, Bankim-Chandra. *Krishnakanta's will*. Translated from the Bengali by J. C. Ghosh. New York, New Directions, 1962 P (Unesco Collection of Representative Works — Indian Series)
One of the earliest Indian social novels, portraying Bengali life in the late 19th century.

Contemporary Indian short stories. 2 vols. New Delhi, Sahitya Akademi, 1959-67 Series I, selected by Krishna Kripalani. Series II, ed. Bhabani Bhattacharya. Stories translated from all the official Indian regional languages plus several written in English. They cover a wide range of subjects, and throw an interesting light on current tastes.

FORSTER, Edward Morgan. *A passage to India*. London, New York, Harcourt, 1924 (and repr.); 1949 P (and repr.)
A classic novel which explores the contact of western and Indian cultures.

GUPTA, Bhairav Prasad. *Gange, o ma mère*. Traduit du hindi par Nicole Balbir. Paris, Gallimard, 1967 P (Collection Du Monde Entier)
A Hindi novel.

JHABVALA, Ruth Prawer. *The householder*. London, Murray; New York, Norton, 1960
A novel of urban life in modern India, by a leading writer.

KABIR, Humayun (ed.) *Green and gold: stories and poems from Bengal.* Norfolk, Conn., New Directions, 1959
A noted selection.

KAUR, Prabhjot. *Plateau: poems.* London, Asia Publishing House, 1966
An award-winning collection; many of the translations are the author's.

KUNHAPPA, Murkot. *Three bags of gold, and other Indian folk tales.* Bombay, London, New York, Asia Publishing House, 1964

MADGULKAR, Vyankatesh Digambar. *The village had no walls.* Tr. Ram Deshmukh. London, 1958 (and repr.); New York, Taplinger, 1966 P
A prize-winning vivid novel of the problems of rural life, based on the experiences of its author, who was a teacher in a village and is a well-known Marathi writer.

MARKANDAYA, Kamala. *Nectar in a sieve.* New York, John Day, 1954; New American Library, 1956 P (Signet Books)
A moving novel of Indian village life, by a leading woman novelist.

MISRA, Vidya Niwas (ed.) *Modern Hindi poetry.* Bloomington, Indiana University Press, 1965 (Unesco Collection of Contemporary Works – Indian Series)
An interesting anthology; translated and partially "recreated" into English poetry by six American poets.

NARAYAN, R. K. *The financial expert.* London, Methuen, 1952; New York, Farrar, 1953; 1959 P
An excellent novel by a major Indian writer in English.

NARAYAN, R. K. *Gods, demons and other great tales from Indian myth and legend.* New York, Viking, 1964; 1967 P
Indian legends skilfully "retold" and sometimes adapted by the famous Indian novelist.

NARAYAN, R. K. *The guide.* London, Methuen; New York, Viking, 1958; New American Library 1966 P (Signet Books)
An excellent amusing picaresque novel set in South India.

NARAYAN, R. K. *The vendor of sweets.* New York, Viking, 1967

PILLAI, Thakazhi. *Chemeen.* Tr. Narayana Menon. London, Gollancz; New York, Harper, 1962 (Unesco Collection of Representative Works – Indian Series)
This powerful and vividly told story of life and love among the fishermen of Kerala in South India won the highest Indian literary prize.

PILLAI, Thakazhi. *Un amour indien.* Tr. N. Balbir. Paris, Mercure de France, 1965 (Collection Unesco d'Oeuvres Représentatives – Série Indienne)
See preceding note.

*PREMCHAND. *The gift of a cow:* a translation of the Hindi novel, *Godaan,* by Gordon C. Roadarmel. London, Allen & Unwin, 1968; Bloomington, Indiana University Press, 1969 (Unesco Collection of Representative Works – Indian Series)
A portrayal of social and economic tensions in an Indian village; this is probably the best work of the most famous Hindi novelist. Premchand has greatly influenced most later writers in Hindi in both style and subject (lower and middle classes, clash of values, and social change). The translation is excellent.

PREMCHAND. *The world of Premchand.* Short stories translated from Hindi by David Rubin. London, Allen & Unwin; Bloomington, Indiana University Press, 1969 (Unesco Collection of Representative Works – Indian Series)
A selection of stories, most of which were not previously translated into English.

RAESIDE, I. M. P. (ed.) *The rough and the smooth.* Calcutta, London, New York, Asia Publishing House, 1967
Translations of Marathi short stories.

RAO, Raja. *Kanthapura.* New York, New Directions, 1963
A widely praised novel (first published in 1938) describing the impact of Gandhi's struggle for independence on an Indian village.

*RAO, Raja. *The serpent and the rope.* New York, Pantheon, 1963
A remarkable "self-portrait of the South Indian Brahmin psyche," this is a novel exploring the relationship of an Indian and a Frenchwoman. Beautifully written.

RAU, Santha Rama. *Home to India.* New York, Harper, 1945; Englewood Cliffs, N.J., Scholastic, 1963 P
A gaily written autobiography of a westernized Indian girl's return to India and the attendant problems.

SINGH, Gopal. *The unstruck melody: poems.* London, Asia Publishing House, 1968
Very interesting free verse, translated by the author from his own Panjabi originals.

SWAMINATHAN, K. *The plough and the stars.* Ed. K. Swaminathan, M. P. Periaswami, Thooran and M. R. Perumal Mudaliar. Bombay, London, New York, Asia Publishing House, 1964

Twenty-six modern Tamil (Southern Indian) short stories, preceded by a background survey of the literary and cultural traditions of the region.

TAGORE, Rabindranath. *Collected poems and plays.* London, Toronto, New York, Macmillan, 1956
   The main poetical and dramatic works of the Bengali winner of the Nobel Prize for Literature in 1913. In general, even good translations of his works usually lack the power and charm of the Bengali originals.

TAGORE, Rabindranath. *A flight of swans: poems from Balaka.* Tr. Aurobindo Bose. Rev. ed. London, Murray; New York, Paragon, 1962 (Wisdom of the East series)
   Some of Tagore's best poems. Other volumes of his poetry available in the "Wisdom of the East" series and translated by Aurobindo Bose include two late works: *The herald of spring: poems from Mohua,* 1957, and *The wings of death,* 1960.

TAGORE, Rabindranath. *Cygne.* Tr. P. J. Jouve et K. Nag. Réédité sur la recommandation de l'Unesco à l'occasion du centenaire de la naissance de l'auteur. Paris, Stock, 1961
   See preceding note.

TAGORE, Rabindranath. *Gitanjali* (Song offerings). A collection of prose translations made by the author from the original Bengali. London, Toronto, Macmillan, 1913, repr. 1965 (Unesco Collection of Representative Works — Indian Series)
   Tagore's fame in the western world originated with this short book.

TAGORE, Rabindranath. *L'offrande lyrique.* Traduction de l'anglais et introduction par André Gide. Paris, Gallimard, 1914 P (and repr.) (Collection Du Monde Entier)
   See preceding note.

TAGORE, Rabindranath. *Gorâ.* Traduction de M. Glotz, entièrement revue sur le texte bengali par P. Fallon. Paris, Laffont, 1961 (Collection Unesco d'Oeuvres Représentatives — Série Indienne)
   Perhaps the best of Tagore's novels.

TAGORE, Rabindranath. *The housewarming and other selected writings.* Ed. Amiya Chakravarty. Tr. Mary Lago and Tarun Gupta. New York, New American Library, 1965 P
   This inexpensive book is good value: it consists mainly of translations of short stories, but also contains some poetry and two plays.

TAGORE, Rabindranath. *One hundred and one: poems.* [Ed. Humayun Kabir.] London, Asia Publishing House, 1966

A well-chosen and interesting selection of poetry composed over a period of 60 years by the great Bengali poet, and translated into English by various Indian authors.

TAGORE, Rabindranath. *Souvenirs d'enfance.* Traduit du bengali par Christine Bossennec et Rajishswari Datta. Paris, Gallimard, 1964 (Collection Unesco d'Oeuvres Représentatives – Série Indienne) (Collection Du Monde Entier)

*TAGORE, Rabindranath. *A Tagore reader.* Ed. Amiya Chakravarty. London, Toronto, New York, Macmillan, 1961; Boston, Beacon, 1966 P (Unesco Collection of Representative Works – Indian Series)
   Excellent selections from a broad range of Tagore's works – poems, plays, letters, and literary criticism. Some of the translations from the Bengali are by Tagore himself.

TAGORE, Rabindranath. *Le vagabond et autres histoires.* Traduit du bengali par Christine Bossennec et Kamaleswar Bhattacharya. Paris, Gallimard, 1962 (Collection Unesco d'Oeuvres Représentatives – Série Indienne) (Collection Du Monde Entier)
   French versions of several other works by Tagore (mostly translated from the English in the 1920s) are available from Éditions Gallimard, Paris.

4 RELIGION AND IDEAS[†]

a/Religion: General Works

*de BARY, William Theodore (comp.) *Sources of Indian tradition.* Compiled by Wm. T. de Bary, Stephen Hay, Roy Weiler [and] Andrew Yarrow. New York, Columbia University Press; Toronto, Oxford University Press, 1958 (and repr.); 2 vols., 1964 P (Introduction to Oriental Civilizations series)
   An excellent selection of texts intended "to provide the general reader with an understanding of the intellectual and spiritual traditions" of India and Pakistan. Includes pieces not only of religious and philosophical, but also of political, social, and economic interest, from antiquity to the present.

*RADHAKRISHNAN, Sarvepalli. *East and West in Religion.* London, Allen & Unwin; New York, Macmillan, 1933 (and repr.)
   Notable essays by the famous Indian thinker who became president of India.

RADHAKRISHNAN, Sarvepalli. *Eastern religions and western thought.* Oxford, Clarendon Press, 1939; New York, Toronto, Oxford University Press, 1940; 1959 P

[†]Many classical religious works will be found in the preceding section, "Indian literature in translation."

An apologia by a leading modern Indian thinker, viewing and interpreting Hindu ideas through the prism of European thought.

RÉGNIER, Rita. *L'Inde et les pays indianisés*. Paris, Bloud & Gay, 1963 P (Collection Religions du Monde)
A brief and elementary sketch of Indian religions, written for laymen.

Les religions de l'Inde. Traduit de l'allemand par L. Jospin. 3 vols. Paris, Payot, 1962-66 P (Collection Bibliothèque Historique, Les Religions de l'Humanité)
Tome 1: *Védisme et hindouisme ancien*, par Jan Gonda. Tome 2: *L'hindouisme récent*, par Jan Gonda. Tome 3: *Buddhisme et jaïnisme*, par A. Bareau. A competent detailed description.

TAGORE, Rabindranath. *The religion of man*. London, Allen & Unwin, 1930, repr. 1953 C&P; New York, Macmillan, 1931, repr. 1958; New York, Beacon, 1961 P
Tagore's religious views, set out in these Hibbert lectures of 1930, help to explain his poetry.

WEBER, Max. *The religion of India: the sociology of Hinduism and Buddhism*. Tr. & ed. Hans H. Gerth and Don Martindale. New York, Free Press (Macmillan); Toronto, London, Collier-Macmillan, 1958; 1967 P
This famous sociological study contains keen insights in placing Indian religions in their general sociological contexts. Since this book was first published in 1921, much evidence has, however, appeared which contradicts the idealized picture presented.

b/Hinduism (including Vedism)

ARCHER, William George. *The loves of Krishna in Indian painting and poetry*. London, Allen & Unwin; New York, Macmillan, 1957; New York, Grove, 1958 P
Krishna's activities are a favourite theme in Indian culture. This well-illustrated book examines their place in poetry and art.

ELIADE, Mircea. *Le Yoga: immortalité et liberté*. Paris, Payot, 1954
An introduction to the principles of Yoga for intellectual westerners.

ELIADE, Mircea. *Yoga: immortality and freedom*. Tr. Willard R. Trask. New York, Pantheon, 1958
See preceding note.

*EMBREE, Ainslie T. (ed.) *The Hindu tradition*. New York, Modern Library (Random House); Toronto, Random House, 1966 (Readings in Oriental Thought series)

A very useful selection of the basic writings of the Hindu tradition over 3000 years, arranged chronologically. Mainly religious, literary, and philosophical. Each section is preceded by an introduction setting the passage(s) in historical and cultural perspective. The absence of interpretive notes is a disadvantage.

GATHIER, Émile. *La pensée hindoue: étude suivie d'un choix de textes.* Paris, Seuil, 1960 (Collection Les Univers)
Covers classical and modern Hinduism, and makes comparisons with Christianity.

MAHADEVAN, T. M. P. *Outlines of Hinduism.* 2nd ed. Bombay, Bharatiya Vidya Bhavan, 1960 P
The author has a "genuine respect for devotional practice and gives a frankly protagonistic presentation." It thus counterbalances Zaehner's *Hinduism* (below).

MORGAN, Kenneth (ed.) *The religion of the Hindus.* New York, Ronald, 1953
Interesting essays by modern Hindus on various aspects of Hinduism, with a selection of passages from Hindu scriptures. According to one critic, the essays "shirk the issue of the gap between norm and actuality."

PARRINDER, Geoffrey. *Upanishads, Gītā and Bible: a comparative study of Hindu and Christian scriptures.* London, Faber, 1962
A fairly useful study written in terms intelligible to the layman.

RADHAKRISHNAN, Sarvepalli. *The Hindu view of life.* London, Allen & Unwin, 1927; repr. 1961 C&P
An Indian philosopher's popular account of Hinduism for the western reader.

*RENOU, Louis. *L 'hindouisme.* 4ᵉ éd. Paris, Presses Universitaires de France, 1966 P (Collection "Que sais-je?")
A good introductory guide.

*RENOU, Louis (ed.) *Hinduism.* New York, Braziller, 1961; Washington Square Press, 1963 P (Great Religions of Modern Man series)
A good preliminary guide, consisting of 40 informative pages of historical introduction to Hinduism as a religion and as a society, followed by 39 passages judiciously selected from notable religious texts dating from classical times to the present.

*RENOU, Louis. *Religions of ancient India.* London, Athlone Press; New York, De Graff, 1953 (Jordan Lectures in Comparative Religion)
This lecture is an authoritative survey of Vedism, Hinduism, and Jainism but does not include Buddhism.

SEN, Kshiti Mohan. *Hinduism.* Harmondsworth, Baltimore, Penguin, 1961
A Hindu scholar's summary of Hinduism's beliefs, practices, and historical
development followed by extracts from four Hindu scriptures.

SEN, Kshiti Mohan. *L'Hindouisme.* Tr. M. et L. Jospin. Paris, Payot, 1962 (Collection Petit Bibliothèque Payot)
See preceding note.

WOOD, Ernest. *Yoga.* Harmondsworth, Baltimore, Penguin, 1959 P (Pelican
Books)
Discusses yoga's philosophy of striving for "liberation," and its practices;
also describes yoga exercises for use in the West.

*ZAEHNER, R. C. *Hinduism.* 2nd ed. London, Toronto, New York, Oxford
University Press, 1962; 1966 P (Home University Library series; Galaxy Books)
A good outline of major Hindu beliefs and a review of modern developments in Hinduism. Counterbalances Mahadevan's *Outlines of Hinduism*
(above).

c/Buddhism †

BACOT, Jacques. *Le Bouddha.* Paris, Presses Universitaires de France, 1947
(Collection Mythes et Religions)
An outline treatment.

BAREAU, A. *Bouddha.* Paris, Seghers, 1962 (Collection Philosophes de Tous
les Temps)
The origins of Buddhism, with a life of the Buddhá and extracts from early
Buddhist texts.

BROWN, Donald Mackenzie (ed.) *The white umbrella: Indian political thought
from Manu to Gandhi.* Berkeley, University of California Press; London, Cambridge University Press, 1953; 1958 P (and repr.)
A useful textbook selection. Good sectional introductions.

CH'EN, Kenneth Kuan Shêng. *Buddhism: the light of Asia.* Woodbury, N.Y.,
Barron, 1968 C&P (Barron's Compact Studies of World Religions)
A solid work, more comprehensive than Conze's book (below) but shows
less insight. Includes special chapters on Buddhism in several countries and
Buddhist art and ceremonies.

---

†General and Indian Buddhism only. Books on Buddhist developments in other individual
countries are listed under those countries in parts III D, IV B (subsection 6b), and IV C
(subsection 6).

*CONZE, Edward. *Buddhism: its essence and development.* Oxford, Cassirer, 1951; London, Faber, 1963; New York, Harper, 1959 P (and repr.) (Harper Torchbooks)
    A short yet comprehensive, lucid and scholarly introduction to Buddhist ideas and practice.

*CONZE, Edward. *Le bouddhisme dans son essence et son développement.* Paris, Payot, 1952 (Collection Bibliothèque Scientifique)
    See preceding note.

CONZE, Edward. *Buddhist meditation.* London, Allen & Unwin, 1956 (and repr.) (Ethical and Religious Classics of East and West series)
    Meditation lies at the heart of Buddhism. This is a clear and informative anthology of classical Buddhist texts on the subject.

CONZE, Edward (comp. & tr.) *Buddhist scriptures.* Harmondsworth, Baltimore, Penguin, 1959
    A good anthology of texts showing the main features of Buddhism.

*CONZE, Edward (ed.) *Buddhist texts through the ages.* Translated from Pali, Sanskrit, Chinese, Tibetan, Japanese and Apabhramsa. Edited in collaboration with I. B. Horner, D. Snellgrove, A. Waley. New York, London, Harper, 1964 P (repr. of Oxford and New York, Philosophical Library, 1954 ed.) (Harper Torchbooks)
    A selection representing the major schools of Buddhism; can be effectively used in conjunction with Conze's *Buddhism: its essence and development* (above), which provides the necessary background.

CONZE, Edward. *Buddhist thought in India.* London, Allen & Unwin, 1962
    An important work by a leading scholar in the field.

*de BARY, William Theodore (ed.) *The Buddhist tradition.* New York, Modern Library, 1969
    A good short selection of Buddhist texts. Most of them appeared previously in the same editor's excellent sourcebooks, cited elsewhere in this reading guide: (1) *Sources of Indian tradition,* (2) *Sources of Chinese tradition,* and (3) R. Tsunoda's *Sources of the Japanese tradition.*

FOUCHER, Alfred Charles Auguste. *La vie du Bouddha.* Paris, Payot, 1949 P (Collection Bibliothèque Historique)
    An original attempt at a scholarly biography by a noted archaeologist.

FOUCHER, Alfred Charles Auguste. *The life of the Buddha, according to the ancient texts and monuments of India.* Abridged translation by Simone Brangier Boas. Middletown, Conn., Wesleyan University Press, 1963
    See preceding note.

FOUCHER, Alfred Charles Auguste. *Les vies antérieures du Bouddha, d'après les textes et les monuments de l'Inde*. Choix de contes. Paris, Presses Universitaires de France, 1955 (Publications du Musée Guimet, Collection Bibliothèque de Diffusion)
   An attractive selection of fables and legends.

HAMILTON, Clarence Herbert (ed.) *Buddhism: a religion of infinite compassion. Selections from Buddhist literature.* Indianapolis, New York, Bobbs-Merrill, 1952 P (Library of Literal Arts series)
   A representative introductory selection of non-philosophical passages from standard Buddhist texts.

MORGAN, Kenneth William (ed.) *The path of the Buddha: Buddhism interpreted by Buddhists.* New York, Ronald, 1956
   It should be made clear that the "interpreters" are all contemporary Buddhists.

MURTI, T. R. V. *The central philosophy of Buddhism.* London, Allen & Unwin, 1955
   "A masterly study of the Mâdhyamika school."

RAHULA, Walpola. *L'enseignement du Bouddha, d'après les textes les plus anciens.* Étude suivie d'un choix de textes. Paris, Seuil, 1961
   A lucid account of the basic principles of Buddhism, followed by a selection of illustrative texts. The author is a Buddhist monk from Ceylon.

RAHULA, Walpola. *What the Buddha taught.* 2nd ed. Bedford, England, Gordon Fraser, 1967
   See preceding note.

SANGHARAKSHITA, Bhikshu. *The Three Jewels: an introduction to Buddhism.* London, Rider, 1967
   "A readable and reliable account by an Englishman who has been a Buddhist monk for twenty years, mostly in India."

*SCHUON, Frithjof. *In the tracks of Buddhism.* Translated from the French by Marco Pallis. London, Allen & Unwin, 1968
   Essentials of Buddhism described with clarity, using comparisons with western religious thought. Emphasis on Japanese Buddhism.

THOMAS, Edward Joseph (ed. & tr.) *The Perfection of Wisdom: the career of the predestined Buddhas.* Tr. E. J. Thomas. London, Murray; New York, Paragon, 1952 (Wisdom of the East series)
   Extracts from Mahayana Buddhist scriptures on the nature of those who are to become Buddhas.

WARREN, Henry Clarke (ed. & tr.) *Buddhism in translations: passages selected from the Buddhist sacred books*, translated from the Pali. Cambridge, Mass., Harvard University Press, 1896, repr. 1953; 1963 P (Harvard Oriental series) (Atheneum)
> Well-chosen extracts bring out clearly the traditional Buddhist teachings on many subjects.

WOODWARD, F. L. (tr.) *Some sayings of the Buddha*. London, Toronto, New York, Oxford University Press, 1925 (and repr.) (World's Classics series)
> A good selection from the Pali canon of Buddhism.

ZURCHNER, Erik. *Buddhism: its origin and spread in words, maps and pictures*. London, Routledge, 1962
> An extremely elementary outline.

d/Other Religions

ĀDI GRANTH. *Selections from the sacred writings of the Sikhs*. Tr. Trilochan Singh [and others]. Revised by George S. Fraser. London, Allen & Unwin, 1960 (and repr.) (Unesco Collection of Representative Works — Indian Series)
> A notable translation from the Ādi Granth, the scripture of the Sikh religion, which owes its origin in the 15th century to the meeting of Hinduism and Islam.

ARCHER, John Clark. *The Sikhs in relation to Hindus, Moslems, Christians and Ahmadiyyas: a study in comparative religion*. Princeton, Princeton University Press, 1946
> The minority religious communities have not yet been adequately studied in a comparative way. The Ahmadiya sect of Islam was founded in the Panjab in 1879.

NĀNAK (1st guru of the Sikhs). *Hymns of Guru Nanak*. Tr. Khushwant Singh. New Delhi, Orient Longmans, 1969 C&P (Unesco Collection of Representative Works — Indian Series)
> Panjabi religious poetry by the founder of the Sikh sect (1469-1538).

TISSERANT, Eugène. *Eastern Christianity in India: a history of the Syro-Malabar Church from the earliest time to the present day*. Authorized adaption from the French by E. R. Hambye. Bombay, Orient Longmans; Toronto, London, Longmans, 1957
> Mainly the Christian history of the Malabar region (revised from the French original of 1941).

e/Philosophy and Thought

CHATTERJEE, Satischandra. *An introduction to Indian philosophy.* By Satischandra Chatterjee and D. M. Datta. 5th ed. Calcutta, University of Calcutta, 1954
   A good short outline.

GHOSHAL, Upendra Nath. *A history of Indian political ideas: the ancient period and the period of transition to the Middle Ages.* 3rd ed. Bombay, Toronto, Oxford University Press, 1959
   Hindu political theories before the Muslim period; a standard work.

*GLASENAPP, Helmuth von. *La philosophie indienne. Initiation à l'histoire de l'Inde et à ses doctrines.* Tr. A.-M. Esnoul. Paris, Payot, 1951 (Collection Bibliothèque Scientifique)
   An excellent presentation by an outstanding scholar. Major section headings: Historical development; the Great systems; the Main problems regarding the conception of the world; Indian philosophy and western philosophy.

History of philosophy, eastern and western. Sponsored by the Ministry of Education, Government of India. 2 vols. London, Allen & Unwin, 1952-53 (and repr.)
   Vol. I is devoted mainly to Indian philosophy, with brief surveys of Chinese and Japanese thought.

MOORE, Charles A. (ed.) *The Indian mind. Essentials of Indian philosophy and culture.* Honolulu, East-West Center Press (University of Hawaii Press), 1967
   A selection of articles by leading "establishment" modern thinkers showing "the fundamentals of the Indian mind as expressed in its great philosophies, religions, social thought and practices" (Editor). Intelligible to educated laymen with a philosophic bent.

NARAVANE, Vishwanath Shridhar. *Modern Indian thought: a philosophical survey.* London, Asia Publishing House, 1965

POTTER, Karl H. *Presuppositions of India's philosophies.* Englewood Cliffs, N.J., Prentice-Hall, 1963
   "One of the few treatments of Indian philosophy on a thematic and problem basis familiar to Western philosophers."

RADHAKRISHNAN, Sarvepalli (ed.) *Contemporary Indian philosophy.* Ed. S. Radhakrishnan and J. H. Muirhead. 2nd ed. London, Allen & Unwin; New York, Macmillan, 1952 (Muirhead Library of Philosophy series)
   Essays by leading contemporary Indian philosophers.

RADHAKRISHNAN, Sarvepalli. *Indian philosophy.* 2nd ed. 2 vols. London, Allen & Unwin; New York, Macmillan, 1929; repr. 1959 (Muirhead Library of Philosophy series)

A well-known interpretation (at times a reinterpretation) of the Indian tradition of philosophy; the influence of western ideas is obvious in this presentation.

RADHAKRISHNAN, Sarvepalli. *A source book in Indian philosophy.* By S. Radhakrishnan and Charles A. Moore. Princeton, Princeton University Press, 1957; 1967 P

A useful selection of translations from ancient, classical, and two modern Indian philosophical works, arranged for the non-Indian philosophical reader.

SAIYIDAIN, Khwaja Ghulam. *The humanist tradition in Indian educational thought.* London, New York, Asia Publishing House; Toronto, Ryerson, 1966

A leading Indian educationist examines the educational ideas of such men as Tagore, Iqbal, Gandhi, Abul Kalam Azad, and Zakir Husain.

SAMARTHA, S. J. *Introduction to Radhakrishnan: the man and his thought.* New York, Association Press, 1964 C&P

A study of Sarvepalli Radhakrishnan, a leading modern Hindu thinker, who was elected president of India in 1962.

SMART, Ninian. *Doctrine and argument in Indian philosophy.* London, Allen & Unwin, 1964 (Muirhead Library of Philosophy series)

A good treatment of the major classical systems of Indian philosophy and a comparison of their treatment of various general religious and philosophical problems, such as causation and the existence of God. Avoids Indian technical terminology.

5 ARTS AND CRAFTS, ARCHITECTURE, AND SCIENCE

ARCHER, William George. *India and modern art.* London, Allen & Unwin, 1959

An interesting study of painting in India in the first half of the 20th century.

ARCHER, William George. *Indian miniatures.* Greenwich, Conn., New York Graphic Society, 1960 (Great Masters of the Past series)

One hundred miniatures (half in colour) from the 12th to the 18th centuries, with brief descriptions.

ARCHER, William George. *Indian painting: fifteen color plates.* London, Toronto, New York, Oxford University Press, 1957

ARCHER, William George. *Painting of the Sikhs.* London, Her Majesty's Stationery Office, 1966 (Victoria and Albert Museum, Monograph series)
An excellent introduction to Sikh painting.

*AUBOYER, Jeannine. *Les arts de l'Inde et des pays indianisés.* Paris, Presses Universitaires de France, 1968 (Collection Les Neufs Muses)
This introduction is particularly good in setting out the essential characteristics of India, and the place of the arts within the context of its civilization. The period up to the Guptas (about the year 1000) is well covered; the subsequent period is treated more sketchily. A shorter English version of the same text but with more and better illustrations appears in the collective volume *The oriental world: India and Southeast Asia* in the inexpensive series "Landmarks of the World's Art" (London, Hamlyn; New York, McGraw-Hill, 1967).

AUBOYER, Jeannine. *Arts et styles de l'Inde.* Paris, Larousse, 1951 (Collection Arts, Styles et Techniques)

AUBOYER, Jeannine. *Introduction à l'étude de l'art de l'Inde.* Roma, Istituto Italiano per il Medio ed Estremo Oriente, 1965 (Serie Orientale Roma)
A scholarly discussion of factors in Indian life and history which have affected the development of its art.

BARNOUW, Erik. *Indian film.* By Erik Barnouw and S. Krishnaswamy. New York, Columbia University Press, 1963
A history of one of the major and most distinctive film industries in Asia.

BOWERS, Faubion. *The dance in India.* New York, Columbia University Press, 1953
A standard introductory work on Indian classical and folk dances.

BROWN, Percy. *Indian architecture.* Vol. 1: *Buddhist and Hindu periods.* 3rd ed. Bombay, Taraporevala, 1956
A standard work for the Buddhist and Hindu monuments.

BUSSAGLI, Mario. *Indian miniatures.* London, Toronto, New York, Hamlyn, 1969 (Cameo series)
Seventy-three fine miniatures in colour (with short accompanying text). Excellent artistic value at a low price.

GARGI, Balwant. *Folk theatre of India.* Seattle, London, University of Washington Press, 1964

A well-written description of nine traditional rural types of folk drama. They are entirely different from the classical theatre.

GOETZ, Hermann. *India: five thousand years of Indian art.* 2nd ed. London, Toronto, Methuen; New York, Crown, 1964 (Art of the World series)
Quite a good survey, illustrated entirely in colour.

HAMBLY, Gavin. *Cities of Mughal India: Delhi, Agra and Fatehpur Sikri.* Photographs by Wim Swaan. London, Elek; Toronto, Ryerson, 1968
Text describes in outline the history of the Mughal dynasty. The superb illustrations, mainly Mughal paintings and photographs of their architecture, illustrate the life and surroundings of the emperors.

KRAMRISCH, Stella. *The art of India: traditions of Indian sculpture, painting, and architecture.* 3rd ed. London, Phaidon Press; New York, New York Graphic Society, 1965
A learned introductory essay of 50 pages, interpreting the symbolism of Indian art, particularly its relationship to religion. 180 fine illustrations, mainly Hindu and Buddhist sculpture, with notes.

KRAMRISCH, Stella. *Arts de l'Inde: traditions de la sculpture, de la peinture et de l'architecture.* Tr. Anne-Marie Esnoul. Paris, Massin, 1955
See preceding note.

RAWSON, Philip. *Indian sculpture.* London, Studio Vista; New York, Dutton, 1966 P
An inexpensive, well-illustrated general introduction.

RAWSON, Philip S. *Indian painting.* London, Zwemmer; Toronto, Burns & MacEachern; New York, Universe, 1961
From prehistoric cave paintings to the 19th century. A good text, lavishly illustrated entirely in colour.

RAWSON, Philip S. *La peinture indienne.* Tr. Georges Lambin. Paris, Tisné, 1961
See preceding note.

*ROWLAND, Benjamin. *The art and architecture of India: Buddhist, Hindu, Jain.* 3rd ed. Harmondsworth, Baltimore, Penguin, 1967 (Pelican History of Art series)
Useful, though rather dry. Many black and white photographs.

SECKEL, Dietrich. *The art of Buddhism.* [Tr. Ann E. Keep.] London, Toronto, Methuen, 1964 (Art of the World series)

Divided into two main sections: (1) the spread of Buddhist art through Asia, country by country; (2) types and forms (e.g. temples, the Buddha image, symbolism). Well illustrated, good maps.

SECKEL, Dietrich. *L'Art du bouddhisme, migration et transformation.* Tr. J.-P. Simon. Paris, Albin Michel, 1964
See preceding note.

WELCH, Stuart C. *The art of Mughal India: paintings and precious objects.* [Catalogue of an exhibition shown in Asia House, 1964] New York, Asia Society, 1963
Eighty-eight fine reproductions, with introductory essays and descriptions that lay heavy stress on the "Indianness" of Mughal art, and seek to minimize its Persian and Turkish tradition.

WELCH, Stuart C. *Gods, thrones and peacocks.* By Stuart Cary Welch and Milo Cleveland Beach. New York, Asia Society, 1965 C&P
Mughal and Rajput paintings (15th to 19th centuries) excellently described in this well-illustrated exhibition catalogue.

6 MODERN INDIA

AZAD, Abul Kalam, Maulana. *India wins freedom: an autobiographical narrative.* New York, Toronto, Longmans, 1959
A controversial book by a major Muslim leader in India.

BETTELHEIM, Charles. *L'Inde indépendante.* Paris, Colin, 1962
A fully documented economic, political, and social survey of India since 1947, with very heavy emphasis on the economy.

BIARDEAU, Madeleine. *Inde.* Paris, Seuil, 1958 P (Collection Petite Planète)
A vivid impressionistic mosaic picture of Indian life: a highly readable (although over-simplified) short text interspersed with remarkable photographs. Suitable as a painless first introduction.

BIARDEAU, Madeleine. *India.* Tr. F. Carter. London, Studio Vista; New York, Viking, 1961 P (and repr.)
See preceding note.

BRECHER, Michael. *Nehru: a political biography.* London, Toronto, New York, Oxford University Press, 1959; [abridged ed.] Boston, Beacon, 1962 P
A notable study of the political architect of modern India.

BROWN, Donald Mackenzie (ed.) *The nationalist movement: Indian political thought from Ranade to Bhave.* Berkeley, University of California Press, 1961 C&P
Selected writings of nine Indian nationalist leaders of the present century.

BROWN, William Norman. *The United States and India and Pakistan.* 2nd ed. Cambridge, Mass., Harvard University Press, 1963 (American Foreign Policy Library series)
A sound general work on the historical and cultural factors affecting present-day developments in India and Pakistan, including a review of their foreign policies.

CHAUDHURI, Nirad C. *The autobiography of an unknown Indian.* London, Toronto, New York, Macmillan, 1951
Mirrors the political, cultural, and social life of 20th century British India, as seen from the inside by a perceptive Indian. Interesting and well observed.

CROCKER, Walter. *Nehru: a contemporary's estimate.* London, Allen & Unwin; New York, Oxford University Press, 1966
A good, relatively short account, neither idealized nor debunking, of one of modern India's chief architects and her first prime minister. The author is an Australian who knew and admired Nehru but was not unaware of his faults.

DAS, Durga. *India, from Curzon to Nehru and after.* London, Collins, 1969
This autobiography of a notable Indian journalist describes India since 1900. The author knew many of the chief political figures personally.

ÉTIENNE, Gilbert. *Les chances de l'Inde.* Paris, Seuil, 1969 P (Collection Esprit, Frontière Ouverte)
A study of contemporary India with particular emphasis on economic factors.

FISCHER, Louis. *Gandhi: his life and message for the world.* New York, Toronto, New American Library; London, New English Library, 1954 P (and repr.) (Mentor Books)
A popular short life.

*FISCHER, Louis. *The life of Mahatma Gandhi.* New York, Harper, 1950; London, Cape, 1951; New York, Collier, 1962 P
Probably the best biography of the outstanding Indian of the century.

GANDHI, Mohandas Karamchand. *All men are brothers: life and thoughts, as told in his own words.* New York, London, Columbia University Press; Paris, Unesco, 1958
   A selection of his writings on non-violence, religion, education, etc.

GANDHI, Mohandas Karamchand. *Tous les hommes sont frères:* Vie et pensées du Mahatma Gandhi d'après ses oeuvres. Textes choisis par Krishna Kripalani, tr. Guy Vogelweith. Paris, Gallimard, 1969 (Collection Idées)
   See preceding note.

GANDHI, Mohandas Karamchand. *An autobiography, or the Story of my experiments with truth.* Tr. M. Desai. New York, Beacon, 1957 P
   A candid self-analysis, down to 1920.

GANDHI, Mohandas Karamchand. *Expériences de vérité, ou Autobiographie.* Tr. G. Belmont. Paris, Presses Universitaires de France, 1950
   Preceded by excellent study of Gandhi by Pierre Meile. See preceding note.

GANDHI, Mohandas Karamchand. *The essential Gandhi: his life, work, and ideas.* An anthology, edited by Louis Fischer. New York, Toronto, Random House, 1962; 1963 P (Vintage Books)
   Quotations of Gandhi's views on many topics, arranged by subject.

GRIFFITHS, Percival Joseph. *Modern India.* 4th ed. London, Benn; New York, Praeger, 1965 (Nations of the Modern World series)
   A short historical survey followed by a detailed examination of political and economic affairs since 1947, written for laymen by a former Indian civil servant.

LACOMBE, Olivier. *Gandhi, ou la force de l'âme.* Paris, Plon, 1964 P (Collection La Recherche de l'Absolu)
   A useful study of Gandhi's ideas.

LAMB, Beatrice Pitney. *India: a world in transition.* [3rd ed.] New York, Praeger, 1968 C&P
   An enthusiastic approach suitable for college students and others without any previous knowledge. Explains contemporary India with constant reference to its past.

LAMB, Beatrice Pitney. *L'Inde: un monde en transition.* Verviers (Belgique), Gérard; Québec, Kasan; Paris, Inter, 1966 P (Collection Marabout Université)
   See preceding note.

LEWIS, Martin Deming (ed.) *Gandhi, maker of modern India?* Boston, Heath, 1965 P (Problems in Asian Civilizations series)
    Various Indian writers evaluate Gandhi.

MOON, Penderel. *Gandhi and modern India.* London, English Universities Press, 1968; New York, Norton, 1969 (Teach Yourself History series)
    A perceptive biography, which places Gandhi in the context of the development of India.

MORRIS-JONES, W. H. *The government and politics of India.* London, Hutchinson, 1964; Garden City, N.Y., Doubleday, 1967 P (Anchor Books)
    An excellent analysis.

NAIPAUL, Vidiadhar Surajprasad. *An area of darkness.* London, Deutsch, 1964
    A masterly autobiographical account of a sensitive Trinidad Indian's reactions on visiting the land of his ancestors.

NEHRU, Jawaharlal. *Toward freedom: the autobiography of Jawaharlal Nehru.* Boston, Beacon, 1958 P (and repr.)
    A revealing self-portrait (first published in 1941) which is important to an understanding of the forces which shaped India.

NEWBY, Eric. *Slowly down the Ganges.* London, Hodder, 1966; New York, Scribner, 1967
    An entertaining travel book by a well-informed traveller with a historical sense and a sophisticated and ironical sense of humour.

PALMER, Norman. *The Indian political system.* Boston, Houghton, 1961 C&P
    A survey of the federal, state, and local structure of government as well as of political parties and policies.

PANIKKAR, Kavalam M. *The foundations of new India.* London, Allen & Unwin, 1963
    An outspoken Indian politician, statesman, and historian discusses the transformation of India leading to independence.

PARK, Richard Leonard. *India's political system.* Englewood Cliffs, N.J., Prentice-Hall, 1967 P
    An acute analysis of the decision-making process and government performance.

PAYNE, Robert. *The life and death of Mahatma Gandhi.* New York, Dutton; Toronto, Clarke Irwin, 1969
    A full-scale biography, well written and admiring, though not entirely uncritical.

SMITH, Donald Eugene. *India as a secular state.* Princeton, Princeton University Press, 1963 C&P
  A pioneer study of the relationship between the secular state of India and religion in its institutional forms.

SRINAVAS, Mysore Narasimhachar. *Social change in modern India.* Berkeley, University of California Press, 1966
  An acute analysis of social change in modern India, by a leading Indian sociologist.

TINKER, Hugh. *India and Pakistan: a short political guide.* [US edition subtitled: *a political analysis.*] [2nd ed.] London, Pall Mall, 1967; New York, Praeger, 1968 C&P
  A good study of contemporary politics, with a guide to further reading.

WILCOX, Wayne A. *India, Pakistan and the rise of China.* New York, Walker; Toronto, McLeod, 1964 P (Walker Summit series)
  A political science approach; seven perceptive lectures for a television audience, followed by a "reference" section of maps, tables, and bibliography.

WOODCOCK, George. *Kerala: a portrait of the Malabar coast.* London, Faber, 1967
  A good narrative account of a little-known coastal state of southwest India. Both history and present conditions are described.

ZINKIN, Taya. *Challenges in India.* London, Chatto; Toronto, Clarke Irwin, 1966
  A sympathetic but critical examination of India's current problems. Includes good chapters on corruption, the difficult position of Muslims in India, caste, women, new standards, and finally "What India could be like."

*ZINKIN, Taya. *India.* London, Thames & Hudson, 1965; New York, Walker, 1966 C&P (New Nations and Peoples series)
  An effective elementary presentation. The first third of the book deals with India before independence (1947); the remainder with the subsequent period and problems of modern India.

D OTHER LANDS OF SOUTH AND SOUTHEAST ASIA

1 GENERAL WORKS

BASTIN, John (ed.) *The emergence of modern Southeast Asia, 1511-1957.* Englewood Cliffs, N.J., Prentice-Hall, 1967 C&P
Thirty assorted readings gathered from a wide variety of old and recent books and articles.

BASTIN, John. *A history of modern Southeast Asia: colonialism, nationalism, and decolonization.* By John Bastin and Harry J. Benda. Englewood Cliffs, N.J., London, Prentice-Hall, 1968 C&P (Spectrum Books)
A short work combining colonial and social history: the intrusion of the West and the Southeast Asian response.

BONE, Robert C. *Contemporary Southeast Asia.* New York, Toronto, Random House, 1962 P (and repr.)
A sketch of the historical background and major problems now affecting the whole area.

BUCHANAN, Keith. *The Southeast Asian world: an introductory essay.* London, Bell, 1967
Examines in layman's terms the basic facts of geography, history, and the social and religious background of the region from Burma to the Philippines.

*CADY, John Frank. *Thailand, Burma, Laos and Cambodia.* Englewood Cliffs, N.J., Prentice-Hall, 1966 C&P (The Modern Nations in Historical Perspective series)
These four countries share the same branch of Buddhist tradition. For its size this little book is very informative on the many features which have united and divided them from antiquity to the present.

*COEDÈS, George. *Les états hindouisés d'Indochine et d'Indonésie.* 3ᵉ éd. Paris, Boccard, 1964
The major synthesis of early Southeast Asian history (up to the arrival of the Portuguese at the beginning of the 16th century).

*COEDÈS, George. *The Indianized states of Southeast Asia.* Ed. Walter F. Vella. Tr. Susan Brown Cowing. Honolulu, East-West Center Press, 1968
See preceding note.

*COEDÈS, George. *Les peuples de la péninsule indochinoise.* Paris, Dunod, 1962 P

A valuable cultural history of Burma, Thailand, Laos, Cambodia, and Vietnam, down to the 19th century, with emphasis on the usually neglected earlier period.

*COEDÈS, George. *The making of South East Asia*. Tr. H. M. Wright. London, Routledge; Berkeley, University of California Press, 1966; 1969 P
    See preceding note.

DOBBY, Ernest Henry George. *Southeast Asia*. 8th ed. London, University of London Press; Mystic, Conn., Verry, 1964
    A standard geography in three parts: physical geography; cultural and social geography of each political unit; social geography of the region as a whole.

*FISHER, Charles. *South-east Asia: a social, economic and political geography*. 2nd ed. London, Methuen; New York, Dutton, 1965; New York, Barnes & Noble, 1967
    A detailed country-by-country description.

GRISWOLD, Alexander B. *Burma, Korea, Tibet*. By A. B. Griswold, Chewan Kim and Peter H. Pott. London, Toronto, Methuen, 1964 (Art of the World series)
    Three uneven art surveys, illustrated with fine colour plates.

HALL, Daniel George Edward (ed.) *Historians of South-east Asia*. London, Toronto, New York, Oxford University Press, 1961 (Historical Writing on the Peoples of Asia series)
    An important series of essays, dealing with the indigenous writings of the peoples of Southeast Asia in a variety of languages, and western historical writing on the area.

*HALL, Daniel George Edward. *A history of South-east Asia*. 3rd ed. London, Toronto, Macmillan; New York, St. Martin's, 1968
    The best comprehensive standard work on the history of Burma, Thailand, Indochina, Malaysia, Indonesia, and the Philippines. Goes down to the early 1950s.

*HARRISON, Brian. *South-east Asia: a short history*. 3rd ed. London, Toronto, Macmillan; New York, St. Martin's, 1966
    A good short introduction, not overburdened with names or dates.

HAY, Stephen N. (ed.) *Southeast Asian history: a bibliographic guide*. Ed. Stephen N. Hay and Margaret H. Case. New York, Praeger, 1962
    A useful introductory outline of 632 titles, with notes consisting largely of quotations from book reviews. Omits some important material.

KAHIN, George McTurnan (ed.) *Governments and politics of Southeast Asia.* 2nd ed. Ithaca, Cornell University Press, 1964
  Good detailed political studies of Thailand, Burma, Indonesia, Malaysia, Vietnam, Laos, Cambodia, and the Philippines by regional experts.

KARNOW, Stanley. *Southeast Asia.* By Stanley Karnow and the Editors of Life [magazine]. New York, Time-Life, 1967 (Life World Library series)
  A simple (and at times simplistic) popular account, from an American viewpoint, profusely illustrated. Good bibliography.

KHÔI, Lê Thánh. *Histoire de l'Asie du Sud-est.* Paris, Presses Universitaires de France, 1959 (Collection "Que sais-je?")
  Brief but helpful.

LACH, Donald Frederick. *Southeast Asia in the eyes of Europe: the 16th century.* Chicago, University of Chicago Press, 1968 P (Phoenix Books)
  An interesting selection of comments by European writers of the 16th century on the "natives" and their countries.

PURCELL, Victor. *The Chinese in Southeast Asia.* 2nd ed. London, Toronto, New York, Oxford University Press (for Royal Institute of International Affairs), 1965
  The standard work on Chinese settlements outside China. Chapters deal in turn with the Chinese in Burma, Siam, Indochina (Vietnam, Cambodia, Laos), Malaysia, Borneo, Indonesia, and the Philippines.

PURCELL, Victor. *The revolution in Southeast Asia.* London, Thames & Hudson, 1962 (Great Revolutions series)
  A well-informed popular account of the changes which have taken place in the region in the past half-century, seen in the context of the local history. The author has had 40 years of administrative and scholarly experience in the area.

PURCELL, Victor. *South and East Asia since 1800.* Cambridge, New York, Cambridge University Press, 1965 P
  A short but solid appraisal of each country's progress from the colonial period, through nationalism to independence.

RAWSON, Philip S. *The art of Southeast Asia: Cambodia, Vietnam, Thailand, Laos, Burma, Java, Bali.* London, Thames & Hudson, 1967; New York, Praeger, 1967 C&P
  An inexpensive, richly illustrated outline, rather short on text, showing the development of Indian art in the lands neighbouring India. The *nature* of the changes it underwent could have been more explicitly brought out.

ROBEQUAIN, Charles. *Le monde malais.* Paris, Payot, 1946 P
  A very competent work, with emphasis on social geography. Partly out of date, but still useful.

ROBEQUAIN, Charles. *Malaya, Indonesia, Borneo and the Philippines.* A geographical, economic, and political description. 2nd ed. Tr. E. D. Laborde. London, New York, Toronto, Longmans, 1958
Translation of *Le monde malais* (above). See preceding note.

SCHECTER, Jerrold. *The new face of Buddha: Buddhism and political power in Southeast Asia.* New York, Coward-McCann; Toronto, Longmans, 1967
A journalist describes the activist Buddhism in many lands of Southeast Asia in the 1960s.

TARLING, Nicholas. *A concise history of Southeast Asia.* New York, London, Praeger, 1966 C&P
Southeast Asian history interpreted as a "frontier area" united in its diversity by being open to a variety of external influences. Concentrates on the period since 1760, especially the political aspects.

TILMAN, Robert O. (ed.) *Man, state, and society in contemporary Southeast Asia.* New York, Praeger, 1969 C&P
Aspects of the changing societies of nine countries in the region since World War II are examined in this good collection of college-level readings, extracted from the works of experts.

2 TIBET, NEPAL

DALAI LAMA. *My land and my people: the autobiography of his holiness the Dalai Lama.* Ed. David Howarth. London, Weidenfeld, 1962
The Dalai Lama, the main spiritual leader of Tibet, has been a refugee in India since the Chinese annexed his country in 1959.

DAVID-NEEL, Alexandra (comp. & tr.) *Textes tibétains inédits.* Paris, La Colombe, 1952 P
Extracts from a variety of classical texts — proverbs, novels, plays, poetry, philosophy, biography — with informative introductions.

DUNCAN, Marion H. *Love songs and proverbs of Tibet.* London, Mitre, 1961
An interesting collection, including 672 proverbs divided by subject.

FÜRER-HAIMENDORF, Christof von. *The Sherpas of Nepal: Buddhist highlanders.* London, Murray; Berkeley, University of California Press, 1964
An anthropologist describes this Himalayan people who have participated in most of the mountaineering expeditions.

HARRER, Heinrich. *Seven years in Tibet.* Translated from the German by Richard Graves. London, Hart-Davis; New York, Dutton, 1953 C&P

An interesting autobiographical account of the years 1943 to 1950, by a German who became tutor and confidant to the then 14-year-old Dalai Lama. Contains much interesting general information on Tibet.

HARRER, Heinrich. *Sept ans d'aventures au Tibet.* Traduit de l'allemand par H. Daussy. Paris, Arthaud, [195-] P
See preceding note.

HOFFMANN, Helmut. *The religions of Tibet.* Tr. Edward Fitzgerald. London, Allen & Unwin; New York, Macmillan, 1961

KARAN, Pradyumna P. *The Himalayan kingdoms: Bhutan, Sikkim and Nepal.* Princeton, Van Nostrand, 1963 P
The main historical, economic, and political features factually outlined.

LALOU, Marcelle. *Les religions du Tibet.* Paris, Presses Universitaires de France, 1957 P (Collection Mythes et Religions)
A short but useful outline of the current state of knowledge, including an evaluation of the influence of pre-Buddhic religions in Tibet.

LI, Tieh-tseng. *Tibet: today and yesterday.* New York, Bookman, 1960
A good history of Tibet based primarily on Chinese sources; particularly strong on the last two centuries.

MARAINI, Fosco. *Secret Tibet.* Tr. Eric Mosbacher. London, Hutchinson; New York, Grove, 1952
A travelogue which pays considerable attention to Tibet's religious tradition and its present life and customs. Readable though not scholarly; beautifully illustrated.

MARAINI, Fosco. *Tibet secret.* Tr. Juliette Bertrand. Paris, Arthaud, 1958 P (Collection Exploration)
See preceding note.

MI-LA-RAS-PA. *The message of Milarepa.* New light upon the Tibetan way. A selection of poems translated from the Tibetan by Sir Humphrey Clarice. London, Murray; New York, Grove, 1958 (Wisdom of the East series)
Wisdom in poetry by the "Saint Francis of Tibet."

MORRIS, John. *A winter in Nepal.* London, Hart-Davis, 1963
An excellent travel book by a man who really knows Nepal and the Gurkhas. Well illustrated.

RICHARDSON, Hugh Edward. *Tibet and its history.* London, Toronto, Oxford University Press, 1962. US edition entitled: *A short history of Tibet.* New York, Dutton, 1962

Main emphasis on 20th century history (particularly foreign relations) but there is an outline of the earlier period.

SHAKABPA, W. D. *Tibet: a political history*. New Haven, London, Yale University Press; Montreal, McGill University Press, 1967
This book by a former Tibetan official offers new and useful information. Especially detailed on the past century.

SNELLGROVE, David L. *Buddhist Himalaya*. Oxford, Cassirer; New York, Philosophical Library, 1957
Religion in Tibet.

*SNELLGROVE, David L. *A cultural history of Tibet*. By David Snellgrove [and] Hugh Richardson. London, Weidenfeld; New York, Praeger, 1968
The new standard history. Many photographs.

*STEIN, Rolf Alfred. *La civilisation tibétaine*. Paris, Dunod, 1962 (Collection Sigma)
Probably the best survey available.

THUBTEN JIGME NORBU. *Tibet is my country*. By Thubten Jigme Norbu as told to Heinrich Harrer. Translated from the German by Edward Fitzgerald. London, Hart-Davis, 1960; New York, Dutton, 1961
Autobiography of the Dalai Lama's brother; an interesting account of the traditional life of Tibet as seen from the inside.

3 CEYLON

ARASARATNAM, S. *Ceylon*. Englewood Cliffs, N.J., Prentice-Hall, 1964 C&P
A handy brief outline of Ceylon's history and the varying racial and religious elements that have combined to make its culture.

BAILEY, Sidney Dawson. *Ceylon*. London, New York, Hutchinson, 1952 P (Hutchinson's University Library series)
Brief but still useful, though getting out of date.

FARMER. B. H. *Ceylon: a divided nation*. London, Toronto, New York, Oxford University Press, 1963 P (Institute of Race Relations)
A booklet mainly concerned with language-group relations in modern times, but with introduction on the earlier period.

JEFFRIES, Charles. *Ceylon: the path to independence*. London, Pall Mall; New York, Praeger, 1963
A history of Ceylon by a British Colonial Office official who was closely concerned with its evolution to independence.

*LUDOWYK, Evelyn Frederick Charles. *The modern history of Ceylon.* London, Weidenfeld; New York, Praeger, 1966 (Asia-Africa series)
A good survey.

LUDOWYK, Evelyn Frederick Charles. *The story of Ceylon.* London, Faber, 1962
A popular presentation, divided into three equal parts: ancient, old, and modern.

PAKEMAN, Sidney Arnold. *Ceylon.* London, Benn; New York, Praeger, 1964 (Nations of the Modern World series)
A good outline of the history of Ceylon to the present time, and a review of its social, cultural, and economic life.

REYNOLDS, C. H. B. (comp.) *An anthology of Sinhalese literature up to 1815.* Edited with an introduction by C. H. B. Reynolds. London, Allen & Unwin; New York, Pegasus, 1971 (Unesco Collection of Representative Works – Ceylon Series)
A comprehensive selection, including some important Buddhist writing.

WILLIAMS, Harry. *Ceylon: pearl of the East.* 2nd ed. London, Hale, 1963
A sympathetic "popular" description.

4 BURMA

BYLES, Marie M. *Journey into Burmese silence.* London, Allen & Unwin, 1962
An informative account of the country and of Burmese Buddhism, by an Australian who has lived in Burmese meditation centres.

CADY, John Frank. *A history of modern Burma.* Ithaca, Cornell University Press, 1958 (and repr.)
Detailed coverage of the last century and a half, especially political history since World War I.

*HALL, Daniel George Edward. *Burma.* 3rd ed. London, Toronto, Hutchinson; New York, Hillary, 1960
A reliable and very informative little book covering Burma's history, culture, and social, political, and economic life, mainly in the British period.

HLA PE (comp. & tr.) *Burmese proverbs.* London, Murray; New York, Paragon, 1962 (Wisdom of the East series) (Unesco Collection of Representative Works – Burmese Series)
A selection of 496 proverbs, placed in their cultural context in a good introductory outline of Burmese history and culture.

HTIN AUNG, U. *Burmese drama: a study with translations of Burmese plays.*
Calcutta, London, New York, Oxford University Press, 1957 (repr. of 1937 ed.)
An informative doctoral study.

HTIN AUNG, U. (ed. & tr.) *Burmese monk's tales.* Collected, translated and
introduced by Maung Htin Aung. New York, London, Columbia University
Press, 1966
Good-humoured 19th century "folk tales" invented for educational purposes by Buddhist monks.

HTIN AUNG, U. *A history of Burma.* New York, London, Columbia University
Press, 1967
A traditionalist and "patriotic" account of Burma's history, which rejects
recent research and western historical methods.

KING, Winston Lee. *A thousand lives away: Buddhism in contemporary Burma.*
Cambridge, Mass., Harvard University Press, 1964
A shrewd examination of current Burmese Buddhist thought by a sympa-
thetic Protestant historian of religion.

MI MI KHAING. *Burmese family,* by Mi Mi Khaing. 1st American ed. Bloomington, London, Indiana University Press, 1962
A charmingly written autobiography by a lady, which gives an excellent
picture of traditional Burmese family life and character.

[SCOTT, James George] *The Burman: his life and notions.* By Shway Yoe.
New York, Norton, 1963 P
A very readable account of all aspects of traditional Burmese life, first published in 1882 by a Scotsman who was a civil servant in Burma for over 30
years.

SPIRO, Melford E. *Burmese supernaturalism: a study in the explanation and
reduction of suffering.* Englewood Cliffs, N.J., Prentice-Hall, 1967 (Prentice-
Hall College Anthropological series)
In spite of Buddhism, animism survives as the folk religion of the Burmese
masses. An anthropologist describes in detail how it permeates their lives.

TINKER, Hugh. *The Union of Burma: a study of the first years of independence.* 4th ed. London, Toronto, New York, Oxford University Press, 1967
A detailed examination.

5 THAILAND

*BLANCHARD, Wendell. *Thailand: its people, its society, its culture*. New Haven, Human Relations Area Files 1958 (and repr.)
    A mine of information, but rather dry reading.

BUSCH, Noel F. *Thailand: an introduction to modern Siam*. Princeton, Van Nostrand, 1959 C&P (Asia Library series)
    A rather simple general introduction.

DE YOUNG, John E. *Village life in modern Thailand*. Berkeley, University of California Press, 1955
    A competent sociological study.

FISTIÉ, Pierre. *L'évolution de la Thaïlande contemporaine*. Paris, Colin, 1967 (Collection Cahiers de la Fondation Nationale des Sciences Politiques — Relations Internationales)
    Far more detailed than the author's other book (below). Although it is mainly a study of political development, other aspects are not excluded.

FISTIÉ, Pierre. *La Thaïlande*. Paris, Presses Universitaires de France, 1963 P (Collection "Que sais-je?")
    A compressed history, mainly political.

INSOR, D. *Thailand: a political, social and economic analysis*. London, Allen & Unwin; New York, Praeger, 1963
    A popularly written general survey of the present state of the country, with particular emphasis on politics and economics.

KAUFMAN, Howard Keva. *Bangkhuad: a community study in Thailand*. Locust Valley, N.Y., Augustin, 1960 (Monographs of the Association for Asian Studies)
    Village life observed.

KHUN CHANG, Khun Phèn. (*La femme, le héros et le vilain*). Poème populaire thaï. Tr. J. Kasem Sibunruang. Paris, Presses Universitaires de France, 1960 (Collection Unesco d'Oeuvres Représentatives — Série Thaïlandaise)

SCHWEISGUTH, P. *Étude sur la littérature siamoise*. Paris, A.-Maisonneuve, 1951
    A valuable work covering the whole of Thai literature since the 13th century. Contains numerous extracts in translation; but is a bibliography with commentary rather than a literary history.

SMITH, Ronald Bishop. *Siam: or, the history of the Thais from the earliest times to 1569 A.D.* Bethesda, Md., Decatur Press, 1966 P
This volume and its continuation (below) are devoted mainly to political history, and are arranged and written in an unusually old-fashioned way. Includes observations of early European travellers.

SMITH, Ronald Bishop. *Siam: or, the history of the Thais from 1569 A.D. to 1824 A.D.* Bethesda, Md., Decatur Press, 1967 P
See preceding note.

6 CAMBODIA (KHMER), LAOS

*BERVAL, René de (ed.) *Présence du Royaume Lao.* Saigon, France-Asie, 1956 P
A very interesting general work consisting of articles published in three numbers of the Saigon French monthly *France-Asie.* Many of the contributors are famous scholars. Contains exhaustive but unannotated bibliography.

*BERVAL, René de (ed.) *Kingdom of Laos: the land of the million elephants and of the white parasol.* Saigon, France-Asie, 1959 P
See preceding note.

BRIGGS, Lawrence Palmer. *The ancient Khmer empire.* Philadelphia, American Philosophical Society, 1951 (Transactions of the American Philosophical Society)
An outstanding history, with full bibliography.

DAUPHIN-MEUNIER, Achille. *Histoire du Cambodge.* 2e éd. Paris, Presses Universitaires de France, 1968 P (Collection "Que sais-je?")
A very sketchy political history.

GITEAU, M. *Histoire du Cambodge.* Paris, Didier, 1962 P
A rather dry and inadequate summary.

*GROSLIER, Bernard Philippe. *Angkor, hommes et pierres.* 2e éd. Grenoble, Paris, Arthaud, 1965 (Collection Les Imaginaires)
A standard work on the remarkable Khmer civilization of mediaeval Cambodia in the Middle Ages, with numerous fine illustrations.

*GROSLIER, Bernard Philippe. *Angkor: art and civilization.* By Bernard Groslier and Jacques Arthaud. Tr. Eric Earnshaw Smith. 2nd ed. London, New York, Praeger, 1966
See preceding note.

GROSLIER, Bernard Philippe. *Indochine.* Geneva, Nagel, 1966 (Collection Archaeologia Mundi)

A thoughtful work on the knowledge yielded by the archaeology and art of Indochina (defined to include present-day Burma, Thailand, Malaya, Cambodia, Laos, and Vietnam). Beautifully illustrated. Complements the same author's *Indochine: carrefour des arts* (below).

GROSLIER, Bernard Philippe. *Indochina.* Tr. James Hogarth. London, Muller, 1967

See preceding note. Complements the same author's *Indochina: art in the melting-pot of races* (below).

GROSLIER, Bernard Philippe. *Indochine, carrefour des arts.* (*Interindien*). Paris, Albin Michel, 1961 (Collection L'Art dans le Monde, Civilisations non-européennes)

A notable work. Deals mainly with the plastic arts and architecture up to the coming of the Europeans. Includes the great Khmer art of Angkor.

GROSLIER, Bernard Philippe. *Indochina: art in the melting-pot of races.* Tr. George Lawrence. London, Toronto, Methuen; New York, Crown, 1962 (Art of the World series)

See preceding note.

*LE BAR, Frank M. (ed.) *Laos: its people, its society, its culture.* Ed. Frank M. LeBar and Adrienne Suddard. [2nd ed.] New Haven, Human Relations Area Files, 1967

An excellent general introduction to many facets of Laos, for reference use.

MARTINI, François. *Contes populaires inédits du Cambodge.* Recueillis et traduits par F. Martini et S. Bernard. Paris, G.-P. Maisonneuve, 1946

MIGOT, André. *Les Khmers: des origines d'Angkor au Cambodge d'aujourd'-hui.* Paris, Le Livre Contemporain, 1960 (Collection L'Aventure du Passé)

PARMENTIER, Henri. *L'art du Laos.* 2 vols. Hanoi, École Française d'Extrême-Orient; Paris, A.-Maisonneuve, 1954

An authoritative work. The second volume consists entirely of plates illustrating the text volume.

PHOUVONG, Thao. *Initiation à la littérature laotienne.* Hanoi, École Française d'Extrême-Orient, 1948-49

PYM, Christopher. *The ancient civilization of Angkor.* New York, Toronto, New American Library; London, New English Library, 1968 P (Mentor Books)

A popular treatment.

STEINBERG, David J. (ed.) *Cambodia: its people, its society, its culture.* 2nd ed. Rev. Herbert H. Vreeland. New Haven, Human Relations Area Files, 1959 (Survey of World Cultures series)

Contains much information in an accessible though uninspiring form, concerning Cambodian history, contemporary society, politics, and economics. Too many generalizations.

THIERRY, Solange. *Les Khmers.* Paris, Seuil, 1964 P (Collection Le Temps qui court)

Impressionistic, evocation through numerous photographs.

TOYE, Hugh. *Laos: buffer state or battleground.* London, New York, Toronto, Oxford University Press, 1968

A largely successful "attempt to relate the current problem of Laos to its historical sources."

7 VIETNAM

Anthologie de la poésie vietnamienne. Paris, Les Éditeurs Français Réunis, 1969 P

Poetry from the last seven centuries, although most of it is modern. Heavy representation of nationalist and communist poets.

AUVADE, Robert. *Bibliographie critique des oeuvres sur l'Indochine française: un siècle d'histoire et d'enseignement.* Paris, G.-P. Maisonneuve, 1965

150 well-selected books and articles (mostly French), usefully annotated. Many of the recommended titles are now out of print, but it is still one of the best works of its type. Another guide to material in both English and French is Joseph Coates, *Bibliography of Vietnam* (Washington, 1964).

BAIN, Chester A. *Vietnam: the roots of conflict.* Englewood Cliffs, N.J., Prentice-Hall, 1967 C&P

For the novice this is a helpful moderate-sized history since ancient times, and an interpretation of the recent period in the light of the past.

BUTTINGER, Joseph. *Vietnam: a political history.* New York, Praeger, 1968

Fairly detailed; from ancient times to the present. An abridgement of his three large documented volumes *The smaller dragon* (1958) and *Vietnam: a dragon embattled* (1967).

CADIÈRE, Leopold Michel. *Croyances et pratiques religieuses des Vietnamiens.* 2e éd. Saigon, École Française d'Extrême-Orient, 1958 (Publications de l'École Française d'Extrême-Orient)

The most learned and best work on the subject; includes Buddhism, Confucianism, Taoism, and spirit worship, seen in their sociological context.

CHESNEAUX, Jean. *Contribution à l'histoire de la nation vietnamienne.* Paris, Editions Sociales, 1954 (La Culture et les Hommes)
General and cultural history, mainly from the 19th century to about 1950, from an "anticolonialist" viewpoint.

CHESNEAUX, Jean. *The Vietnamese nation: a contribution to history.* Tr. Malcolm Salmon. Sydney, Australia, Current Book Distributors, 1966 P
Revised, abridged version of the French original (above), updated to about 1960.

CHESNEAUX, Jean. *Le Vietnam: études de politique et d'histoire.* Paris, Maspéro, 1968 P
A series of informed essays.

DEVILLERS, Philippe. *Viet Nam, de la guerre française à la guerre américaine.* Par Philippe Devillers et Jean Lacouture. Paris, Seuil, 1969
A balanced, rather detailed account of the Vietnam problem from 1946 to 1954, with particular attention to its international ramifications.

DUNCANSON, Dennis J. *Government and revolution in Vietnam.* London, New York, Toronto, Oxford University Press (for the Royal Institute of International Affairs), 1968
A thorough study, with excellent historical background, and a critique of recent policies. The author has wide experience in the area and knows several of the languages, including Chinese and Vietnamese.

DURAND, Maurice. *Introduction à la littérature vietnamienne.* Par Maurice Durand et Nguyen Tran Huan. Paris, G.-P. Maisonneuve, 1969 (Collection Unesco, Introductions aux Littératures Orientales)

FALL, Bernard B. *Street without joy.* 4th ed. Harrisburg, Pa., Stackpole, 1964
This work, *The two Viet-Nams* (below), and *Viet-Nam witness* (below), are important political and military accounts of Vietnam since 1946 by a sharp, on-the-spot observer.

FALL, Bernard B. *Indochine, 1946-1962: chronique d'une guerre révolutionnaire (Street without joy).* Adapté de l'américaine par Serge Ouvaroff. Paris, Laffont, 1962
See preceding note.

FALL, Bernard B. *The two Viet-Nams: a political and military analysis.* 2nd ed. New York, London, Praeger, 1964 (and repr.)
A balanced examination by an experienced observer.

FALL, Bernard B. *Viet-Nam witness, 1953-66.* New York, Praeger; London, Pall Mall, 1966
See preceding note.

HO-CHI-MINH. *Oeuvres choisies.* Paris, Maspéro, 1967 P
Selections made by a communist organization from Ho's works between 1922 and 1967, showing the Vietnamese revolutionary leader's basic views; includes several of his poems.

HONEY, Patrick J. *Genesis of a tragedy: the historical background to the Vietnam war.* London, Benn; Toronto, General, 1968 P
An excellent outline of the history of Vietnam since antiquity, in an 80-page booklet.

HUARD, Pierre Alphonse. *Connaissance du Viêt-nam.* Par Pierre Huard et Maurice Durand. Paris, Imprimerie Nationale; Hanoi, École Française d'Extrême-Orient, 1954
A good general account of traditional life till the beginning of the 20th century. Separate chapters discuss such topics as social life, war, the peasants, clothing, food, music, and literature.

KHÔI, Lê Thánh. *Le Viet-Nam: histoire et civilisation, le milieu et l'histoire.* Paris, Editions de Minuit, 1955
This book's considerable value is reduced by a Marxist slant.

LACOUTURE, Jean. *Hô Chi Minh.* Paris, Seuil, 1967
A biography, by a sympathetic observer, of the remarkable North Vietnamese communist leader.

LANCASTER, Donald. *The emancipation of French Indochina.* London, New York, Toronto, Oxford University Press (for Royal Institute of International Affairs), 1961
The first third of this book concerns the period from the arrival of Christian missionaries until the Japanese occupation in World War II. The remainder deals with the nationalist period — a valuable, rather detailed account.

MASSON, André. *Histoire du Vietnam.* 3e éd. Paris, Presses Universitaires de France, 1967 P (Collection "Que sais-je?")
A useful cultural history for laymen by a noted scholar; shows the main currents, rather than attempting to chronicle the facts in detail.

NEWMAN, Bernard. *Background to Viet-Nam.* New York, 1965; New York, New American Library, 1966 P
This well-written book explains the historical, social, political, and religious factors which are essential to an understanding of the current problems of Vietnam.

NGUYEN-DINH-THI. *Front du ciel.* Adaptation française et présentation de Madeleine Riffaud. Paris, Julliard, 1968
According to the translator, this is the first complete novel translated from Vietnamese. It is a combination war diary and love story by a North Vietnamese pilot.

NGUYÊN-DU. *Kim vân-kiêu.* Traduit du vietnamien par Xuân-Phuc et Xuân-Viêt. Paris, Gallimard, 1961 P (Collection Connaissance de l'Orient) (Collection Unesco d'Oeuvres Représentatives – Série Vietnamienne)
Probably the most popular piece of Vietnamese literature, this novel in verse, or epic, concerns the frustration of true love by the prevailing social system. The poet (1765-1820) is one of the major classical authors.

NGUYÊN-DU. *Vaste recueil de légendes merveilleuses.* Traduit du vietnamien par Nguyen-Tran-Huan. Paris, Gallimard, 1962 P (Collection Connaissance de l'Orient) (Collection Unesco d'Oeuvres Représentatives – Série Vietnamienne)

NHAT-HANH, Thich. *Vietnam: lotus in a sea of fire.* New York, Hill, 1967 P
A good description of the relationship of Buddhism with Vietnamese culture in the past, and the present situation.

RAFFEL, Burton (ed. & tr.) *From the Vietnamese: ten centuries of poetry.* New York, October House, 1968
A slim volume of short poems freely but attractively translated, with a brief general introduction to the forms of Vietnamese poetry.

SMITH, Ralph. *Viet-Nam and the West.* London, Toronto, Heinemann, 1968
An examination of Vietnamese history from 1858 to 1963 leads the author to conclude that western failure to understand the gulf between Vietnamese and western logic is responsible for many of the present problems.

8 MALAYSIA

ALLEN, Richard. *Malaysia – prospect and retrospect: the impact and aftermath of colonial rule.* London, New York, Toronto, Oxford University Press, 1968
After a good historical introduction the work is devoted mainly to political developments in Southeast Asia since 1945. Sir Richard Allen was British ambassador to Burma 1956-62.

FISTIÉ, Pierre. *Singapour et la Malaisie.* Paris, Presses Universitaires de France, 1960 P (Collection "Que sais-je?")
A sound brief introduction covering history and contemporary politics and economics.

*GOULD, James W. *The United States and Malaysia.* Cambridge, Mass., Harvard University Press; London, Oxford University Press, 1969 (American Foreign Policy Library series)
A very useful introduction not only to the history, but also to the culture and society of Malaysia. The title is quite misleading (less than 20 pages out of 250 are directly devoted to American relations). Good annotated chapter of "Suggested Reading."

GULLICK, J. M. *Malaysia.* London, Benn; New York, Praeger, 1969 (Nations of the Modern World series)
Mainly on the period since World War II, with strong emphasis on economics.

MILLER, Harry. *The story of Malaysia.* London, Faber; New York, Praeger, 1965
A popularly written book by a journalist with long experience in Malaya.

PURCELL, Victor. *Malaysia.* London, Thames & Hudson, 1965; New York, Walker, 1965 C&P (New Nations and Peoples series)
A clear, rather elementary introduction to many aspects of Malaysian life, with main emphasis on the present period.

PURCELL, Victor. *The memoirs of a Malayan official.* London, Toronto, Cassell; New York, International Publications Service, 1965
An interesting autobiography by an English colonial civil servant who spent many years in the area.

RICE, Oliver (ed.) *Modern Malay verse: 1946-1961.* Selected by Oliver Rice and Abdullah Majid. Tr. Abdullah Majid, Ashraf, and Oliver Rice. Kuala Lumpur, Toronto, London, New York, Oxford University Press, 1963 P
Representative verses by six contemporary poets, with a brief informative introduction on Malay poetry by James Kirkup.

SCHULTZ, George F. (ed.) *Vietnamese legends and other tales.* Adapted from the Vietnamese. Rutland, Vt., Tuttle, 1965 P

TREGONNING, K. G. *A history of modern Malaya.* Singapore, Eastern Universities Press (for University of London Press) [Tokyo pr.], 1964 (History of Modern South-east Asia series)
An attempt to see Malayan history "from within."

TREGONNING, K. G. *A history of modern Sabah (North Borneo 1881-1963).* 2nd ed. Singapore, University of Malaya Press (for University of Singapore Press); London, Toronto, New York, Oxford University Press, 1965 P
A scholarly history with a rather "Asian" interpretation, by an Australian scholar.

TREGONNING, K. G. *Malaysia and Singapore.* 2nd ed. Melbourne, Cheshire, 1966
Brief work on modern Malaysia to 1965.

TREGONNING, K. G. *North Borneo.* London, Her Majesty's Stationery Office, 1960 (and repr.) (Corona Library series)
A well-illustrated popular and optimistic introduction to the history and present condition of modern North Borneo.

*WANG, Gungwu (ed.) *Malaysia: a survey.* London, Pall Mall; New York, Praeger, 1964
A very useful collection of basic factual material, geographical and human, historical, social and cultural, economic and political.

WINSTEDT, Richard Olof (comp.) *Malay proverbs,* chosen and introduced by Richard Winstedt. London, Murray; New York, Paragon, 1950 (and repr.) (Wisdom of the East series)
Arranged by subject, with a first-rate introduction comparing Malay proverbs with those of other cultures.

*WINSTEDT, Richard Olof. *Malaya and its history.* 7th ed. London, Hutchinson, 1966 P
A short but authoritative outline.

*WINSTEDT, Richard Olof. *The Malays: a cultural history.* 5th ed. London, Routledge, 1961
A sound general review, less political than the preceding work, and good on customs.

*WINSTEDT, Richard Olof. *Les moeurs et coutumes des Malais.* Paris, Payot, 1952 P
A sound general review of the cultural history of Malaya.

9 INDONESIA

ANWAR, Chairil. *Selected poems.* Tr. Burton Raffel and Nurdin Salam. New York, New Directions, 1962 P (World Poets series)
Verse by a leading Indonesian poet, who died in 1949.

BRUHAT, Jean. *Histoire de l'Indonésie.* 2ᵉ éd. Paris, Presses Universitaires de France, 1968 (Collection "Que sais-je?")
A standard short history.

CALDWELL, Malcolm. *Indonesia.* London, New York, Toronto, Oxford University Press, 1968 P (Modern World series)

A short account of Dutch colonization and its consequences, and an examination of present-day Indonesia and its prospects.

DAMAIS, Louis Charles (ed. & tr.) *Cent deux poèmes indonésiens (1925-1950).* Paris, A.-Maisonneuve, 1965 (Collection Unesco d'Oeuvres Représentatives — Traductions d'Oeuvres d'Auteurs Contemporains)

GEERTZ, Clifford. *The religion of Java.* New York, Free Press of Glencoe; London, Toronto, Collier-Macmillan, 1960; 1964 P
  An interesting study of the various elements which together make up the religious and cultural life in a small Muslim town.

GRANT, Bruce. *Indonesia.* Harmondsworth, Baltimore, Penguin, 1967 P
  A competent general account of Indonesia's past history and culture and present-day situation by a journalist.

HENDON, Rufus S. (tr.) *Six Indonesian short stories.* New Haven, Yale University Southeast Asia Studies [Distributor: Detroit, Cellar Bookshop], 1968 P
  Six high-quality stories written in the 1940s and 1950s.

HOLT, Claire. *Art in Indonesia: continuities and change.* Ithaca, Cornell University Press, 1967
  An outstanding study from ancient to modern art, with a strong emphasis on the artistic continuity that is expressed in Indonesian art and drama. Valuable appendices give synopses of epics illustrated in sculpture, painting, dance, and drama, and the texts of several plays.

KARTINI, Raden Adjeng. *Letters of a Javanese princess.* Tr. Agnes Louise Symmers. Edited with an introduction by Hildred Geertz. New York, Norton, 1964 P (Unesco Collection of Representative Works — Indonesian Series)
  Social and cultural change in Java (as a result of westernization) as observed by a regent's daughter in letters written 1899 to 1905. First published 1920.

KARTINI, Raden Adjeng. *Lettres de Raden Adjeng Kartini: Java en 1900.* Choisies et traduites par Louis Charles Damais. Introduction et notes de Jeanne Cuisinier. Paris, La Haye, Mouton, 1960 (École Pratique des Hautes Études. Sorbonne. 6ᵉ section. Sciences Economiques et Sociales. Le Monde d'Outre-Mer Passé et Présent. 2ᵉ série. Documents) (Collection Unesco d'Oeuvres Représentatives — Série Indonésienne)
  See preceding note.

*LEGGE, John David. *Indonesia.* Englewood Cliffs, N.J., Prentice-Hall, 1964 C&P
  The various historical and cultural factors (Hindu, Islamic, and European) that have influenced Indonesia's development and lie behind her present tensions are well analysed.

LUBIS, Mochtar. *Twilight in Djakarta.* Tr. Claire Holt. New York, Vanguard, 1964
A critical social novel set in Djakarta in the recent past.

*McVEY, Ruth T. (ed.) *Indonesia.* [2nd ed.] New Haven, Human Relations Area Files, 1967 (Yale University, Southeast Asia Studies series) (Survey of World Cultures series)
A reliable survey and reference book on many aspects of Indonesia's history, culture, and present condition.

MINTZ, Jeanne S. *Indonesia: a profile.* Princeton, Toronto, London, Van Nostrand, 1961 (Asia Library series)
An elementary introduction, with good annotated bibliography.

NIEUWENHUIZE, Christoffel Anthonie Olivier van. *Aspects of Islam in postcolonial Indonesia.* The Hague, van Hoeve, 1958
A sociological study. In spite of the book's title, it also contains a useful account of both the pre-Muslim background and Islam before the departure of the Dutch.

PALMIER, Leslie H. *Indonesia.* London, Thames & Hudson; New York, Walker, 1965 (New Nations and Peoples series)
A competent, illustrated survey for the general reader.

RAFFEL, Burton (ed.) *Anthology of modern Indonesian poetry.* Berkeley, University of California Press; London, Cambridge University Press, 1964; Albany, State University of New York Press, 1968 P (Asian Literature Program of the Asia Society)
A good introduction to the major poets of a literature which made a complete break with its past about 1920 to develop a modern literary language.

RAFFEL, Burton. *The development of modern Indonesian poetry.* Albany, State University of New York Press, 1967
A pioneer study of the main trends and poets, with numerous translations.

*TEEUW, A. *Modern Indonesian literature.* The Hague, Nijhoff, 1967 (Koninklijk Instituut voor Taal-, Land- en Volkenkunde)
An excellent critical and historical treatment of the period since 1920.

VLEKKE, Bernard Hubertus Maria. *Nusantara: a history of Indonesia.* 2nd ed. Hague, van Hoeve, 1959; Chicago, Quadrangle, 1960
The standard history to the time of its publication.

WAGNER, Frits A. *Indonesia: the art of an island group.* London, Toronto, Methuen; Cleveland, World, 1959 (and repr.) (Art of the World series)

A wide-ranging historical survey of the "arts" of Indonesia, not only painting, sculpture, and architecture but also music, drama, and literature. Numerous excellent colour plates.

WAGNER, Frits A. *Indonésie, l'art d'un archipel.* Tr. I. Vromen. Paris, Michel, 1959 (Collection L'Art dans le Monde)
See preceding note.

10 PHILIPPINES

CASPER, Leonard (comp.) *New writing from the Philippines: a critique and anthology.* Syracuse, N.Y., Syracuse University Press, 1966
A representative collection of Filipino belles lettres in English, introduced by a survey of Filipino literature and a detailed critical analysis.

CASTILLO Y TUAZON, Teofilo del. *Philippine literature, from ancient times to the present.* [By] Teofilo del Castillo y Tuazon [and] Buenaventura S. Medina, Jr. Quezon City (Philippines), Teofilo del Castillo, 1966
An informed pedestrian review of the totality of Philippine literature in many of its languages since antiquity, with numerous extracts translated into English from the vernaculars, particularly Tagalog and Spanish, and original works in English.

CORPUZ, Onofre D. *The Philippines.* Englewood Cliffs, N.J., Prentice-Hall, 1965 C&P (Spectrum Books)
A simply written, brief interpretation of the main themes of Philippine history and a survey of its present social and political situation.

KUHN, F. *The Philippines: yesterday and today.* By F. Kuhn and D. Kuhn. New York, Holt, 1966
Another useful general work.

NELSON, Raymond. *The Philippines.* London, Thames & Hudson, 1968 (New Nations and Peoples series)
Half the book is devoted to geography and to the history of pre-independence times; the remainder to a description of present-day Philippine society, culture, politics, and economics. Better on economics than on history.

RAVENHOLT, Albert. *The Philippines: a young republic on the move.* Princeton, Van Nostrand, 1962 P
An excellent introductory cultural and historical outline.

SCHURZ, William Lytle. *The Manila galleon.* New York, Dutton, 1939, repr. 1959 C&P

The story of the annual Spanish galleon voyages for trade between the Philippines and Mexico, from the 16th to the 19th century.

WILLOQUET, Gaston. *Histoire des Philippines.* Paris, Presses Universitaires de France, 1961 (Collection "Que sais-je?")

A short outline, followed by an economic social and political survey of the islands in the recent past.

IV The Far East

*Including Mongolia.
†Excluding religious and philosophical (classified in subsection 6 below).
‡Including translations of some texts.
§Chinese and Japanese developments. For general works on Buddhism see part III, subsection C4c.
¶Including history and criticism of drama.

*For Buddhism (Japanese and Chinese) see above subsection B6b. For general works on Buddhism, see part III, subsection C4c.

INTRODUCTION

The Far East, in spite of its diverse elements, is generally regarded by the outside world as an entity. Yet China, Japan, and the peninsula of Korea which lies between them are very different from one another. All these countries have separate ancient languages, and their peoples and cultures are quite distinct. Nevertheless, the widespread impression that they have much in common does have a basis in cultural reality and is not based simply on certain physical features shared by these peoples: the indelible impress of Chinese civilization marks them all.

The Chinese are an immensely talented people, whose history has been continuously documented for more than 3000 years. In the past century China has been going through what is perhaps the greatest social and spiritual upheaval of its existence. The whole world is bound to be greatly affected by this turmoil among a people which constitutes one-quarter of mankind, whose current population of 800 million is now rising by some 15 million a year, and whose numbers appear likely to increase further in geometrical progression. What China has thought, said, and done has already for millennia had great relevance for much of the world.

In contrast with the often abstract and metaphysical speculations and mystico-philosophical preoccupations of Indian civilization, with its emphasis on the individual, the Chinese have throughout their long history attached major importance to the social and societal aspects of civilization. A pervasive sense of ethics, morality, duty, and discipline has been the particular contribution of Confucianism, while the individualistic and quietist element – also traditional in China – has been provided largely by Taoism. Rationality and practicality, skill and inventiveness, have been characteristic and permanent features of Chinese civilization.

The history of China is marked by frequent struggles against external, non-Chinese, northern and northwestern neighbours. The sequence was: Huns, Turks, Mongols and Manchus, and in the past century westerners, representing the commercial and industrial interests of European nations and America. The country has also been periodically racked by internal strife, in which north China and the south have often been at odds. In spite of changes of dynasty, the cultural unity of China has been maintained, and modern China, communist though it be, is still clearly the descendant of the civilization of the north Chinese Shang, the first authenticated major Chinese dynasty. The language and script of the present day are visibly a development of those used more than three and a half millennia ago. Over 2500 years ago the Chinese social and moral order was already firmly rooted in family obligations and an agricultural way of life, and these remained at the foundations of Chinese society until the beginning of the communist period. Intellectual patterns crystallized. Confucianism and Taoism were established as the main schools of thought, and great literature was being written. The political unity of north and south China was achieved in the 3rd century B.C.; in the following four centuries, under the Han dynasty, the Chinese Empire reached a high standard of organizational efficiency, thanks to a superlative civil service, which was to be the backbone of the empire for most of its subsequent history. The remarkable economic and cultural progress, and particularly the flowering of classical scholarship, literature, and art, brought the Han period the acclaim of later generations as a golden age. In spite of the centuries of political chaos which followed the collapse of that dynasty in 221, a vigorous intellectual life continued to flourish. Buddhism arrived from India and rapidly established itself, in modified form, as an integral element of Chinese civilization. New cultural heights were reached under the T'ang dynasty (618-907). The arts of reading and writing became widespread, and literature flourished. Artistic, scholarly, and economic progress continued unabated under the Sung dynasty (960-1280), and more important still was the revival of Confucianism in a new form ("neo-Confucianism") which was to survive essentially as the spiritual and intellectual foundation of the Chinese way of life and thought, until its overthrow by the Chinese Communists in the present century.

Contacts between China and the outside world have been intermittent. The Mongols, who breached China's frontiers in the 13th century and established their own rule, initially had comparatively close links with their Mongol brethren in the west, who controlled Persia, Asia Minor, and most of Central Asia as well as large tracts of what is now Russia. This was the age when Marco Polo and other travellers brought back to Europe much more accurate information about China than had been available previously. The Chinese, for their part, gained some knowledge of the "barbarians" to the west, but seem to have thought Europe and the Europeans much less interesting than the European barbarians found them. Under the Ming, from the 14th to the 17th centuries, Chinese ships plied the seas as far west as the coasts of Arabia and Africa, but afterwards the Chinese lost interest in such distant lands. The isolation which developed reached its culmination under the last dynasty, the Ch'ing (1644-1912), when China became almost completely cut off – intellectually from all non-Confucian currents and commercially from foreign trade. Foreigners were regarded with deep suspicion. However, from the middle of the 19th century, the Chinese were compelled, by the pressure of European naval and military power, to grant a privileged position to European merchants. Realizing the need for modern (i.e. European) weapons if they were to survive, the Chinese government sent young officers to Europe for training. The young men later came back with more than a knowledge of the requisite technology and European languages. Their vocabulary included such dangerous foreign terms as "democracy" and "reform." Frustrated in their attempts to bring about changes, the would-be reformers became revolutionaries. In 1912, as a result of their efforts, the ancient Chinese Empire passed into history. The successor was the Chinese Republic, with Sun Yat-sen, the leader of the revolutionaries, as first president. The initial decade of Nationalist China was a very difficult one. China's weakness in facing foreign pressures, its defeats on the battlefield and at the conference table, brought about widespread disillusionment among the many who had expected an instant millennium. In this atmosphere was born the Chinese Communist party (1921). Gaining strength and prestige by intensive guerilla activity against the Japanese during the Second World War, the Communists finally took over China in 1949 and proclaimed a People's Republic. Under the leadership of Mao Tse-tung, the Chinese have been engaged in a complete reconstruction of their society, economically and socially. In place of the family and the region, the nation or people are now to be the focus of personal loyalties. It is intended that traditional values based on Confucian ideas should be replaced by the ideals of Marxist-Leninism as interpreted by Mao Tse-tung, whose little Red Book of *Thoughts* has become a new Holy Writ. Mao's ideas have moulded the minds of a complete generation. The communalization of agriculture and the massive increase in industrialization in the past 20 years are transforming China. The future consequences are incalculable.

Chinese culture had an enormous effect on the Japanese at a formative period of their history, and, with varying intensity, in later times also. The origins of the Japanese people remain rather obscure, but they appear to have migrated to Japan from the steppes of northeastern Asia via Korea. Some two thousand years ago they were already organized into small clan states under priestly kings, practising a polytheistic religion, which was essentially nature-worship. It was termed Shinto (literally "the way of the gods") by the adherents of Buddhism, which had penetrated Japan in the 6th century as a Chinese, rather than an Indian, religion. Confucianism also came to Japan from China. These two imported systems had a profound influence on all subsequent Japanese thinking and were, in time, considerably modified in their Japanese environment. The European Middle Ages were the formative period of Japanese identity and culture. Japan experienced massive cultural influence from China during the T'ang age of Chinese might and splendour. This was less the result of direct Chinese activity than the work of the many Japanese Buddhists who went to study in China. On their return to Japan they would enthusiastically spread the ideals, attitudes, and arts of China, the homeland of their new faith. In every sphere, from religion to government, and from land tenure to aesthetics, the Japanese took over or adapted Chinese models. "Adapted" is a key word here. The geographical isolation of Japan, combined with certain historical circumstances, the persistence of ancient Japanese traditions and other complex psychological factors, ensured that the borrowed materials were transmuted and took on distinctive (i.e. Japanese) characteristics. Chinese influences remained continuous throughout most of Japanese history. Educated Japanese men were at all periods connoisseurs of Chinese literature in the original language, and themselves wrote classical Chinese for literary purposes. The women, however, were generally much less educated and their ignorance of Chinese obliged them to write in Japanese. And so it happened that women were the pioneers of Japanese literature. The first important works were partly fictional diaries and long novels, peppered with poetry. These began to appear in the late 10th century.

About that time, the real political power began to pass to the warrior class, a new élite which was to dominate society until the 20th century. However, the military men continued to show external respect for the trappings of royalty, even during the long periods when the central government had very little effective power. The bureaucrat-scholar was for over 2000 years the linchpin of the whole Chinese political system and the major creator and arbiter of literature and taste generally. In Japan, on the contrary, the civil service was held in but small esteem and had little power. Cultural standards were set largely by the provincial warrior aristocracy, which was bound together by personal loyalties and family ties. Appreciation of the military virtues is reflected in the many tales of great battles, which are a major theme in Japanese literature. In most activities of public life and society, until the 20th century, the Japanese looked for leadership almost automatically to the warrior class. Even in religion and thought the military mentality was influential, although Japanese folk beliefs and traditions also played their part in the modification of imported ideas. Thus, some of the doctrines of historic Buddhism became almost unrecognizably transformed; a case in point is the doctrine of *nirvāna*, which in popular Japanese Buddhism became a paradise for the soul of the individual. Zen Buddhism, imported from China in the 12th century, was particularly favoured by the warriors, very possibly because of its emphasis on the attainment of insight through physical and mental discipline rather than through scholarly study.

Local war lords shared the power for several centuries until central government was restored under the auspices of the Tokugawa family of generals at the beginning of the 17th century and peace was maintained until the middle of the 19th. It was their policy to insulate Japan from external contacts, which were regarded as disruptive, or at least potentially so. Not until the middle of the 19th century was Japan reopened to outside influences and trade, henceforth mainly European and American. But from then on modernization became the essential government policy, and a rapid transformation took place in the economic, military, and educational fields, which gradually led to social changes. Real political westernization has, however, been much more superficial. Great industrial and commercial combines and the nationalistic militarism of the élite were the major political factors, until they were checked by the defeat of Japan in the Second World War. Since that time the army has been much less powerful but the combines remain a major force.

During the past generation Japanese society has been changing very much internally. There has been a weakening of traditional ethics and norms, and concomitantly an increasing alienation of youth and an alarming rise in crime. Another aspect of the spiritual and social disorientation associated with rapid westernization is the rise of many "new religions," especially since the Second World War. Politically, Japan's post-war ideal has become "non-involvement" in political adventures and an almost single-minded concentration on economic progress, as well as a strong urge to become the bridge between Asia and the western world. Culturally, there have been very interesting developments in the arts, especially in literature, films, and architecture. Japanese novels and short stories, a blend of traditional and western elements, have won international acclaim and have been translated into many languages. Recent Japanese architecture has shown outstanding imagination in the use of modern materials. Western and traditional elements have combined to produce a vigorous and distinctive hybrid modern Japanese culture.

Korea is now the home of over 40 million people. Since it first came under Chinese domination a little over 2000 years ago Chinese influence has been massive and sustained. Confuciansim and Buddhism have both become deeply ingrained in Korean consciousness and were major factors in developing and maintaining a sense of unity in Korea, superseding the ancient clan loyalties. Korea remained united from the 7th century until 1945. It was self-governing but recognized Chinese suzerainty and developed a distinctive traditional culture, largely based on Chinese elements but with a decided cachet of its own – one that is visible to the outsider even in the art and architecture. As with Japan and China, the traditional civilization of Korea has been shaken to its foundations by the advent of western ideas, economics, and weapons since the latter part of the 19th century.

The works cited in this final portion of the book testify to the great diversity in the historical and cultural development and experience undergone by hundreds of millions of men of different stocks inhabiting a vast area of the globe and extending over millennia of time. Yet there is an unmistakable cohesion: it is provided by that remarkable expression of the human spirit called Chinese civilization.

A GENERAL WORKS

BEASLEY, William Gerald (ed.) *Historians of China and Japan.* Ed. W. G.
Beasley and E. G. Pulleyblank. London, Toronto, New York, Oxford University Press, 1961 (School of Oriental and African Studies, University of London:
Historical Writing on the Peoples of Asia series)
  Important essays on Far Eastern historiography, historians, and history.

BECKMANN, George M. *The modernization of China and Japan.* New York,
Harper, 1962
  A good study. The first sections describe the traditional societies; the remainder the transition and the modern period, relating these to international developments.

BUHOT, Jean. *Chinese and Japanese art, with sections on Korea and Vietnam.*
Ed. Charles McCurdy. Tr. Remy Inglis Hall. New York, Praeger, 1967; Garden
City, N.Y., Doubleday, 1967 P (Anchor Books)
  A very helpful work; the art is treated country by country, each subdivided
by art form.

*CHESNEAUX, Jean. *L'Asie orientale aux XIXe et XXe siècles: Chine, Japon,
Inde, Sud-est asiatique.* Paris, Presses Universitaires de France, 1966 (Collection
Nouvelle Clio)
  An excellent introduction to the historical problems of Asia, and the state
of research. A good guide to further reading.

CLYDE, Paul Hibbert. *The Far East: a history of the impact of the West on
Eastern Asia.* 4th ed., by P. H. Clyde and B. F. Beers. Englewood Cliffs, N.J.,
Prentice-Hall, 1966
  A good well-documented study.

Encyclopédie de la Pléiade. Histoire de l'Art. Tome 1: *Art non-chrétien.* Paris,
Gallimard, 1961
  Contains: Buhot, Jean: *Extrême-Orient.* A very useful country-by-country
description, each subdivided by art form.

*FAIRBANK, John King. *East Asia: the modern transformation.* [By] John K.
Fairbank, Edwin O. Reischauer, Albert M. Craig. Boston, Houghton; London,
Allen & Unwin, 1965
  Probably the best history of China, Japan, and Korea since the middle of
the 19th century. Constitutes vol. 2 of *A History of East Asian civilisation*;
vol. 1 is *East Asia: the great tradition,* by Edwin O. Reischauer and J. K.
Fairbank (below). Contains an excellent annotated bibliography.

The Far East and Australasia, 1970. A survey and directory of Asia and the
Pacific. London, Europa, 1970

An extremely valuable general reference work, especially for political and economic matters, with introductory essays on historical, economic, and other topics by experts. (A revised edition is issued annually.) The area covered includes Afghanistan in the west and Soviet Central Asia in the north.

FITZGERALD, Charles Patrick. *A concise history of East Asia.* London, Toronto, Heinemann; New York, Praeger, 1966 C&P
Covers China, Japan and Korea, and Southeast Asia, with attention to social factors. Useful.

GREENE, Fred. *The Far East.* New York, Rinehart, 1957
Modern political history of China, Japan, India and Pakistan, and Southeast Asia, with emphasis on international relations.

KIM, Young Hum. *East Asia's turbulent century, with American diplomatic documents.* New York, Appleton-Century-Crofts, 1966 P
International relations of China, Japan, and Korea, 1840-1965, with emphasis on the role of the United States.

LATOURETTE, Kenneth Scott. *A short history of the Far East.* 4th ed. New York, Macmillan; Toronto, London, Collier-Macmillan, 1964 (and repr.)
A standard introductory work, now becoming somewhat dated, which also deals with India and Southeast Asia. (Despite the title, not so short — over 750 large pages.)

LEE, Sherman E. *A history of Far Eastern art.* London, Thames & Hudson, 1964; New York, Abrams, 1965
A beautifully illustrated general history, covering China, Japan, Korea, Southeast Asia, and Indonesia.

MORRIS, Ivan. *Madly singing in the mountains: an appreciation and anthology of Arthur Waley.* Ed. Ivan Morris. London, Allen & Unwin, 1970
By his excellent translations of Chinese and Japanese literature Waley was for over half a century the best popularizer of Far Eastern literature in the West. One-third of this book is devoted to Morris's "appreciation," the remainder to a selection from Waley's translations and essays.

*PEFFER, Nathaniel. *The Far East: a modern history.* Ann Arbor, University of Michigan Press; Toronto, Ambassador, 1958
A good standard introductory history, over-simplified at times.

PICARD, Robert. *Les compagnies des Indes: route de la porcelaine.* [Par] R. Picard, J.-P. Kerneis, Y. Bruneau. Paris, Arthaud, 1966

A well-illustrated and interesting account of the merchant companies of various European nations engaged in the East India and China trade, especially for porcelain, from the 16th century onwards.

*REISCHAUER, Edwin O. *East Asia: the great tradition.* By Edwin O. Reischauer and John K. Fairbank. 2nd ed. Boston, Houghton, 1960; London, Allen & Unwin, 1961
An outstanding introduction to the history of China, Korea, and Japan until the middle of the 19th century. Excellent annotated bibliography. Constitutes vol. 1 of *A history of East Asian civilization.* For the sequel see J. K. Fairbank, *East Asia: the modern transformation* (above).

THORP, Willard L. (ed.) *The United States and the Far East.* 2nd ed. Englewood Cliffs, N.J., Prentice-Hall, 1962 P
Good surveys of American foreign policy on Japan, Korea, communist China, and Taiwan.

UPJOHN, Everard M. *Histoire mondiale de l'art.* Tome 5: *L'Orient et l'Extrême-Orient.* [Par] Everard M. Upjohn, Paul S. Wingert [et] Jane Gaston Mahler. Verviers (Belgique), Gérard; Québec, Kasan; Paris, Inter, 1966 P (Collection Marabout Université)
This volume gives a helpful outline of many major features of oriental art. (English original in *History of World Art,* New York, Oxford University Press, 2nd ed., 1958.)

B CHINA

1 REFERENCE WORKS

*DAVIDSON, Martha. *A list of published translations from Chinese into English, French and German: literature exclusive of poetry.* Washington, American Council of Learned Societies, 1952
A very useful bibliography of translations made before the middle of the 20th century.

*GENTZLER, J. Mason. *A syllabus of Chinese civilization.* New York, London, Columbia University Press, 1968 P (Companions to Asian Studies series)
Inexpensive up-to-date guidance for teachers and students of introductory courses. Contains historical outlines, together with annotated listing of recommended elementary readings in English. Marked emphasis on institutional history.

GOODRICH, Luther Carrington. *A syllabus of the history of Chinese civilization and culture.* By L. C. Goodrich and H. C. Fenn. 6th ed. New York, The China Society of America, 1958
Handy orientation for beginners. Lists topics with brief bibliographies.

*HERRMANN, Albert. *An historical atlas of China.* [2nd ed.] General editor: Norton Ginsburg. Prefatory essay by Paul Wheatley. Chicago, Aldine; Edinburgh, Edinburgh University Press, 1966
The most useful atlas of its kind now available. Excellent introduction by Wheatley on the problems of historical cartography.

*HUCKER, Charles O. *China: a critical bibliography.* Tucson, University of Arizona Press, 1962
A work which is very helpful both to beginners and to advanced readers. Intelligent critical annotations to the 2300 references (western-language books and articles, some quoted more than once under different subject headings). Non-specialists will find the brief orientational introductions to each topical section very useful.

*WEITZMAN, David L. *Chinese studies in paperback.* Berkeley, McCutchan, 1967 P
A handy booklet aiming to list all paperbacks available (i.e. non-selective). Summarizes each book's contents, while avoiding value judgments. Books grouped by subjects. Compiler draws attention to the paucity of books on literature and the other arts and science, as compared with the relatively large number of collections of political documents and works on the Sino-Soviet dispute.

2 GENERAL WORKS

*Aspects de la Chine. Causeries faites à la Radiodiffusion française dans le cadre de l'Heure de Culture française ... Par E. Balazs [et al.]. 3 vols. Paris, Presses Universitaires de France, 1959-62 P (Tome 1-2: Publications du Musée Guimet. Tome 3: Centre d'Études de Politique Étrangère)
> A first-class introduction for the general reader to traditional and modern China in all its apsects. Tome 1-2: Langue, histoire, religions, philosophie, littérature, arts. Tome 3: Époque contemporaine.

CRESSEY, George Babcock. Land of the 500 million: a geography of China. New York, Toronto, McGraw-Hill, 1955
> An excellent general geography.

CRESSEY, George Babcock. Géographie humaine et économique de la Chine. Préface et traduction de Charles Mourey. Paris, Payot, 1939 P (Collection Bibliothèque Géographique)
> See preceding note.

*DAWSON, Raymond Stanley (ed.) The legacy of China. Oxford, Clarendon Press; Toronto, New York, Oxford University Press, 1964
> This series of articles by various experts surveys "the legacy of traditional Chinese civilization." It forms an admirable introduction for the general reader. Good coverage of philosophy and religious thought, literature, art, science, and government.

*EICHHORN, Werner. Chinese civilization: an introduction. Tr. Janet Seligman. London, Faber; New York, Praeger, 1969
> This is an excellent work for laymen. Deals particularly with intellectual and social (rather than political) history, to the late 13th century. Good chapters on the Chinese theatre, novel, and the impact of Europe on Chinese intellectuals.

*FAIRBANK, John King. The United States and China. [2nd ed.] Cambridge, Mass., Harvard University Press; New York, Viking; Toronto, Macmillan, 1958 (and repr.) C&P (Compass Books)
> An outstanding general introduction to modern China, much wider in scope than the title implies. A well-annotated comprehensive bibliography provides excellent orientation on most aspects of Chinese history and civilization at all periods. Highly recommended.

FEUERWERKER, Albert (ed.) Modern China. Englewood Cliffs, N.J., Prentice-Hall, 1964 C&P (Spectrum Books)
> Twelve useful articles by various experts, introducing major aspects of China in the last hundred years, as illustrations of its transition to a modern society.

HUARD, Pierre Alphonse. *Chine d'hier et d'aujourd'hui: civilisation, arts, techniques.* Par Pierre Huard et Ming Wong. Paris, Horizons de France, 1960
> This handsome volume covers Chinese civilization briefly in all its aspects. With an abundance of good illustrations to enliven the text, it is a painless introduction to China's past and present for the non-specialist.

LATOURETTE, Kenneth Scott. *The Chinese: their history and culture.* 4th ed. New York, Macmillan; London, Toronto, Collier-Macmillan, 1964 (and repr.)
> A rather old-fashioned standard general work, with good annotated bibliographies.

LI, Dun J. (ed.) *The essence of Chinese civilization.* Princeton, Van Nostrand, 1967
> An excellent selection of passages from Chinese authors of many periods arranged under the following headings: philosophy and religion, government, economics, family and society. Connecting editorial material too thin.

LIN, Yutang. *My country and my people.* [2nd ed.] London, Heinemann, 1939, repr. 1956
> A lively and readable book for the general reader, which seeks to show the "spirit" of the Chinese.

3 HISTORY AND SOCIAL SCIENCES[†]

BALAZS, Étienne. *Chinese civilization and bureaucracy.* Tr. H. M. Wright. Ed. Arthur F. Wright. New Haven, London, Yale University Press, 1964 C&P
> Outstanding studies on Chinese institutions (bureaucracy, feudalism, fairs, towns, land ownership, etc.), history, and thought.

BAWDEN, Charles R. *The modern history of Mongolia.* London, Weidenfeld; New York, Praeger, 1968 (Asia-Africa series)
> From the 17th century to modern communist times.

BODDE, Derk. *China's cultural tradition: what and whither?* New York, Toronto, London, Holt, 1957 P (and repr.) (Source Problems in World Civilization series)
> A good booklet examining basic features of Chinese culture, particularly sociological.

BODDE, Derk. *China's gifts to the West.* Washington, American Council on Education, 1942
> This interesting booklet (still in print) mentions such items as silk, tea, pa-

[†]Including Mongolia.

per, printing, explosives, and games which Europe borrowed from China in the Middle Ages and later.

BUCK, Pearl S. *The good earth.* New York, Simon & Schuster, 1931 (and repr.); Pocket Books; Washington Square; Grosset; [no dates, all P]
   The life of a Chinese peasant family in the 1920s is the subject of this famous novel, which won the Nobel Prize for its author. It is perhaps the best of her many sympathetic works on China.

CHESNEAUX, Jean. *Introduction aux études d'histoire contemporaine de Chine, 1898-1949.* Par Jean Chesneaux et John Lust. La Haye, Paris, Mouton, 1965
   A useful work.

CHESNEAUX, Jean. *Les sociétés secrètes en Chine, XIXe et XXe siècles.* Paris, Julliard, 1965 (Collection Archives)
   A valuable survey.

CH'IEN, Tuan-sheng. *The government and politics of China.* Cambridge, Mass., Harvard University Press, 1950
   Covers all Chinese history, but emphasizes the modern period. A useful work.

DAVID-NEEL, Alexandra. *Quarante siècles d'expansion chinoise.* Paris, La Palatine, 1964 P
   A brief survey by a notable expert and stylist.

DAWSON, Raymond Stanley. *The Chinese chameleon: an analysis of European conceptions of Chinese civilization.* London, Toronto, New York, Oxford University Press, 1967
   A good study, showing how China has been viewed by Europeans, both friendly and hostile, from Marco Polo's time to the present.

EBERHARD, Wolfram. *A history of China.* Tr. E. W. Dickes. 2nd ed. London, Routledge; Berkeley, University of California Press, 1960 (and repr.)
   A somewhat interpretative social history, incorporating the results of recent research, especially in archaeology.

EBERHARD, Wolfram. *Histoire de la Chine, des origines à nos jours.* Tr. George Deniker. Paris, Payot, 1952 (Collection Bibliothèque Historique)
   See preceding note.

ENNIN, *Ennin's diary.* Tr. Edwin O. Reischauer. New York, Ronald, 1955
   A systematic account of Chinese life in the 9th century, recorded by a contemporary Japanese Buddhist traveller. The information is well interpreted in Reischauer's companion volume (below) *Ennin's travels.*

ENNIN. *Journal d'un voyageur en Chine au IXe siècle.* Traduction et introduction de Roger Lévy. Paris, Albin Michel, 1961
    See preceding note.

*FITZGERALD, Charles Patrick. *China: a short cultural history.* 3rd ed. London, Cresset; New York, Praeger, 1961 (and repr.) C&P
    A recommended introduction to Chinese cultural history, down to the 19th century.

FRANKE, Wolfgang. *China and the West.* Tr. R. A. Wilson. Oxford, Blackwell, 1967; New York, Harper, 1967 P
    A short work for the general reader, dealing mainly with Chinese ideas about, and knowledge of, the West in the past 450 years.

GARDNER, Charles Sidney. *Chinese traditional historiography.* Cambridge, Mass., Harvard University Press, 1938, repr. 1961
    A small but influential analysis; interest not limited to Sinologists.

GERNET, Jacques. *La Chine ancienne.* Paris, Presses Universitaires de France, 1964 P
    A short lucid social and economic history, down to the foundation of the empire in 221 B.C.E.

GERNET, Jacques. *Ancient China, from the beginnings to the Empire.* Tr. Raymond Rudorff. London, Faber; Berkeley, University of California Press, 1968
    See preceding note.

GERNET, Jacques. *La vie quotidienne en Chine à la veille de l'invasion mongole (1250-1276).* Paris, Hachette, 1959 (Collection La Vie Quotidienne)
    A good description of the main everyday features of traditional Chinese civilization, especially as lived in the contemporary capital, Hangchow.

GERNET, Jacques. *Daily life in China on the eve of the Mongol invasion, 1250-1276.* Tr. H. M. Wright. New York, Macmillan, 1962
    See preceding note.

*GOODRICH, Luther Carrington. *A short history of the Chinese people.* 3rd ed. New York, Harper, 1959; 1963 P; with a final chapter by W. A. C. Adie: London, Allen & Unwin, 1969 C&P
    Probably the best really short history; some emphasis on material culture.

*GROUSSET, René. *Histoire de la Chine.* Paris, Fayard, 1942; Club de Libraires de France, 1957
    A cultural history of traditional China for the layman; very readable, though rather superficial.

*GROUSSET, René. *The rise and splendour of the Chinese Empire.* Tr. Anthony Watson-Gandy and Terence Gordon. London, Bles, 1952; Berkeley, University of California Press, 1953; 1962 P
  Translation of preceding work. See previous note.

HAHN, Emily. *China only yesterday, 1850-1950: a century of change.* Garden City, N.Y., Doubleday, 1963; London, Weidenfeld, 1964
  History in chatty style. Readable though rather novelettish, but contains much information based on good sources.

HO, Ping-ti. *The ladder of success in imperial China: aspects of social nobility, 1368-1911.* New York, London, Columbia University Press, 1962; New York, Wiley, 1964 P (Columbia University, Studies of the East Asian Institute) (Science Editions)
  An interesting and original study of the social stratification and the changing composition of the ruling classes in Chinese society.

HOLT, Edgar. *The Opium Wars in China.* London, Putnam; Chester Springs, Pa., Dufour, 1964
  A popular treatment of the wars in the mid-19th century which first opened up China to western trade and ideas.

HUCKER, Charles O. *Chinese history: a bibliographic review.* Washington, American Historical Association; New York, Macmillan, 1962 P (Service Center for Teachers of History Publications)
  Handy bibliographic essay, discussing and evaluating English language books on Chinese history.

HUCKER, Charles O. *The traditional Chinese state in Ming times (1368-1644).* Tucson, University of Arizona Press, 1961 P
  A readable essay on government in traditional China, also applicable in general to the following two and a half centuries.

HUDSON, Geoffrey Francis. *Europe and China: a survey of their relations from the earliest times to 1800.* Boston, Beacon, 1961 P [repr. of 1931 ed.]
  A sound book on commercial and cultural relations.

KIRBY, Edward Stuart. *Introduction to the economic history of China.* London, Allen & Unwin; New York, Macmillan, 1954
  A good short survey.

LACH, Donald Frederick. *China in the eyes of Europe: the 16th century.* Chicago, University of Chicago Press, 1968 P (Phoenix Books)
  The impact of China on Europe.

LAMB, Harold. *Genghis Khan, the emperor of all men.* New York, Doubleday, 1952; Toronto, New York, Bantam, 1960 P
A lively though romanticized biography of the 13th century Mongol world conqueror.

LANG, Olga. *Chinese family and society.* New Haven, Yale University Press; London, Oxford University Press, 1946; repr. Hamden, Conn., Shoestring Press, 1968
A classic sociological study.

LANG, Olga. *La vie en Chine.* Tr. Aline Chalufour. Paris, Hachette, 1950 (Collection La Vie Quotidienne)

LEVENSON, Joseph Richard. *China: an interpretative history, from the beginnings to the fall of Han.* By Joseph R. Levenson and Franz Schurmann. Berkeley, University of California Press, 1969
A stimulating re-examination of the main currents of Chinese history to the 3rd century; 130 very interesting pages.

LÉVY, Roger. *Trente siècles d'histoire de Chine.* Paris, Presses Universitaires de France, 1967 P
A rather superficial survey, sketching the main elements of Chinese history in 300 small pages.

LI, Dun J. *The ageless Chinese: a history.* New York, Scribner, 1965 C&P
A college textbook covering the whole of Chinese history.

LOEWE, Michael. *Everyday life in early imperial China during the Han period, 202 B.C. – A.D. 220.* London, Batsford; New York, Putnam, 1969
A competent elementary book.

LOEWE, Michael. *Imperial China: the historical background to the modern age.* London, Allen & Unwin; New York, Praeger, 1966
An informative survey for the non-specialist of the main features of Chinese history and culture, down to about 1850. Chapters include social distinctions, government, operation of the economy, growth of cities, and relations with foreign peoples.

LUNG, Chang. *La Chine à l'aube du XXᵉ siècle.* Les relations diplomatiques de le Chine avec les puissances depuis la guerre sino-japonaise jusqu'à la guerre russo-japonaise. Paris, Nouvelles Editions Latines, 1962
Fairly detailed.

McALEAVY, Henry. *The modern history of China.* London, Weidenfeld; New York, Praeger, 1967 C&P (Asia-Africa series)
A balanced, mainly political, history of the past century and a quarter.

MASPÉRO, Henri. *La Chine antique.* Nouvelle éd. revue ... par Paul Demiéville. Paris, Presses Universitaires de France, 1965 (Collection Annales du Musée Guimet, Bibliothèque d'Études)
A standard work on the history and culture of the Chou period (to about 256 B.C.).

MASPÉRO, Henri. *Histoire et institutions de la Chine ancienne, des origines au XIIe siècle apres J.-C.* Par Henri Maspéro et Étienne Balazs. Texte revisé par Paul Demiéville. Paris, Presses Universitaires de France, 1967 (Collection Annales du Musée Guimet, Bibliothèque d'Études)
An outstanding work by two major scholars, addressed to the non-specialist.

*MASPÉRO, Henri. *Les institutions de la Chine.* Par Henri Maspéro et Jean Escarra. Paris, Presses Universitaires de France, 1952
Political, social, economic, and intellectual institutions throughout China's history surveyed in this valuable work for the layman.

NING, Lao T'ai-t'ai. *A daughter of Han: the autobiography of a Chinese working woman.* [By] Ida Pruitt, from the story told her by Ning Lao T'ai-t'ai. Stanford, Stanford University Press, 1967 C&P (repr. of 1945 ed.)
Interesting in itself and excellent for its lively descriptions of Chinese daily life between 1867 and 1938.

PELISSIER, Roger. *La Chine entre la scène.* Paris, Julliard, 1963
History, both political and cultural, in the form of well-chosen selections from contemporary writers, visitors, and journalists who visited China.

PELISSIER, Roger. *The awakening of China, 1793-1949.* Ed. & tr. Martin Kieffer. London, Secker, 1966; New York, Putnams; Toronto, Longmans, 1967 (History in the Making series)
A translation of the preceding work.

REISCHAUER, Edwin Oldfather. *Ennin's travels in T'ang China.* New York, Ronald, 1955
A systematic description of 9th century China, derived from the Diary of Ennin (see above, entry under Ennin) translated by Reischauer.

SCHAFER, E. H. *The vermillion bird: T'ang images of the south.* Berkeley, University of California Press, 1967
The literary and artistic genius of China in a talented era (7th to 9th centuries) reflected in a fine work.

SCHURMANN, Franz. *The China reader.* Edited, annotated and with introductions by Franz Schurmann and Orville Schell. 3 vols. New York, Toronto, Random House, 1967 C&P (Vintage Books)

Vol. 1: *Imperial China: the decline of the last dynasty and the origins of modern China* — the 18th and 19th centuries. Vol. 2: *Republican China: nationalism, war and the rise of communism, 1911-1949.* Vol. 3: *Communist China ... 1949 to the present.* This documentary history, consisting of selections from contemporary accounts and the writings of leading scholars and interpreters of China, provides the general reader with important background information for understanding modern China.

*TENG, Ssu-yü. *China's response to the West: a documentary survey, 1839-1923.* By Ssu-yü Teng [and] John K. Fairbank. Cambridge, Mass., Harvard University Press; London, Oxford University Press, 1954 C&P; New York, Atheneum, 1963 P
Sixty-five important documents with introductions setting them in their historical perspective. Essential reading for this topic.

WALEY, Arthur. *The Opium War through Chinese eyes.* London, Allen & Unwin, 1958; New York, Macmillan, 1959; Stanford, Stanford University Press, 1968 P
A well-written account giving contemporary views on the wars between 1839 and 1860 which broke the traditional isolation of China. For the western viewpoint see Edgar Holt's work (above).

4 HISTORY OF CHINESE LITERATURE

BIRCH, Cyril (ed.) *Chinese communist literature.* New York, London, Praeger, 1963
Papers by various authors on the problems of literature in communist China.

BISHOP, John Lyman (ed.) *Studies in Chinese literature.* Cambridge, Mass., Harvard University Press, 1965 C&P (Harvard-Yenching Institute Studies)
Articles by noted scholars on a wide range of literary subjects.

HSIA, Chih-tsing. *The classic Chinese novel: a critical introduction.* New York, London, Columbia University Press, 1968 (Companions to Asian Studies series)
A detailed study of six major classical Chinese novels, containing long extracts in translation and a comparison with western classics. Good bibliography.

*HSIA, Chih-tsing. *A history of modern Chinese fiction, 1917-57.* With an appendix on Taiwan by Tsi-an Hsia. New Haven, London, Yale University Press, 1961
A good analysis of ideas and detailed critical evaluation of the main authors.

HU, Pin-ching. *Li Ch'ing-chao.* New York, Twayne, 1966 (Twayne's World Authors series)

    Biography of a notable 12th century Chinese poetess who specialized in *ts'u* (lyrics or poetry for singing), with translation of her extant work. The author also analyses the nature of Chinese poetry.

KALTENMARK, Odile. *La littérature chinoise.* [2ᵉ éd.] Paris, Presses Universitaires de France, 1967 P (Collection "Que sais-je?")

    A very summary general survey, inadequate in explanation of basic ideas, but has the virtue of brevity.

KALTENMARK, Odile. *Chinese literature.* Tr. Anne-Marie Geoghegan. New York, Walker, 1963 C&P

    See preceding note.

*LIU, James J. Y. *The art of Chinese poetry.* London, Routledge; Chicago, University of Chicago Press, 1962; 1966 P

    An excellent explanation of Chinese poetics for western readers.

LIU, Wu-chi. *An introduction to Chinese literature.* [By] Liu Wu-chi. Bloomington, London, Indiana University Press, 1966

    A useful work for westerners. Emphasis is on the major writers, literary styles, and movements only. Includes helpful partly annotated bibliography for further reading.

LU, Hsün. *A brief history of Chinese fiction.* Peking, Foreign Languages Press, 1959

    A standard social-critical work (1920-24) covering both classical and colloquial fiction.

*MARGOULIÈS, Georges. *Histoire de la littérature chinoise: poésie.* Paris, Payot, 1948 P (Collection Bibliothèque Historique)

    A general history of the traditional genres, illustrated by translations of Chinese poems.

*MARGOULIÈS, Georges. *Histoire de la littérature chinoise: prose.* Paris, Payot, 1949 P (Collection Bibliothèque Historique)

    A general historical account of artistic prose.

*SCOTT, Adolphe Clarence. *The classical theatre of China.* London, Allen & Unwin; New York, Macmillan, 1957

    A detailed description of the history and many other aspects of the traditional theatre by a noted expert.

SCOTT, Adolphe Clarence. *An introduction to the Chinese theatre.* New York, Theatre Arts Books, 1959 P

A discussion for non-specialists of theatre techniques, and the outlines of 20 popular plays.

*SCOTT, Adolphe Clarence. *Literature and the arts in twentieth century China.* Garden City, Doubleday, 1963 P; London, Allen & Unwin, 1965
A useful non-technical outline of literature, theatre and dance, cinema, painting, architecture, sculpture, and music. About 20 pages are devoted to each topic.

*WATSON, Burton. *Early Chinese literature.* New York, Columbia University Press, 1962 C&P
A good survey of Chinese writing on history, philosophy, and poetry down to the 2nd century. Helpful select bibliographies.

WELLS, Henry W. *The classical drama of the Orient.* Bombay, London, New York, Asia Publishing House, 1965
A series of studies on the aims, methods, and conventions of classical Chinese and Japanese drama.

5 CHINESE LITERATURE IN TRANSLATION[†]

a/General and Mixed Works

BELPAIRE, Bruno (comp. & tr.) *Anthologie d'écrivains chinois.* Paris, Presses Universitaires de France, 1957
A selection from writers of the T'ang period (7th to 9th centuries).

*BIRCH, Cyril (comp. & ed.) *Anthology of Chinese literature, from early times to the fourteenth century.* Associate editor Donald Keene. New York, Grove, 1956 P (and repr.); Harmondsworth, Penguin, 1967 P (Unesco Collection of Representative Works — Chinese Series)
A good selection of representative pieces of most genres (excluding philosophy and religion), with excellent introductory essays to the volume and to the individual sections. Successful translations by various hands. Probably the best general anthology of its kind in English.

GILES, Herbert Allen (ed.) *Gems of Chinese literature.* 2 vols. (in 1). New York, Paragon; New York, Dover, 1965 P (repr. of 2nd [1923] ed.)
Chinese prose and verse, translated in a pleasant, slightly old-fashioned style. The originals date from ca. 550 B.C. to 1650 A.D.

LIN, Yutang (ed. & tr.) *Translations from the Chinese.* Cleveland, World, 1963 P

[†]Excluding religious and philosophical literature (for these see subsection 6 below).

A good selection of prose and poetry of all kinds, which express aspects of the Chinese personality; arranged by subject.

LU, Hsün. *Selected works*. 4 vols. Peking, Foreign Languages Press, 1956-60
Short stories, criticism, and other works of the writer and social critic (1881-1936) who is revered as the patron saint of literature by the Chinese communists.

*MARGOULIÈS, Georges. *Anthologie raisonnée de la littérature chinoise*. Paris, Payot, 1948 P (Collection Bibliothèque Historique)
Short passages, prose and poetry, from all periods, arranged by subject. Long introductory orientation for the general reader.

MEUWESE, Catherine (comp. & tr.) *L'Inde du Bouddha, vue par des pèlerins chinois sous la dynastie Tang (VIIe siècle)*. Présentation d'Étiemble. Texte établi et annoté par Catherine Meuwese. Paris, Calmann-Lévy, 1968
Mainly devoted to the travels of an observant Chinese Buddhist pilgrim, Hsüan-tsang (Xuan-zang, d. 664). Includes his travels in Central Asia. For an English account, see Arthur Waley's *The real Tripitaka* (below).

MIRSKY, Jeannette (ed. & tr.) *The great Chinese travelers*. New York, Pantheon, 1964
Descriptions of the non-Chinese world, as seen by Chinese travellers, written from ancient times until the 19th century.

WALEY, Arthur. *The real Tripitaka*. London, Allen & Unwin, 1952
The first half of this book deals very enjoyably with the life and travels of Hsüan-tsang, the great Chinese Buddhist pilgrim to India in the 7th century.

b/Historical Works

SSU-MA, Ch'ien. *Records of the historian*. Selected and translated by Burton Watson. New York, London, Toronto, Oxford University Press, 1969 P
Extracts from the earliest major history of China, compiled in the 1st century B.C., and considered as a model for historians until modern times. (Watson has made a more complete translation, entitled *Records of the Grand Historian of China*, 2 vols. New York, Columbia University Press, 1961; there is a complete French translation in 6 vols.: *Les mémoires historiques de Se-ma Ts'ien*, tr. Edouard Chavannes, Paris, A.-Maisonneuve 1967, repr. of 1905 ed.)

c/The Novel, Short Story, and Folk Tale

BAUER, Wolfgang (ed. & tr.) *The golden casket: Chinese novellas of two millennia*. Translated by Christopher Levenson from Wolfgang Bauer's and Herbert Franke's German version. New York, Harcourt, 1964; Harmondsworth, Penguin, 1967 P

Forty-six short stories by a wide range of authors. An excellent selection of a traditional form, these novellas date from the 3rd pre-Christian century to the 18th century.

CHIN-P'ING-MEI. *Chin P'ing Mei, the Adventurous history of Hsi Men and his six wives.* New York, Putnam, 1940 (and repr.); Capricorn, 1960 P
Popular anonymous novel, written late in the 16th century. Amusing, if somewhat pornographic, satire on the moral degeneracy of contemporary Chinese society.

EBERHARD, Wolfram (ed.) *Folktales of China.* Chicago, University of Chicago Press; London, Routledge, 1965 (Folktales of the World series)
An interesting selection, grouped according to types, by a leading scholar in Chinese folklore.

FÊNG, Mêng-lung. *Stories from a Ming collection.* Translations of Chinese short stories published in the 17th century, by Cyril Birch. London, Bodley Head, 1958; Bloomington, Indiana University Press, 1959; New York, Grove, 1968 P (Unesco Collection of Representative Works – Chinese Series)
Six enjoyable stories from one of the best periods of Chinese story-writing.

HU, Wan-ch'un. *Man of a special cut.* Peking, Foreign Languages Press, 1963 P
These nine stories by a contemporary steel worker and short-story writer are devoted to the noble struggle of the working class and provide a picture of government-approved writing.

JENNER, W. J. F. (comp.) *Modern Chinese short stories.* Tr. W. J. F. Jenner and Gladys Yang. London, Toronto, New York, Oxford University Press, 1970 P (Oxford Paperbacks)
Twenty stories by leading writers of the past half-century reflect the enormous changes in styles and interests during the period.

KAO, Yu-pao. *My childhood.* Peking, Foreign Languages Press, 1960 P
Autobiographical novel describing the events which transformed Chinese village life in North China from the pre-war period to the communist take-over.

LI, Ju-chen. *Flowers in the mirror.* Tr. & ed. Lin Tai-yi. Berkeley, University of California Press; London, Owen, 1965
A well-known 19th century historical travel novel which satirized contemporary society.

LI, Yü. *Jou pu tuan: the prayer-mat of flesh.* Tr. Richard Martin. New York, Grove, 1963; 1966 P
An erotic, humorous, and satirical novel illustrating the manners of the somewhat decadent period in which it was written (early 17th century).

LIN, Yutang (ed.) *Famous Chinese short stories*. New York, Simon & Schuster, 1948; New York, Washington Square, 1954 P
Twenty good tales from different periods, arranged by type.

LIU, E. *The travels of Lao Ts'an*. Translated from the Chinese by Harold Shadick. Ithaca, Cornell University Press, 1952; 1966 P
Classic modern satirical novel of life in China at the beginning of the 20th century, more critical of bureaucracy than even of corruption.

LIU, E. *L'Odyssée de Lao Ts'an*. Par Lieou Ngo. Tr. Cheng Tcheng. Paris, Gallimard, 1964 P (Collection Connaissance de l'Orient) (Collection Unesco d'Oeuvres Représentatives — Série Chinoise)
See preceding note.

LO, Kuan-chung. *San Kuo, or Romance of the Three Kingdoms*. Translated from the Chinese by Charles H. Brewitt-Taylor. 2 vols. Rutland, Vt., Tuttle, 1959 (repr. of 1925 ed.)
A popular historical novel about the 3rd century, attributed to the 14th century writer Lo Kuan-chung.

LU, Hsün. *Old tales retold*. Peking, Foreign Languages Press, 1961 P
Satirical retelling of old legends which criticize social institutions.

LU, Hsün. *Selected stories of Lu Hsun*. 2nd ed. Tr. Yang Hsien-yi and Gladys Yang. Peking, Foreign Languages Press, 1963
The author (1881-1936) was perhaps the most influential writer of the 20th century. A leftist politically, he developed a new style of realism breaking with the classical tradition. His stories often contain biting satire and social criticism. The Foreign Languages Publishing House in Peking also publishes English and French translations of the works of many other communist and left-wing Chinese writers.

LU, Hsün. *The true story of Ah Q*. Peking, Foreign Languages Press, 1953
A comical novel.

LU, Hsün. *La véritable histoire de Ah Q*. Tr. Paul Jamati. Paris, Editions Française Réunis, 1953
See preceding note.

MAO, Tun. *Midnight*. Tr. Hsü Meng-hsiung. Peking, Foreign Languages Press, 1957
A representative novel of the communist era, describing bourgeois life in Shanghai, about 1930. The author, a revolutionary and literary man, has been minister of culture in China.

MAO, Tun. *Minuit.* Par Mao-Dun. Pékin, Éditions en Langues Etrangères, [195-]
See preceding note.

PA, Kin. *The family.* By Pa Chin. Tr. Sidney Shapiro. Peking, Foreign Languages Press, 1958
The generation gap in Szechuan at the beginning of the 20th century. Most of the heroes of this author's works are young revolutionaries, and his writings were very popular with Chinese students in the 1930s and 1940s.

P'U, Sung-ling. *Contes extraordinaires du pavillon du loisir.* [Par] P'ou Songling. Introduction par Yves Hervouet. Traduit par une équipe de traducteurs. Paris, Gallimard, 1909
A 17th century collection of short stories about ghosts and other supernatural creatures greatly admired for its literary style.

SHEN, Fu. *Chapters from a floating life.* Tr. Shirley M. Black. London, New York; Toronto, Oxford University Press, 1960
Reminiscences of a minor 18th century official, mainly about his deep and moving love for his wife and his personal problems. Has been very popular in China since it was "rediscovered" in 1877.

SHEN, Fu. *Six récits au fil inconstant des jours.* Traduit du chinois par P. Ryckmans. Bruxelles, Larcier, 1966
A good translation of the work described above.

SHUI-HU CHUAN. *All men are brothers.* Tr. Pearl S. Buck. 3rd ed. 2 vols. London, Methuen; New York, Grove, 1957 P
A great traditional Chinese picaresque adventure novel of the Robin Hood type.

*TS'AO, Chan. *Dream of the red chamber.* By Tsao Hsueh-chin, with a continuation by Kao Ou. Translated from the Chinese by Chi-chen Wang. New York, Twayne, 1958
This famous 18th century novel, a family saga and romance, gives a vivid picture of middle-class Chinese society and civilization in traditional China.

TS'AO, Chan. *Dream of the red chamber.* By Tsao Hsueh-chin. Translated and adapted by Chi-chen Wang. Garden City, N.Y., Doubleday, 1958 P; London, Vision, 1963
An abridged translation.

TS'AO, Chan. *Le rêve du pavillon rouge.* (Hong-leou mong). Traduit en allemand par Franz Kuhn. Version française établie par Armel Guerne. Tome 2. Paris, Guy le Prat, 1964 (Collection Unesco d'Oeuvres Représentatives — Série Chinoise)
See first entry under this author.

TSAO, Y. *Bright skies.* Tr. Chang Pei-chi. Peking, Foreign Languages Press, 1960

A sample of communist Chinese drama. "It describes how ... the doctors and professors of a medical college ... with the help of the Party, gradually shake off their old ideology of subservience to the U.S." (Editor's note).

WALEY, Arthur. *Ballads and stories from Tun-Huang: an anthology.* London, Allen & Unwin; New York, Macmillan, 1960

Ninth century popular literature racily translated in the Waley manner.

WU, Ch'eng-en. *Monkey.* Tr. Arthur Waley. London, Allen & Unwin, 1942 (and repr.); New York, John Day; New York, Grove, 1958 P

Entertaining 16th century picaresque folk epic in the form of a satirical novel. First-rate translation.

d/Poetry

CH'U TZ'U. *Ch'u Tz'ŭ: the Songs of the South: an ancient Chinese anthology.* Tr. David Hawkes. Oxford, Clarendon Press; Toronto, New York, Oxford University Press, 1959; Boston, Beacon, 1962 P (Unesco Collection of Representative Works – Chinese Series)

A 2nd century collection of beautiful allegorical poetry, with an undertone of bitterness. Notable translation.

DAVIS, Albert Richard (ed.) *Penguin book of Chinese verse.* Verse translations by Robert Kotewall and Norman L. Smith. Harmondsworth, Baltimore, Penguin, 1962 P (and repr.)

A very small selection of poetry from the earliest times to the 20th century, preceded by a note on the forms of Chinese verse and brief biographies of poets.

*DEMIÉVILLE, Paul (comp.) *Anthologie de la poésie chinoise classique.* Paris, Gallimard, 1962 P (Connaissance de l'Orient) (Collection Unesco d'Oeuvres Représentatives – Série Chinoise)

An excellent broad selection.

FRODSHAM, J. D. (comp.) *An anthology of Chinese verse: Han Wei Chin and the northern and southern dynasties.* Translated and annotated by J. D. Frodsham, with the collaboration of Ch'eng Hsi. Oxford, Clarendon Press; Toronto, New York, Oxford University Press, 1967 (The Oxford Library of East Asian Literatures series)

A valiant attempt at the translation of poems from a formative period of Chinese verse (206 B.C. to 618 A.D.). The cultural background and the major poetic themes are set out in a good introduction.

FRODSHAM, J. D. *The murmuring stream*. The life and works of the Chinese nature poet Hsieh Ling-yün (385-433), Duke of K'ang-Lo. 2 vols. Kuala Lumpur, University of Malaya Press; London, New York, Toronto, Oxford University Press, 1969

> Vol. 1 contains the biography of the first great nature poet, translations from his verse, and a comparison with the work of other poets.

GRAHAM, Angus Charles (tr.) *Poems of the late T'ang*. Harmondsworth, Baltimore, Penguin, 1965 (Unesco Collection of Representative Works — Chinese Series)

> A good translation of poems by seven poets of the 8th and 9th centuries, preceded by an interesting essay on the problems of translating Chinese poetry. On the latter, compare with James Liu, *The art of Chinese poetry*, 1962 (above, subsection 4).

GUILLERMAZ, Patricia (comp. & tr.) *Poésie chinoise contemporaine*. Paris, Seghers, 1962

> An interesting selection in translation.

*HSU, Kai-yu (ed. & tr.) *Twentieth century Chinese poetry: an anthology*. Tr. & ed. Kai-yu Hsu. Garden City, N.Y., Doubleday, 1963; 1964 P

> These verses by 44 poets from the beginnings of modern poetry (1918) to the rise of the "new" folk poetry (1958) mirror modern China's changing ideals and ideas. Good.

JENYNS, Soame (tr.) *Selections from the Three Hundred Poems of the T'ang dynasty*. London, Murray; New York, Paragon, 1940 (and repr.) (Wisdom of the East series)

> Poetry from a favourite anthology of T'ang dynasty poets (7th to 9th centuries), arranged by topic.

PAYNE, Robert (ed.) *The white pony: an anthology of Chinese poetry*. New York, Day, 1947; London, Allen & Unwin, 1949; New York, Toronto, New American Library, 1960 P (Mentor Books)

> A good selection of poems of all periods, translated by various (and unequal) hands. Biographical introductions to the poets.

SU, Shih. *Su Tung-p'o: selections from a Sung dynasty poet*. Translated and with an introduction by Burton Watson. New York, London, Columbia University Press, 1965 P (Unesco Collection of Representative Works — Chinese Series)

> Readable translations of 85 poems on many subjects by the greatest poet (d. 1101) of the Sung dynasty.

T'AO, Ch'ien. *T'ao the hermit.* Sixty poems, translated by William Acker. London, Thames & Hudson; New York, Vanguard, 1952
   Some of China's finest nature poetry, by a 4th/5th century poet.

*WALEY, Arthur (tr.) *Chinese poems.* London, Allen & Unwin; New York, Macmillan, 1946, repr. 1962; 1964 P. American edition entitled *Translations from the Chinese.*

WALEY, Arthur. *The life and times of Po Chü-i, 772-846 A.D.* London, Allen & Unwin; New York, Macmillan, 1949
   Biography of a great Chinese poet and fine translations of many of his poems. Many of these reappear in Waley's *Chinese poems* (above).

WALEY, Arthur. *The poetry and career of Li Po.* London, Allen & Unwin; New York, Macmillan, 1950 (and repr.) (Ethical and Religious Classics of East and West series)
   An 8th century Taoist poet who is very popular in the West. This excellent study and translation of some of his poetry is done with Waley's usual skill.

WALEY, Arthur. *Yuan Mei, eighteenth century Chinese poet.* London, Allen & Unwin; New York, Macmillan, 1956; New York, Grove, 1956 P
   Enjoyable biography of a "lovable, witty, generous, affectionate, hot-tempered, wildly prejudiced man."

e/Drama

HSIUNG, Shih-i (ed. & tr.) *Lady Precious Stream: an old Chinese play, done into English according to its traditional style.* 10th ed. London, Methuen, 1950 (and repr.)
   An English adaptation (1934) of a popular Chinese ("commercial") drama.

KUO, Mo-jo. *K'iu yuan,* par Kouo Mojo. Traduit du chinois par Liang Pai-tchin. Paris, Gallimard, 1957 (Collection Connaissance de l'Orient)
   A modern play.

LI, Tche-houa (ed. & tr.) *Le signe de patience et autres pièces du théâtre des Yuan.* Traduction, introduction et notes de Li Tche-houa. Paris, Gallimard, 1963 (Collection Connaissance de l'Orient) (Collection Unesco d'Oeuvres Représentatives — Série Chinoise)
   Plays of the 13th and 14th centuries.

SCOTT, Adolphe C. (comp. & tr.) *Traditional Chinese plays.* Translated, described and annotated by A. C. Scott. Madison, University of Wisconsin Press, 1967

Skilful interpretation of two popular traditional plays: "Ssu Lang visits his mother" and "The butterfly dream."

WANG, Shih-Fu. *The romance of the western chamber.* Tr. S. I. Hsiung. Intro. C. T. Hsia. New York, London, Columbia University Press, repr. 1968 C&P (Unesco Collection of Representative Works – Chinese Series)
    A famous 13th century romantic play. C. T. Hsia, a noted literary critic, has added a useful introduction to this pre-World-War-II translation.

6 RELIGION AND IDEAS[†]

a/General Works

BRIÈRE, O. *Fifty years of Chinese philosophy, 1898-1948.* Translated from the French by Lawrence G. Thompson. Edited, with an introduction, by Dennis J. Doolin. New York, Praeger, 1965 P
    A good scholarly review.

CHAI, Ch'u. *The story of Chinese philosophy.* By Ch'u Chai and Winberg Chai. New York, Washington Square, 1961 P
    Eight ancient Chinese philosophical systems: a readable introduction to the subject.

CHAN, Wing-tsit. *Religious trends in modern China.* New York, Columbia University Press, 1953
    An interesting work.

CHAN, Wing-tsit. *A source book in Chinese philosophy.* Tr. & comp. Wing-tsit Chan. Princeton, Princeton University Press, 1963
    A comprehensive selection of original texts by philosophers from Confucian times to the 20th century, presented with good introductions, suitable for western readers.

*CREEL, H. G. *Chinese thought: from Confucius to Mao Tsê-tung.* Chicago, University of Chicago Press, 1953 (and repr.); New York, New American Library; London, Eyre & Spottiswoode, 1960 P (and repr.) (Mentor Books)
    An excellent and stimulating brief non-technical survey.

CREEL, H. G. *La pensée chinoise, de Confucius à Mao Tseu-Tong.* Tr. Jean-François Leclerc. Paris, Payot, 1955 P (Collection Bibliothèque Historique)
    See preceding note.

[†]Including translations of some texts.

DAY, Clarence Burton. *The philosophers of China, classical and contemporary.* New York, Philosophical Library, 1962; New York, Citadel, 1962 P; London, Owen, 1962
 A good survey, consisting mainly of translated selections. Especially good coverage of modern philosophy.

*DE BARY, William Theodore (ed.) *Sources of Chinese tradition.* New York, Columbia University Press; London, Oxford University Press, 1960; 2 vols. 1964 P (Introduction to Oriental Civilizations series)
 An excellent broad selection of readings in Chinese thought from antiquity to Mao Tse-tung, with illuminating commentaries.

ELIOT, Charles Norton E. *Japanese Buddhism.* 2nd ed. London, Routledge; New York, Barnes & Noble, 1959
 Originally published in 1935, and still a standard work on the history of Japanese Buddhism and the doctrines of its sects, i.e. obsolete but not yet superseded.

FÊNG, Yu-lan. *A history of Chinese philosophy.* By Fung Yu-lan. Tr. Derk Bodde. 2 vols. Princeton, Princeton University Press, 1952-53 (and repr.)
 The standard comprehensive general work.

*FÊNG, Yu-lan. *A short history of Chinese philosophy.* By Fung Yu-lan. Ed. Derk Bodde. New York, Macmillan, 1948 (and repr.); New York, Free Press; London, Toronto, Collier-Macmillan, 1966 P
 An admirable summary of his standard *History of Chinese philosophy.*

*FÊNG, Yu-lan. *Précis d'histoire de la philosophie chinoise.* Par Fong Yeou-Lan. Paris, Payot, 1952 P
 See preceding note.

FENG, Yu-lan. *The spirit of Chinese philosophy.* By Fung Yu-lan. Tr. E. R. Hughes. London, Kegan Paul, 1947; Boston, Beacon, 1962 P
 Themes of Chinese thought to the 13th century, presented by a major contemporary philosopher.

HUGHES, Ernest Richard (ed. & tr.) *Chinese philosophy in classical times.* London, Dent; New York, Dutton, 1942 (and repr.) (Everyman's Library series)
 Good selections from many of the ancient schools, with good introduction by the editor.

HUGHES, Ernest Richard. *Religion in China.* By Ernest Richard Hughes and K. Hughes. London, New York, Hutchinson, 1950
 An introductory outline to Confucianism, Taoism, Buddhism, Islam, and Christianity and finally to religion in 20th century pre-communist China.

MASPÉRO, Henri. *Les religions chinoises.* Paris, Presses Universitaires de France, 1967 P (repr. of 1950 ed.) (Henri Maspéro: Mélanges posthumes sur les religions et l'histoire de la Chine, 1) (Publications du Musée Guimet, Bibliothèque de Diffusion)
  A brief but authoritative survey.

SMITH, David Howard. *Chinese religion.* London, Weidenfeld, 1968
  A helpful non-technical general survey, covering not only the usual ones (Confucianism, Taoism, and Buddhism) but also the ancient, primitive, and folk religions, "western" religions (Christianity, Judaism, and Islam), and religion in communist China.

TA-HSÜEH. *The Great Learning and The Mean-in-action.* Tr. Ernest Richard Hughes. London, Dent, 1942; New York, Dutton, 1943
  A standard translation of two of the Chinese classics.

THOMPSON, Lawrence. *Chinese religion.* Belmont, California, Dickenson, 1969 P
  "An excellent introductory overview of the Chinese religious complex."

WALEY, Arthur. *Three ways of thought in ancient China.* London, Allen & Unwin, 1939, repr. 1964; New York, Macmillan, 1939, repr. Barnes 1953; Garden City, Doubleday, 1956 P (Anchor series)
  A lucid study of Taoism, Confucianism, and "Realism/Legalism," by a comparison of translated extracts from the works of the leaders of these traditions.

WALEY, Arthur. *Trois courants de la pensée chinoise antique.* Les trois plus anciens ouvrages de la philosophie de la Chine: Tchouang Tseu, Mencius et Han Fei Tseu. Tr. George Deniker. Paris, Payot, 1949 P (Collection Bibliothèque Scientifique)
  See preceding note.

WEBER, Max. *The religion of China: Confucianism and Taoism.* Tr. Hans H. Gerth. With an introduction by C. K. Yang. New York, Free Press (Macmillan); London, Toronto, Collier-Macmillan, 1951; 1964 P
  An important 50-year-old sociological study. Largely outdated but still very interesting.

WRIGHT, Arthur F. (ed.) *Studies in Chinese thought.* Chicago, University of Chicago Press, 1953 (and repr.); 1967 P (Comparative Studies in Culture and Civilizations series)
  Nine articles by leading scholars. Some are sufficiently general to be of great interest to the non-specialist.

YANG, Ch'ing-K'un. *Religion in Chinese society: a study of contemporary social functions of religion and some of their historical factors.* Berkeley, University of California Press, 1961; 1967 P

A well-known Chinese sociologist's examination of Chinese religions from a rather unfamiliar angle; not a description of their beliefs and practices but how religious concepts and beliefs have affected the form of Chinese society socially, economically, and politically both in traditional and modern China. Good.

ZENKER, Ernst Victor. *Histoire de la philosophie chinoise.* Tr. G. Lepage. Paris, Payot, 1932 (and repr.) (Collection Bibliothèque Historique)

Still a useful outline.

b/Buddhism[†]

CH'EN, Kenneth K. S. *Buddhism in China: a historical survey.* Princeton, Princeton University Press, 1964

A sound, rather detailed work.

KAPLEAU, Philip. *The three pillars of Zen.* Boston, Beacon, 1967 P

Contains translations of the writings of modern Japanese Zen masters, and interviews with them.

*RENONDEAU, G. *Le bouddhisme japonais: textes fondamentaux,* par Honen, Shinran, Nichiren et Dôgen. Preface et traduction G. Renondeau. Paris, Albin Michel, 1965 (Collection Spiritualités Vivantes — Série Bouddhisme) (Collection Unesco d'Oeuvres Représentatives — Série Japonaise)

Translations of mediaeval Japanese Buddhist texts.

ROBINSON, Richard M. (tr.) *Chinese Buddhist verse.* London, Murray; New York, Grove, 1955 (Wisdom of the East series)

Hymns of various kinds, preceded by a survey of the history and style of Buddhist religious poetry in China, showing its canons of taste and art.

*ROSS, Nancy Wilson (ed.) *The world of Zen: an East-West anthology.* New York, Random House, 1960 P

A successful Zenophile anthology. revealing Zen's broad range, with a valuable introduction which puts the selections in their setting.

The Shinshu Seiten. The Holy Scripture of Shinshu, compiled and published by the Honpa Hongwanji Mission of Hawaii. Honolulu, 1955

The chief sacred writings of the Pure Land sect (Shinshu).

SUZUKI, Daisetz Teitaro. *Manual of Zen Buddhism.* Rev. ed., repr. New York, Grove, 1960 P

[†]I.e. Chinese and Japanese Buddhism. For general works on Buddhism see part III, subsection C4c.

D. T. Suzuki is Zen's major interpreter to the West (in particular of its Rinzai tradition). This book includes extracts from important Zen texts.

SUZUKI, Daisetz Teitaro. *Zen and Japanese Buddhism.* 2nd ed. Tokyo, Japan Travel Bureau; Rutland, Vt., Tuttle, 1961
    A very handy little book, divided into two parts: (1) Zen Buddhism, (2) Japanese Buddhism.

SUZUKI, Daisetz Teitaro. *Zen Buddhism: selected writings of D. T. Suzuki.* Ed. William Barrett. Garden City, N.Y., Doubleday, 1956 P
    A good selection with an excellent introduction by the editor.

WATANABE, Shoko. *Japanese Buddhism: a critical appraisal.* 2nd ed. Tokyo, Kokusai Bunko Shinkokai; New York, Japan Publications, 1964 P (Japanese Life and Culture series)
    Fourteen centuries of Japanese Buddhism, critically discussed by a Japanese Buddhist scholar.

*WATTS, Alan Wilson. *The way of Zen.* New York, Pantheon, 1957; New York, Toronto, New American Library, 1959 P (and repr.) (Mentor Books)
    A rather personal survey of the history, principles, and practice of this form of Buddhism by an enthusiastic westerner.

WATTS, Alan Wilson. *Le bouddhisme Zen.* Tr. P. Berlot. Paris, Payot, 1960 P (Collection Bibliothèque Scientifique)
    See preceding note.

WELCH, Holmes. *The Buddhist revival in China,* with a section of photographs by Henri Cartier-Bresson. Cambridge, Mass., Harvard University Press, 1968 (Harvard East Asian Studies series)
    An examination of the upheavals which Chinese Buddhism has undergone in suddenly being thrust into the modern era. Notable photographs.

WELCH, Holmes. *The practice of Chinese Buddhism, 1900-1950.* Cambridge, Mass., Harvard University Press, 1967 (Harvard East Asian Studies series)
    A detailed description of what it is like to live in Buddhist monasteries, based on interviews with "average" inmates. Excludes doctrinal matters.

WRIGHT, Arthur F. *Buddhism in Chinese history.* Stanford, Stanford University Press; London, Oxford University Press, 1959; New York, Atheneum, 1965 P
    An interesting outline of the rise and fall of Buddhism in China, and an assessment of its impact.

c/Confucianism

CHAI, Ch'u (ed. & tr.) *The sacred books of Confucius and other Confucian classics.* Ed. & tr. Ch'u Chai and Winberg Chai. New York, University Books,

1965. Also issued under title: *The humanist way in ancient China: essential works of Confucianism*. New York, Toronto, London, Bantam, 1965 P
A useful compilation from eight basic Confucian classics. The translations are not all adequate.

CHANG, Chia-sên. *The development of Neo-Confucian thought*, by Carsun Chang. 2 vols. New York, Bookman, 1957-62
A detailed study, covering the post-Confucian period up to the present and containing numerous translated excerpts. The work makes frequent illuminating comparisons with western thought.

CHOW, Yih-ching. *La philosophie morale dans le Néo-Confucianisme*. Paris, Presses Universitaires de France, 1954
Mainly a study of a notable 11th century philosopher, with selected translations.

CHU, Hsi. *Reflections on things at hand: the Neo-Confucian anthology*. Compiled by Chu Hsi and Lü Tsu-ch'ien. Translated with notes by Wing-tsit Chan. New York, London, Columbia University Press, 1967 (Translations from Oriental Classics series) (Unesco Collection of Representative Works — Chinese Series)
The basic work of Neo-Confucianism, compiled in the 12th century; outlines its main doctrines. "It is undoubtedly the most important single work of philosophy produced in the Far East in the second millennium A.D." (Foreword by W. T. de Bary).

*CONFUCIUS. *The Analects of Confucius*. Translated and annotated by Arthur Waley. London, Allen & Unwin; New York, Random House, 1938, repr. 1964; New York, Vintage [Random House], 1968 P (Vintage Books)
An attractive and scholarly translation of a work which has moulded the Chinese people for over 2000 years. Excellent introduction.

CONFUCIUS. *The Analects, or the Conversations of Confucius with his disciples and certain others*. Tr. William Edward Soothill. Ed. Lady Hosie. 2nd ed. London, Oxford University Press, 1937 (and repr.) (World's Classics series)
Another well-known translation which first appeared in 1910.

CONFUCIUS. *The Sayings of Confucius*. Tr. Lionel Giles. London, Murray, 1907 (and repr.); New York, Grove, 1961 P (Wisdom of the East series)
The Analects, abridged and rearranged by topics, with short notes.

CONFUCIUS. *Maximes et pensées*. Tr. C. Pauthier. Paris, A. Silvaire, 1963
A version of the Analects.

CONFUCIUS. *Loen yu: Entretien de Confucius et de ses disciples*. Texte chinois avec traduction française et latine de Séraphin Couvreur. 2ᵉ éd. Paris, Les Belles Lettres, 1949
Scholarly translation of the Analects of Confucius.

CREEL, Herrlee Glessner. *Confucius and the Chinese Way.* New York, Harper & Row, 1960 P (Harper Torchbooks). Original edition entitled *Confucius: the man and the myth* (1949)
   A readable critical study of the great sage.

GRIPEKOVEN, Jeanne. *Confucius et son temps.* Bruxelles, Office de Publicité; Neuchâtel, La Baconnière, 1955

HSÜN-TZU. *Hsün Tzu: basic writings.* Tr. Burton Watson. New York, London, Columbia University Press, 1963 P (Unesco Collection of Representative Works — Chinese Series)
   A well-translated selection from a leading Confucian philosopher of the 3rd century B.C., who took a rather negative view of man's basic nature.

KAIZUKA, Shigeki. *Confucius.* Tr. G. Bownas. London, Allen & Unwin; New York, Macmillan, 1956
   A traditionalist biography and interpretation.

LIN, Yutang. *The wisdom of Confucius.* London, Michael Joseph; New York, Modern Library, 1938 (and repr.)
   The major features of Confucian thought described; followed by a translation of Confucius's *Analects,* and passages from other Confucian works. Good initiation for the layman.

LIN, Yutang. *La sagesse de Confucius,* tr. Th. Bridel-Wasem. Paris, Attinger, 1949
   See preceding note.

LIU, Wu-chi. *A short history of Confucian philosophy.* Harmondsworth, Baltı more, Penguin, 1955 P; New York, Dell, 1964 P
   A good, rather enthusiastic introduction.

LIU, Wu-chi. *La philosophie de Confucius: le courant le plus marquant de la pensée chinoise.* Tr. Raoul Baude. Paris, Payot, 1963 P (Collection Petit Bibliothèque Payot)
   See preceding note.

MENCIUS. *The Book of Mencius.* Tr. Lionel Giles. London, Murray; New York, Grove, 1942 (and repr.) (Wisdom of the East series)
   Knowledge of the sayings of the 4th century thinker, Mencius, has for over 2000 years been part of the intellectual equipment of all Chinese who pretended to even the minimum of education. This is a good abridged translation.

MENCIUS. *Mencius: a new translation, arranged and annotated for the general reader.* By W. A. C. H. Dobson. Toronto, University of Toronto Press; London, Oxford University Press, 1963 P (Unesco Collection of Representative Works — Chinese Series)

> A free translation, partial paraphrase, and interpretation addressed to the non-specialist.

MENCIUS. *Oeuvres de Mengtzeu.* Texte chinois avec traductions française et latine de Séraphin Couvreur. 2e éd. Paris, Les Belles Lettres, 1949

> A scholarly version.

*SHIH-CHING. *The Book of Songs.* Translated from the Chinese by Arthur Waley. 2nd ed. London, Allen & Unwin, 1954; New York, Grove, 1960 P

> A first-class blank verse translation of the ancient anthology *Shih-ching,* one of the five Confucian classics.

WRIGHT, Arthur F. (ed.) *Confucianism and Chinese civilization.* New York, Atheneum, 1964 P

> Twelve studies by leading scholars which, as the editor notes, "illustrate the effects of the Confucian world view ... on the development of Chinese civilization ... [Confucianism is] the central tradition of the massive human achievement we call Chinese civilization."

d/Taoism

CHUANG-TZU. *Chuang Tzu: basic writings.* Tr. Burton Watson. New York, London, Columbia University Press, 1964 P (Unesco Collection of Representative Works — Chinese Series)

> The work of one of the main early figures of Taoism. Watson has also translated the *Complete Works.* New York, London, Columbia University Press, 1968 C&P (Unesco Collection of Representative Works — Chinese Series)

CHUANG-TZU. *Musings of a Chinese mystic: selections from the philosophy of Chuang Tzu.* Ed. Lionel Giles. London, Murray; New York, Paragon, 1906 (and repr.) (Wisdom of the East series)

> Selections from the 19th century translation of Herbert A. Giles, with an introduction to the thought of Chuang-tzu.

CHUANG-TZU. *L'oeuvre complète de Tchouang-tseu.* Traduction, préface et notes de Liou Kia-Hway. Paris, Gallimard, 1969 (Collection Unesco d'Oeuvres Représentatives — Série Chinoise)

> See preceding note.

KALTENMARK, Max. *Lao tseu et le taoïsme.* Paris, Seuil, 1965 (Les Maîtres Spirituels)

> A simple outline of his thought for the general reader.

KALTENMARK, Max. *Lao Tzu and Taoism*. Tr. Roger Greaves. Stanford, Stanford University Press, 1969
    See preceding note.

LAO-TZU
    The *Tao-te ching,* a semi-poetic and somewhat cryptic philosophical work, is the main classic of Taoism. Translations differ considerably. As it is such a basic work, several translations, both English and French, have been cited.

LAO-TZU. *Tao te ching*. Tr. D. S. Lau. Baltimore, Penguin, 1963 P
    A lucid and beautiful translation with a sound historical introduction.

LAO-TZU. *The Way of Lao Tzu (Tao-te ching)*. Translated with introductory essays, comments and notes by Wing-tsit Chan. New York, Bobbs-Merrill, 1963 P (Library of Liberal Arts series)
    The translator used classical commentaries as well as modern research.

*LAO-TZU. *Tao te ching: the Book of the Way and its virtue*. Tr. J. J. L. Duyvendak. London, Murray; New York, Paragon, 1954 (and repr.) (Wisdom of the East series)
    A good modern translation, with a somewhat rationalistic interpretation.

LAO-TZU. *The wisdom of Laotse*. Translated, edited with an introduction and notes by Lin Yutang. New York, Modern Library, 1948 (and repr.); London, Joseph, 1958
    A fine rationalistic translation of the *Tao te-ching,* with selections from Chuang-tzu interspersed.

LAO-TZU. *The Way and its power. A study of the Tao Tê Ching and its place in Chinese thought*. By Arthur Waley. London, Allen & Unwin, 1934 (and repr.); New York, Grove, 1958 P (Evergreen Books) (Unesco Collection of Representative Works – Chinese Series)
    An attractive rather mystical translation in free verse, with a valuable introduction describing the work's place in the context of early Chinese thought.

*LAO-TZU. *Tao tö king: le livre de la voie et de la vertu ...* Tr. J. J. L. Duyvendak. Paris, A.-Maisonneuve, 1953
    A good modern translation with a somewhat rationalistic interpretation.

LAO-TZU. *Tao tö king [Par] Lao Tseu*. Traduit du chinois par Liou Kia-Hway. Paris, Gallimard, 1967 P (Collection Connaissance de l'Orient)

LAO-TZU. *La voie et sa vertu [de] Lao Tseu*. Texte chinois présenté et traduit par Houang Kia-tcheng et Pierre Leyris. Paris, Seuil, 1949
    An informative introduction.

LIEH-TZU. *The Book of Lieh-tzŭ.* Tr. A. C. Graham. London, Murray; New York, Paragon, 1960 (Unesco Collection of Representative Works – Chinese Series) (Wisdom of the East series)
A famous collection of ancient Taoist tales and sayings which makes quite entertaining reading.

LIEH-TZU. *Le vrai classique du vide parfait,* par Lie-tseu. Tr. Benedykt Grynpas. Paris, Gallimard, 1961 (Collection Unesco d'Oeuvres Représentatives – Série Chinoise)
A famous collection of ancient Taoist tales and sayings.

MASPÉRO, Henri. *Le Taoïsme.* Paris, Presses Universitaires de France, 1967 P (repr. of 1950 ed.) (Henri Maspéro: Mélanges posthumes sur les religions et l'histoire de la Chine) (Publications du Musée Guimet, Bibliothèque de Diffusion)
A short but authoritative work.

*VANDIER-NICOLAS, Nicole. *Le Taoisme.* Paris, Presses Universitaires de France, 1965 P (Collection Mythes et Religions)
An excellent brief but comprehensive historical outline.

WELCH, Holmes. *Taoism: the parting of the Way.* Rev. [2nd] ed. Boston, Beacon; Toronto, Saunders, 1966 P (Beacon Paperbacks)
The basic historical account of Taoism, showing its parallel development as a scholarly system and as a folk religion.

WIEGER, Léon (ed. & tr.) *Les pères du système taoiste.* Textes chinois avec traduction française. 2ᵉ éd. Paris, Les Belles Lettres, 1950
Works of Lao-tzu, Lieh-tzu, and Chuang-tzu.

e/Other

HAN FEI TZU. *Han Fei Tzu: basic writings.* Tr. Burton Watson. New York, Columbia University Press, 1964 P (Unesco Collection of Representative Works – Chinese Series)
A main work of 3rd century B.C. "Legalism," a somewhat Machiavellian doctrine of achieving a strong authoritarian state at any price.

MO-TZU. *Mo Tzu: basic writings.* Tr. Burton Watson. New York, London, Columbia University Press, 1963 P (Unesco Collection of Representative Works – Chinese Series)
Readable selections from an important political and social thinker of the 5th century B.C. who favoured both universal love and utilitarianism.

7 ARTS AND CRAFTS, ARCHITECTURE, AND SCIENCE

AUBOYER, Jeannine. *Les arts de l'Asie orientale et de l'Extrême-Orient.* [2ᵉ éd.] Paris, Presses Universitaires de France, 1964 P (Collection "Que sais-je?")
For its very small size, this is an effective summary.

BINYON, Laurence. *Painting in the Far East: an introduction to the history of pictorial art in Asia, especially China and Japan.* 3rd ed. New York, Dover, 1959 P (repr. of 1923 ed.)
Still a good general introductory book; not only studies the works but also interprets their aims.

BOYD, Andrew. *Chinese architecture and town planning, 1500 B.C. – A.D. 1911.* London, Tiranti; Chicago, University of Chicago Press, 1962
A very condensed look at the mainstream of traditional architecture.

*CAHILL, James. *Chinese painting.* Geneva, Skira, 1960. American ed. entitled: *Chinese paintings, xi-xiv centuries.* New York, Crown; Cleveland, World, 1960 (Treasures of Asia series)
Beautiful illustrations together with an excellent informative text by a leading specialist.

*CAHILL, James. *La peinture chinoise.* Tr. Yves Rivière. Genève, Skira, 1960 (Collection Les Trésors de l'Asie)
See preceding note.

CHANG, Isabelle C. *Chinese cooking made easy.* New York, Paperback Library Inc., 1961 P
Chinese cookery is an aspect of traditional Chinese culture. This book contains recipes for 367 Chinese dishes which can be made of ingredients available in North America.

CHIANG, Yee. *Chinese calligraphy: an introduction to its aesthetic and technique.* 2nd ed. Cambridge, Mass., Harvard University Press, 1954
A standard introduction to all aspects of the subject, and its place in the artistic tradition of China.

CHIANG, Yee. *The Chinese eye: an interpretation of Chinese painting.* London, Faber, 1953; Bloomington, Indiana University Press, 1964 P
A well-known popular work on the style of Chinese painting and its relationship to Chinese philosophy and culture.

DRISCOLL, Lucy. *Chinese calligraphy.* By Lucy Driscoll and Toda Kenji. Chicago, University of Chicago Press, 1932; repr. New York, Paragon, 1964

A good introduction to the theory and aesthetics of Chinese writing, for those unfamiliar with the Chinese tradition.

FEDDERSEN, Martin. *Chinese decorative arts: a handbook for collectors and connoisseurs.* Tr. Arthur Lane. 2nd ed. London, Faber, 1961
A very useful general work.

GROUSSET, René. *La Chine et son art.* Paris, Plon, 1951
An introductory work, valuable mainly in showing Chinese art in its cultural setting.

GROUSSET, René. *Chinese art and culture.* Tr. Haakon Chevalier. London, Deutsch; New York, Orion, 1959; New York, Grove, 1961 P
See preceding note.

HUARD, Pierre Alphonse. *La médecine chinoise au cours des siècles.* Par Pierre Huard et Ming Wong. Paris, Dacosta, 1959
The principles of traditional Chinese medicine, its influence, and the impact of western medicine on modern China described non-technically.

HUARD, Pierre Alphonse. *Chinese medicine.* By Pierre Huard and Ming Wong. Tr. Bernard Fielding. London, Weidenfeld; New York, Toronto, McGraw-Hill, 1968 P (World University Library series)
See preceding note.

*JENYNS, Soame. *A background to Chinese painting.* New York, Schocken, 1966 P (repr. of 1935 ed.)
A good introduction to the religious and social setting of Chinese painting. Chapters on the influence of religion, relationship to calligraphy, patronage, materials and technique, treatment of landscape, and the human figure.

JENYNS, Soame. *Ming pottery and porcelain.* London, Faber, 1953
A reliable volume, describing the work of the Ming period (1368-1644).

JENYNS, Soame. *Later Chinese porcelain: the Ch'ing dynasty, 1644-1912.* 2nd ed. London, Faber, 1959
An authoritative history, with numerous plates; a sequel to the preceding volume.

LEE, Sherman E. *Chinese landscape painting.* 2nd ed. Cleveland, Cleveland Museum of Art, 1962
An attractive short introduction.

LIN, Yutang (ed. & tr.) *The Chinese theory of art: translations from the masters of Chinese art.* London, Heinemann, 1967

Interesting translations ranging from the 6th century B.C.E. to the 18th century.

LUZZATO-BILITZ, Oscar. *Oriental lacqueur.* London, Toronto, New York, Hamlyn, 1969
Fine reproductions of Chinese and Japanese work, with short accompanying text. Good value at a low price.

NEEDHAM, Joseph. *The grand titration: science and society in East and West.* London, Allen & Unwin; Toronto, University of Toronto Press, 1969
A series of excellent essays and lectures on the history of Chinese science, and its influence on the rest of the world. Easier for laymen than his definitive work below.

NEEDHAM, Joseph. *Science and civilisation in China.* By Joseph Needham, with the research assistance of Wang Ling. Cambridge, New York, Cambridge University Press, 1954- [in progress]
A remarkable and invaluable detailed pioneer study. Seven volumes are planned, but only vols. 1-4 have appeared so far. Vol. 1: *Introductory orientations.* Vol. 2: *History of scientific thought.* Vol. 3: *Mathematics and the sciences of heaven and earth.* Vol. 4: *Physics and physical technology* (2 vols.).

*PAUL-DAVID, Madeleine. *Arts et styles de la Chine.* Paris, Larousse, 1953 P (Collection Arts, Styles et Techniques)
A rapid survey by periods, from prehistory to the end of the Chinese Empire. The various arts of each period are described in individual sections.

*SICKMAN, Laurence. *The art and architecture of China.* By Laurence Sickman and Alexander Soper. 2nd ed. Harmondsworth, Baltimore, Penguin, 1960 (Pelican History of Art series)
An excellent history of traditional art and architecture with numerous good plates and a useful bibliography.

SIRÉN, Osvald. *The Chinese on the art of painting.* New York, Schocken, 1963 P (repr. of 1936 Peiping ed.)
Classical Chinese texts on Chinese aesthetics, forming a historical survey of painting in the context of Chinese culture.

SPEISER, Werner. *China: spirit and society.* Tr. George Lawrence. London, Toronto, Methuen, 1960; New York, Crown, 1961 (Art of the World series)
Chinese art well described in its cultural setting. All plates are in colour.

SPEISER, Werner. *Chine: esprit et société.* Traduit de l'allemand par Denise van Moppès. Paris, Albin Michel, 1960
See preceding note.

*SULLIVAN, Michael. *A short history of Chinese art.* London, Faber; Berkeley, University of California Press, 1967 C&P
A broad-ranging, up-to-date general survey, dealing not only with painting, sculpture, and architecture but also with the minor arts, and emphasizing the relationship of art forms with their time. One of the best popular introductions.

SULLIVAN, Michael. *Chinese art in the twentieth century.* London, Faber; Berkeley, University of California Press, 1959
A useful work on a neglected area of Chinese art.

*SWANN, Peter C. *The art of China, Korea and Japan.* London, Thames & Hudson; New York, Praeger, 1963 P (and repr.) (World of Art series)
A richly illustrated yet inexpensive historical survey.

*SWANN, Peter C. *L'art de la Chine, de la Corée et du Japon.* Paris, Larousse, 1963 (Collection Le Monde de l'Art)
See preceding note.

WALEY, Arthur. *An introduction to the study of Chinese painting.* New York, Grove, 1958 (repr. of 1923 ed.)
A detailed older but still authoritative standard work.

WATSON, William. *Early civilization in China.* New York, McGraw-Hill, 1966 P
The material culture of China to the 3rd century B.C., described and lavishly illustrated.

*WILLETTS, William. *Chinese art.* New York, Braziller; 2 vols. Harmondsworth, Baltimore, Penguin, 1958 P
A good historical treatment emphasizing the technical means and the social conditions in which they developed rather than the artistic quality of the work. Although all main aspects of Chinese art are supposed to be covered, certain (e.g. painting and calligraphy) are only sketchily discussed.

8 MODERN CHINA

BARNETT, A. Doak. *Communist China in perspective.* New York, Praeger, 1962 P
Three essays, analysing the historical background to Chinese communism, the nature of its revolution in China, and forecasting the future.

BIANCO, Lucien. *Les origines de la révolution chinoise, 1915-1949.* Paris, Gallimard, 1967 P (Collection Idées)
A good conspectus of the background to communist China.

BODDE, Derk. *Peking diary: 1948-1949 – a year of revolution.* New York, Schuman, 1950; London, Cape, 1951; Greenwich, Conn., Fawcett, 1967
> A notable contemporary first-hand account of the communist conquest by a well-known Sinologist.

BRULÉ, Jean-Pierre. *La Chine a vingt ans.* Paris, Fayard, 1969 P (Collection Le Monde sans Frontières)
> A good general overview of the development of the People's Republic in the past generation. The main sections examine the demographic, economic, commercial, military, and nuclear challenges which it poses to the world.

*BUCK, Pearl S. *My several worlds.* New York, John Day, 1954; New York, Pocket Books, [no date] P
> Autobiography of a remarkable American woman who grew up in China; portrays the clash of the old and the new in that country.

*CHAI, Ch'u. *The changing society of China.* By Ch'u Chai and Winberg Chai. New York, New American Library, 1962 P (Mentor Books)
> A handy volume of general information for the layman on many aspects of the historical and social background of China and its changing present.

CH'ÊN, Jerome (ed.) *Mao.* Englewood Cliffs, N.J., London, Prentice-Hall, 1969 C&P (Great Lives Observed series. Spectrum series)
> One of the best little books on its subject. Good introduction by editor followed by (1) a selection of Mao's writings arranged by subject, (2) opinions on Mao expressed by 12 of his contemporaries, Chinese and foreign, and (3) four scholarly evaluations of Mao's role in history. The book concludes with a useful critique of books on Mao and Chinese communism.

CH'ÊN, Jerome. *Mao and the Chinese revolution.* London, Toronto, New York, Oxford University Press, 1965; 1968 P
> An important book for the understanding of modern China, this work achieves its aim of being a dispassionate analysis of Mao's life and times. See also the biography by Stuart Schram (below).

CHESNEAUX, Jean. *Sun Yat-sen.* Paris, Club Français du Livre, 1959 (Collection Portraits de l'Histoire)
> A short biography of the leader of the Chinese revolution which overthrew the ancient Chinese Empire in 1911 and who became the first president of China in 1912, and an evaluation of his place in Chinese history.

*CLUBB, Oliver Edward. *Twentieth century China.* New York, Columbia University Press, 1964; 1965 P
> A balanced survey of Chinese history since 1911, excellent for the layman.

*CROIZIER, Ralph C. (ed.) *China's cultural legacy and communism.* New York, London, Praeger, 1970 (Praeger Library of Chinese Affairs)
> An anthology of writings by westerners and Chinese about the attitude of Chinese communism to China's past. A well-selected, well-organized, and interesting key to understanding modern China.

DEVILLERS, Philippe. *Ce que Mao a vraiment dit.* Paris, Stock, 1968
> Important selections from Mao's speeches, with commentary.

DUBARBIER, Georges. *La Chine du XXe siècle: des Mandchous à Mao.* Paris, Payot, 1965 (Collection Etudes et Documents)
> A survey of the transformation which China has undergone since the end of the Manchu empire.

DUBARBIER, Georges. *Histoire de la Chine moderne.* 3e éd. Paris, Presses Universitaires de France, 1966 P (Collection "Que sais-je?")
> A short general review.

FEUERWERKER, Albert (ed.) *History in communist China.* Cambridge, Mass., London, M.I.T. Press, 1968
> Seventeen papers discussing communist China's attitude to its own history and history-writing. Partly overlaps with Croizier's work (above).

FITZGERALD, Charles Patrick. *The birth of communist China.* Harmondsworth, Baltimore, Penguin, 1965 P; New York, Praeger, 1966
> An informed study and interpretation of China since the establishment of the Republic.

FITZGERALD, Charles Patrick. *The Chinese view of their place in the world.* London, Toronto, New York, Oxford University Press, 1964 P (Chatham House Essays, Royal Institute of International Affairs)
> Thoughtful essays, mostly devoted to the 19th and 20th centuries.

GOMPERTZ, Geoffrey Haviland. *China in turmoil.* London, Dent, 1967
> Interesting account of the "life of the expatriate [i.e. European] communities in Hong Kong and on the coast and rivers of China during the first half of the [20th] century, with special emphasis upon the second quarter." Largely autobiographical.

GREEN, Felix. *China: the country Americans are not allowed to visit.* New York, Ballantine Books, 1962 P
> In spite of the silly subtitle on this paperback edition, this is a well-written, sober, first-hand account of China in the early 1960s by a veteran news commentator. Original edition entitled *Awakened China* (US) and *The Wall has two sides* (British).

GUILLERMAZ, Jacques. *La Chine populaire*. 2ᵉ éd. Paris, Presses Universitaires de France, 1961 P (Collection "Que sais-je?")
>An excellent short survey of the history of Chinese communism and its rule in China.

HAN, Suyin. *The crippled tree: China, biography, history, autobiography*. London, Cape; New York, Putnam, 1965 (and repr.); London, Mayflower, 1968 P
>A biographical evocation of life in changing China, and the impact of the West on the author's family. Highly readable.

HAN, Suyin. *L'arbre blessé*. Paris, Stock, 1966 P
>See preceding note.

HAN, Suyin. *A mortal flower; China: autobiography, history*. New York, Bookman, 1966
>A sequel to the preceding work, covering the years 1928-38.

HAN, Suyin. *Une fleur mortelle*. Paris, Stock, 1967 P
>See preceding note.

HINTON, Harold C. *Communist China in world politics*. Boston, Houghton, 1966
>An informed and detailed survey by a political expert.

HSÜ, Immanuel C. Y. *The rise of modern China*. New York, London, Toronto, Oxford University Press, 1970
>A detailed but fascinating account of China's modernization from the 7th century to the present.

*HU, Ch'ang-tu (ed.) *China: its people, its society, its culture*. New Haven, Human Relations Area Files; London, Mayflower, 1960 (Survey of World Cultures series)
>A comprehensive work on all aspects, with stress on Maoist China and its social and economic life. Good bibliography, partly annotated.

KESSLE, Gun. *Chinese journey*. [By] Gun Kessle and Jan Myrdal. Boston, Beacon, 1967 P
>172 photographs of people at work and play and their physical surroundings in various parts of China, taken during the assembling of material for Myrdal's book *Report from a Chinese village* (below).

KITAGAWA, Joseph M. (ed.) *Understanding modern China*. Chicago, Quadrangle; Toronto, Burns & MacEachern, 1969
>Communist China's actions and motives are frequently puzzling to westerners with different preconceptions and logical inferences. In the 12 essays in this volume experts try to explain.

LATOURETTE, Kenneth Scott. *A history of modern China.* Harmondsworth, Baltimore, Penguin, 1954 (and repr.)
   A brief factual survey of China from the middle of the 19th to the middle of the 20th century.

*LATTIMORE, Owen. *Nomads and commissars: Mongolia revisited.* London, Toronto, New York, Oxford University Press, 1962
   A noted scholar's general description of Mongolia and the Mongols today in the light of their history.

*LATTIMORE, Owen. *Mongolie: nomades et commissaires.* Paris, Seuil, 1966
   See preceding note.

LÉVY, Roger. *Mao Tsö-tong.* Présentation, choix de textes, illustrations. Paris, Seghers, 1965
   A fairly good composite picture including the opinions of Mao's contemporaries and his own words on various subjects.

LEWIS, John Wilson. *Major doctrines of communist China.* New York, Norton, 1964 P
   A collection of texts illustrating many facets of communist Chinese ideology.

LINEBARGER, Paul Myron Anthony. *Far Eastern governments and politics: China and Japan.* [By] Paul M. A. Linebarger, Djang Chu [and] Ardath W. Burks. 2nd ed. Princeton, Toronto, London, Van Nostrand, 1956
   Three political scientists give an expertly detailed examination of the development of government in China and Japan from early times.

MALRAUX, André. *Les Conquérants.* Paris, Club des Libraires de France, 1959; Hachette, 1962
   Malraux's first novel, originally published in 1929, is set in the China of the Kuomintang revolutionaries. The author has written a new postscript on their successors.

MALRAUX, André. *The conquerors.* Tr. Winifred Stephens Whale. Boston, Beacon, 1956 P
   See preceding note.

MAO, Tsê-tung. *Mao Tse-tung: an anthology of his writings.* Edited with an introduction by Anne Fremantle. New York, Toronto, New American Library; London, New English Library, 1962 P (Mentor Books)
   A selection of Mao's writings from 1926 to 1957, showing the development of his thought.

MAO, Tsê-tung. *Mao Tse-toung.* Textes traduits et présentés par Stuart Schram. Paris, Colin, 1963 P (Collection U, Série "Idées Politiques")
A selection, grouped by subject, from the speeches and writings of the moulder of communist China.

MAO, Tsê-tung. *Mao Tse-tung on art and literature.* Peking, Foreign Languages Press, 1960
A selection of Mao's views, which are official guidelines for a whole generation of artists and writers.

MAO, Tsê-tung. *Quotations from Chairman Mao Tse-tung.* Edited with an introductory essay by Stuart R. Schram, foreword by A. Doak Barnett. New York, Bantam, 1967 P; New York, Praeger, 1968
The "Little Red Book" which functions as the sacred scripture of communist China. Good short introduction and a few notes by the editor.

MENDE, Tibor. *China and her shadow.* London, Thames & Hudson, 1961
A well-observed description by a French political scientist after a 15,000 mile tour of communist China.

MENDE, Tibor. *La Chine et son ombre.* Tr. Magdeleine Paz. Paris, Seuil, 1960
See preceding note.

MIGOT, André. *Mao Tsé-toung.* Paris, Planète, 1966 P
A biography which is also a short history of modern China. Well illustrated.

MITCHISON, Lois. *China.* London, Thames & Hudson; New York, Walker, 1966 C&P (New Nations and Peoples series)
A short but fairly balanced popular book on modern China, copiously illustrated.

MOSELEY, George. *China: empire to People's Republic.* London, Batsford, 1968
Useful history 1911-67, for general readers.

MYRDAHL, Jan. *Report from a Chinese village.* New York, Toronto, New American Library; London, New English Library, 1966 P (Mentor Books)
Villagers' stories about their life, told to the author, who then analysed the institutions of the village in 1962. Good photographs. (See also the illustrations in Kessle's *Chinese journey* (above).)

*NORTH, Robert Carver. *Chinese communism.* New York, Toronto, McGraw-Hill; London, Weidenfeld, 1966 P (World University Library series)
A helpful brief historical survey of China in the 20th century. Wider in scope than the title suggests.

NORTH, Robert Carver. *Le communisme chinois.* Texte français de Andrée
Tranchant. Paris, Hachette, 1966 P (Collection L'Univers des Connaissances)
   See preceding note.

NOSSAL, Frederick. *Dateline Peking.* Toronto, Longmans, 1962
   A perceptive Canadian's impressions of modern China while correspondent
   of the Toronto newspaper *Globe and Mail.*

NOSSAL, Frederick. *Méridien de Pékin.* Tr. Jean R. Weiland. Paris, France-
Empire, 1964
   See preceding note.

*PURCELL, Victor. *China.* London, Benn; Mystic, Conn., Verry, 1962 (Nations
of the Modern World series)
   A thoroughly competent account of modern China, with particular emphasis on the traditions which explain its present.

QUIGLEY, Harold S. *China's politics in perspective.* Minneapolis, University
of Minnesota Press; Toronto, T. Allen; London, Oxford University Press, 1962
   From Sun Yat-sen to 1961. Suitable for laymen and college students.

SCHRAM, Stuart R. *Mao Tse-tung.* [2nd ed.] Harmondsworth, Baltimore, Penguin, 1967 P; New York, Simon & Schuster, 1967
   Valuable both as a political biography and as an introduction to the history
   of China in the 20th century. This book and that of Jerome Ch'en (above)
   are the best biographies at present.

SCHWARTZ, Harry. *Communist China.* Chicago, Encyclopaedia Britannica
Press, 1965 P
   A simple short introduction to its role and future.

C JAPAN

1 REFERENCE WORKS

*BORTON, Hugh (ed.) *Japan.* Ithaca, Cornell University Press, 1951
    This book, which consists of articles written by various experts for the *Encyclopedia Americana,* contains information on many aspects of Japan's past and present in a form convenient for the layman.

BORTON, Hugh (comp.) *A selected list of books and articles on Japan in English, French and German.* Compiled by Hugh Borton, Serge Elisséef [and others] [2nd ed.] Cambridge, Harvard University Press (for the Harvard-Yenching Institute), 1954
    A helpful classified listing of 1781 annotated entries, published to the year 1953.

*JAPAN. Mombushō. Nihon Yunesuko Kokunai Iinkai. *Japan: its land, people and culture.* Compiled by Japanese National Commission for Unesco. [2nd ed.] Tokyo, Ministry of Finance Printing Bureau, 1964
    An authoritative and encyclopaedic up-to-date official survey of every aspect of Japan. 900 large pages of facts and 200 pages of illustrations.

*SILBERMAN, Bernard S. *Japan and Korea: a critical bibliography.* Tucson, University of Arizona Press, 1962 P
    An extremely useful book, confined to works in western languages. The entries are arranged by subject, well selected, annotated, and graded, for ease of use by non-specialists. Each section is introduced by a helpful subject review. Contains 1928 entries.

*VARLEY, H. Paul. *A syllabus of Japanese civilization.* New York, London, Columbia University Press, 1968 P (Companions to Asian Studies series)
    Inexpensive guidance for teachers and students of introductory courses. Outlines of Japanese civilization with annotated listing of elementary readings on major topics.

2 GENERAL WORKS

*HALL, John Whitney. *Twelve doors to Japan.* By John Whitney Hall and Richard K. Beardsley. New York, Toronto, McGraw-Hill, 1965
    An excellent introduction to Japan's history, civilization, and present. Chapters cover geography, anthropology, history, language, literature, arts, politics, law, and economics. Select bibliographies to each chapter.

OGRIZEK, Doré. *Le Japon.* Textes de Madeleine Paul-David, Marcel Giuglaris, Jean-Pierre Hauchecorne, Paul Mousset, René Sieffert, Kikou Yamata. Paris, Odé, 1954
A readable illustrated introduction to Japanese culture and history.

*TSUNODA, Ryusaku (comp.) *Sources of the Japanese tradition.* Comp. Ryusaku Tsunoda, Wm. Theodore de Bary, Donald Keene. New York, Columbia University Press; London, Toronto, New York, Oxford University Press, 1958; 2 vols., 1964 P (Records of Civilization: Sources and Studies) (Introduction to Oriental Civilizations) (Unesco Collection of Representative Works — Japanese Series)
Fundamental extracts from Japanese writings of all periods, which constitute an extremely good perspective on the history of Japanese ideas. A first-class anthology.

*WEBB, Herschel. *An introduction to Japan.* 2nd ed. New York, Columbia University Press; London, Oxford University Press, 1957 (and repr.); 1960 P
A very concise yet readable survey of basic information, particularly suitable for use by schools and adult study groups. Chapters on geography, history, government, economy, social life, art, literature, religion. Good select reading lists after each chapter.

3 HISTORY AND SOCIAL SCIENCES

BEASLEY, William Gerald. *The modern history of Japan.* London, Weidenfeld, 1963; 1967 P; New York, Praeger, 1963 C&P (Asia-Africa series)
From the early 19th century to 1962; a lucid survey, with emphasis on social and economic factors.

*BENEDICT, Ruth (Fulton). *The chrysanthemum and the sword: patterns of Japanese culture.* Boston, Houghton, 1946 (and repr.); London, Routledge, 1967; Cleveland, World; New York, Meridian, 1967 P
An interesting and well-written analysis of the Japanese character and traditional ethics and mores.

*BERSIHAND, Roger. *Histoire du Japon, des origines à nos jours.* Paris, Payot, 1959 P (Collection Bibliothèque Historique)
A useful general history with more detail on the past century.

BLACKER, Carmen. *The Japanese enlightenment: a study of Fukuzawa Yukichi.* Cambridge, New York, Cambridge University Press, 1964
The career and ideas of a famous 19th century westernizer.

BORTON, Hugh. *Japan's modern century.* New York, Ronald, 1955
A good history of Japan since 1850, mainly political.

BOXER, Charles Ralph. *The Christian century in Japan, 1549-1650.* Berkeley, University of California Press, 1951
On early missionary work and the resulting development of Christianity in Japan. Also gives a revealing picture of Japan in the 16th and 17th centuries.

BOXER, Charles Ralph. *Jan Compagnie in Japan, 1600-1850: an essay on the cultural, artistic and scientific influence exercised by the Hollanders in Japan from the seventeenth to the nineteenth centuries.* 2nd ed. The Hague, Nijhoff, 1950
A sound study.

BUCK, Pearl S. *The people of Japan.* New York, Simon & Schuster, 1966
A short general book which succeeds in making the Japanese more comprehensible to westerners.

COLE, Wendell. *Kyoto in the Monoyama period.* Norman, University of Oklahoma Press, 1967
A readable evocation of Japan's former capital during its heyday in the 16th century.

COOPER, Michael (ed.) *They came to Japan: an anthology of European reports on Japan, 1543-1640.* Berkeley, University of California Press, 1965
Extracts from European travellers' accounts, arranged under 23 subject headings. Interesting.

DORE, Ronald Philip. *City life in Japan: a study of a Tokyo ward.* London, Routledge; Berkeley, University of California Press, 1958 C&P
An illuminating sociological survey.

DORE, Ronald Philip. *Education in Tokugawa Japan.* London, Routledge; Berkeley, University of California Press, 1965
An important and well-written work on the 17th to 19th centuries.

EMBREE, John F. *Suye Mura, a Japanese village.* Chicago, University of Chicago Press, 1964 P (repr. of 1939 ed.) (Phoenix Books)
Traditional rural life well portrayed in this sociological study.

FRÉDÉRIC, Louis. *La vie quotidienne au Japon à l'époque des Samouraï, 1185-1603.* Paris, Hachette, 1968
An interesting evocation of many aspects of mediaeval Japanese civilization.

GONTHIER, André. *Histoire des institutions japonaises.* Bruxelles, Éditions de la Libraire Encyclopédique, 1956
   Covers the development from early times to the 20th century.

HALL, John Whitney. *Japanese history: new dimensions of approach and understanding.* [2nd ed.] Washington, American Historical Association; New York, Macmillan, 1966 P (Service Center for Teachers of History publication)
   A sound 69-page critical essay on the problems of Japanese history and an evaluation of the works on Japanese history available in English.

HASEGAWA, Nyozekan. *The Japanese character: a cultural profile.* Tr. John Bester. Tokyo, Palo Alto, Kodansha, 1966 (Japanese National Commission for Unesco Publications)
   A valuable historically based examination — more scholarly but less empirical than Kawasaki's book (below).

INOUE, Mitsusada. *Introduction to Japanese history before the Meiji restoration.* [2nd ed.] Tokyo, Kokusai Bunka Shinkokai; New York, Japan Publications, 1968 P (Japanese Life and Culture series)
   A general survey for westerners by a leading Japanese historian, taking account of recent Japanese research.

IWATA, Masakazu. *Ōkubo Toshimichi, the Bismarck of Japan.* Berkeley, University of California Press, 1964
   A biography and study of a notable mid-19th century leader and reformer.

KAWASAKI, Ichiro. *Japan unmasked.* Rutland, Vt., Tuttle; London, Prentice-Hall, 1969 (and repr.)
   A Japanese diplomat tells the secrets of the Japanese character. An excellent self-analysis which makes the Japanese mentality intelligible.

KEENE, Donald. *The Japanese discovery of Europe: Honda Toshiaki and other discoverers, 1720-1798.* [2nd ed.] Stanford, Stanford University Press, 1969 P
   An interesting study of Japanese reaction to western culture, with long extracts in translation from the Japanese.

KIDDER, Jonathan Edward. *Japan before Buddhism.* London, Thames & Hudson; New York, Praeger, 1959 (Ancient Peoples and Places series)
   A lavishly illustrated popular archaeological survey.

LACH, Donald Frederick. *Japan in the eyes of Europe: the 16th century.* Chicago, University of Chicago Press, 1968 P (Phoenix Books)

LENSEN, George Alexander. *The Russian push toward Japan: Russo-Japanese Relations, 1697-1875.* Princeton, Princeton University Press; London, Oxford University Press, 1959
   A solid work.

LESQUILLER, Jean. *Le Japon*. Paris, Sirey, 1966 (Collection L'Histoire du XXe Siècle)
> A detailed general history (mainly political) beginning with the Meiji era a century ago.

MORRIS, Ivan. *The world of the shining prince: court life in ancient Japan*. New York, Knopf; Toronto, Random House, 1964
> Japanese court civilization in a flourishing period, about the 10th century, vividly described on the basis of contemporary writings.

*REISCHAUER, Edwin Oldfather. *Japan, past and present*. 3rd ed. New York, Knopf; Toronto, Random House; London, Duckworth, 1964 (and repr.)
> One of the best short outlines of Japanese history.

*SANSOM, George Bailey. *A history of Japan*. 3 vols. Stanford, Stanford University Press; London, Cresset, 1958-63
> Well-written and reliable — the standard detailed history of pre-modern Japan. Vol. 1, to 1334; vol. 2, 1334-1615; vol. 3, 1615-1867.

*SANSOM, George Bailey. *Japan: a short cultural history*. [2nd] rev. ed. London, Cresset, 1962; New York, Appleton, 1962 (and repr.); Des Moines, Iowa, Meredith, 1962
> Probably the most readable sound general introduction to Japan before the 19th century.

*SANSOM, George Bailey. *The western world and Japan*. London, Cresset; New York, Knopf, 1950
> A first-class examination of western intrusion and influence, 16th to 19th centuries.

SHELDON, Charles David. *The rise of the merchant class in Tokugawa Japan, 1600-1868: an introductory survey*. Locast Valley, N.Y., Augustin (for the Association for Asian Studies), 1958 (Monographs of the Association for Asian Studies)
> Sound economic history.

SILBERMAN, Bernard S. (ed.) *Japanese character and culture: a book of selected readings*. Tucson, University of Arizona Press, 1962
> A useful selection of extracts.

SMITH, Thomas C. *The agrarian origins of modern Japan*. Stanford, Stanford University Press, 1959; New York, Atheneum, 1966 P
> A pioneer work showing how changes in landholding lie behind the development of modern Japan.

STATLER, Oliver. *Japanese inn.* New York, Toronto, Random House; London, Secker, 1961; New York, Pyramid, 1962 P (and repr.)
> The history of an inn since the 17th century is used as a vehicle for painlessly imparting Japanese history since the 16th century. Very readable.

*STORRY, Richard. *A history of modern Japan.* London, Toronto, Cassell, 1960; New York, Barnes & Noble, 1962; Harmondsworth, Baltimore, Penguin, 1965 P (Pelican Books)
> A good outline.

*STORRY, Richard. *Histoire du Japon.* Paris, Fayard, 196– P
> See preceding note.

TREWARTHA, Glenn Thomas. *Japan: a physical, cultural and regional geography.* 3rd ed. Madison, University of Wisconsin Press; London, Methuen, 1965
> A standard geography.

4 HISTORY OF JAPANESE LITERATURE

BERSIHAND, Roger. *La littérature japonaise.* Paris, Presses Universitaires de France, 1956 (Collection "Que sais-je?")
> A useful short historical introduction, with samples of the different genres. Modern literature occupies the second half of the book, and it is rather crowded with detail.

BERSIHAND. Roger. *Japanese literature.* New York, Walker; Toronto, McLeod, 1965 C&P (Walker Sun Books)
> See preceding note.

*BLYTH, Reginald Horace. *Japanese humour.* Tōkyō, Japanese Travel Bureau, 1957
> A lively selection of pieces in prose and verse of many periods, to prove the author's assertion that "the Japanese [are] the most humorous and the most poetic of all nations." Excellent translations.

BLYTH, Reginald Horace. *Oriental humour.* Tokyo, Hokuseido Press, 1959
> Although China and Korea are included, this book concentrates on Japanese humour. Contains poetry, short stories, and literary criticism – full of insight, but somewhat idiosyncratic.

BONNEAU, Georges. *Histoire de la littérature japonaise contemporaine (1868-1938).* Paris, Payot, 1940

A good review. The second half consists of representative selections in translation.

*KEENE, Donald. *Japanese literature: an introduction for western readers.* London, Murray, 1953; New York, Grove, 1955 P (and repr.) (Wisdom of the East series) (Evergreen Books)

An excellent outline for the layman. Describes main features of each genre, but is not crowded with details of authors and titles.

KOKUSAI BUNKA SHINKOKAI. *Introduction to classic Japanese literature.* Tokyo, Kokusai Bunka Shinkokai, 1948, repr. 1959

Useful summaries of 67 famous literary works, with an introduction on the development of Japanese literature. The work below can be considered as a more detailed continuation.

KOKUSAI BUNKA SHINKOKAI. *Introduction to contemporary Japanese literature.* 2 vols. Tokyo, Kokusai Bunka Shinkokai, 1939 (repr. 1958)-1959

Summaries of the prose literary works published since the Meiji era with short biographies of the major and minor writers.

McCLELLAN, Edwin. *Two Japanese novelists: Sōseki and Tōson.* Chicago, London, University of Chicago Press, 1969

The modern Japanese novel was created largely by these two writers of its formative period. Tōson is more lyrical, but Natsume Sōseki is more imaginatively realistic. (See next section for examples.) This is an excellent introduction to their work.

MINER, Earl. *The Japanese tradition in British and American literature.* Princeton, Princeton University Press, 1958; 1966 P

A well-written description of Japanese influences.

NAKAMURA, Mitsuo. *Japanese fiction in the Meiji era.* Tokyo, Kokusai Bunka Shinkokai (The Society for International Cultural Relations), 1966 (Series on Japanese Life and Culture)

A sound critical review of late 19th and early 20th century work.

SIEFFERT, René. *La littérature japonaise.* Paris, Colin, 1961 P

A good outline general literary history.

UEDA, Makoto. *Literary and art theories in Japan.* Cleveland, Press of Western Reserve University, 1967

A valuable discussion on the Japanese contribution to aesthetic theory. Each chapter considers critical comments on an art by a different classical Japanese writer.

5 JAPANESE LITERATURE
IN TRANSLATION

a/General and Mixed Works

*KEENE, Donald (comp. & ed.) *Anthology of Japanese literature from the earliest era to the mid-nineteenth century.* New York, Grove, 1955; 1960 P; London, Allen & Unwin, 1956; 2nd ed. entitled *Japanese literature to the 19th century.* Rev. ed., Harmondsworth, Penguin, 1968 P (Unesco Collection of Representative Works – Japanese Series)

> Probably the best anthology in English of pre-modern Japanese literature. Well translated by various hands. First-class introduction explaining the selections in their historical and cultural setting.

*KEENE, Donald (comp. & ed.) *Modern Japanese literature: an anthology.* New York, Grove, 1956; 1960 P; London, Thames & Hudson, 1957 (Unesco Collection of Representative Works – Japanese Series)

> A successful selection of high-quality literature from the mid-19th to the mid-20th century, in all the main genres. Excellent translations.

REISCHAUER, Edwin Oldfather. *Translations from early Japanese literature.* By Edwin O. Reischauer and Joseph K. Yamagiwa. Cambridge, Mass., Harvard University Press, 1951 (and repr.) (Publications of the Harvard-Yenching Institute)

> Rather literal translations of four mediaeval works give the reader a closer idea of the originals than the more polished free translations of Donald Keene's *Anthology* (above).

b/Historical, Social, and Political Works

GIKEIKI. *Yoshitune: a fifteenth-century Japanese chronicle.* Tr. Helen Craig McCullough. Stanford, Stanford University Press, 1966

> A prose epic of the adventures of Minamoto Yoshitune, a 12th century nobleman-warrior of the Robin Hood type, who has been the subject of many poems, stories, and films.

ŌKAGAMI. *The Ōkagami: a Japanese historical tale.* Tr. Joseph K. Yamagiwa. London, Allen & Unwin, 1967 (Unesco Collection of Representative Works – Japanese Series)

> Romanticized Japanese anecdotal history written in the 11th century and covering the period 850-1025. It has both historical and literary interest.

SEI, Shōnagon. *The Pillow book of Sei Shonagon.* Tr. & ed. Ivan Morris. 2 vols. New York, Columbia University Press; London, Oxford University Press, 1967 (Unesco Collection of Representative Works – Japanese Series)

Sei Shōnagon was a 10th century Japanese court lady who kept a notebook by her pillow in which she jotted down anecdotes, diary entries, poetry, and anything that interested her. This is a complete English translation of that delightful book, with a valuable introduction and scholarly notes.

*SEI, Shōnagon. *The Pillow-book of Sei Shōnagon.* Tr. Arthur Waley. London, Allen & Unwin, 1928, repr. 1957 P; New York, Grove, 1960 P
Selections from the charming book described above, in the excellent translation typical of Waley's work.

*SEI, Shōnagon. *Les notes de chevet de Sei Shônagon, dame d'honneur au palais de Kyoto.* Traduit du japonais par André Beaujard. 2 vols. Paris, Gallimard, 1966 (Collection Connaissance de l'Orient) (Collection Unesco d'Oeuvres Représentatives — Série Japonaise)
See note to the entry before the last (above).

TAIHEIKI. *The Taiheki: a chronicle of medieval Japan.* Tr. Helen Craig McCullough. New York, Columbia University Press; Toronto, London, Oxford University Press, 1959 (Records of Civilization: Sources and Studies series)
Translation of a well-known Japanese popular war epic.

c/The Novel, Short Story, Folk Tale

ABE, Kōbō. *The face of another.* Tr. E. Dale Saunders. New York, Knopf, 1966; London, Weidenfeld, 1969
A very interesting "psychological" novel about a man who creates a new personality for himself.

ABE, Kōbō. *Friends.* Tr. Donald Keene. New York, Grove, 1969
Drama of the "theatre of the absurd." Excellently translated.

ABE, Kōbō. *The ruined map.* Tr. E. Dale Saunders. New York, Knopf; Toronto, Random House, 1969
A first-class avant-garde detective thriller.

ABE, Kōbō. *The woman in the dunes.* Tr. E. Dale Saunders. New York, Knopf; Toronto, Random House; London, Secker, 1964; New York, Berkley, 1965 P (Unesco Collection of Contemporary Works — Asian Series)
A gripping, melodramatic modern novel which won a major Japanese literary award and was made into a very successful film.

AKUTAGAWA, Ryūnosuke. *Exotic Japanese stories ...* 16 unusual tales. Tr. Takashi Kojima and John McVittie. Introduction by John McVittie. New York, Liveright, 1964
An interesting selection, with useful introduction for western readers.

AKUTAGAWA, Ryūnosuke. *Rashomon and other stories.* Tr. Takashi Kojima. New York, Bantam, 1959 P (Unesco Collection of Representative Works — Japanese Series)

Excellent stories by a leading modern Japanese writer (1892-1927). *Rashomon* was made into a film which was widely acclaimed in the West.

AKUTAGAWA, Ryūnosuke. *Rashomon et autres contes.* Traduction et avant-propos de Arimasa Mori. Paris, Gallimard, 1965 (Collection Connaissance de l'Orient) (Collection Unesco d'Oeuvres Représentatives — Série Japonaise)

See preceding note.

DAZAI, Osamu. *No longer human.* Tr. Donald Keene. Norfolk, Conn., New Directions, 1958

A first-class writer's novel on the decline of a man.

DAZAI, Osamu. *La déchéance d'un homme.* Traduit du japonais par Georges Renondeau. Paris, Gallimard, 1962 P (Collection Du Monde Entier)

See preceding note.

DAZAI, Osamu. *The setting sun.* Tr. Donald Keene. New York, New Directions, 1956; London, Peter Owen, 1958

A powerful novel of the breakdown of traditional society.

DAZAI, Osamu. *Soleil couchant.* Traduit du japonais par Henriette de Sarbois et Georges Renondeau. Paris, Gallimard, 1961 P (Collection Du Monde Entier)

See preceding note.

DORSON, Richard Mercer. *Folk legends of Japan.* Rutland, Vt., Tuttle, 1962 (and repr.)

A good collection.

FUTABATEI, Shimei. *Japan's first modern novel: Ukigumo of Futabatei Shimei.* Translation and critical commentary by Marleigh Grayer Ryan. New York, London, Columbia University Press, 1967 (Unesco Collection of Representative Works — Japanese Series)

The major influence of the 19th century Russian novelists is discussed by the translator.

HIBBETT, Howard. *The Floating World in Japanese fiction: tales of Ukiyo and their background.* London, Toronto, New York, Oxford University Press, 1959; New York, Grove, 1960 P

City life among the fashionable, as seen in the new urban literature of the end of the 17th and beginning of the 18th century.

IBUSE, Masuji. *Black rain.* Tr. John Bester. Tokyo, Palo Alto, Kodansha; London, Ward Lock, 1969

A leading Japanese writer's award-winning novel about the effects of the atomic bomb destruction of Hiroshima on ordinary people. Depressing but well done.

IHARA, Saikaku. *Five women who loved love.* Tr. William Theodore de Bary. Rutland, Vt., Tuttle, 1956 C&P
Admirable translation of a group of five stories by the famous 17th century realist novelist. Three of these stories are also translated by Ivan Morris in his introduction to this author's *Life of an amorous woman* (below).

IHARA, Saikaku. *Cinq amoureuses.* Traduit du japonais, préfacé et annoté par G. Bonmarchand. Paris, Gallimard, 1959 (Collection Connaissance de l'Orient) (Collection Unesco d'Oeuvres Représentatives – Série Japonaise)
See preceding note.

IHARA, Saikaku. *The Japanese family storehouse, or, the Millionaire's Gospel modernised ...* Translated from the Japanese by G. W. Sargent. Cambridge, New York, Cambridge University Press, 1959 (University of Cambridge Oriental Publications series)
Thirty-five short stories, embodying practical advice on how to get rich and stay rich, give a vivid picture of 17th century Japanese city life.

IHARA, Saikaku. *The life of an amorous woman, and other writings.* Ed. & tr. Ivan Morris. London, Chapman, 1963; Corgi Books, 1965 P; New York, New Directions, 1963 C&P
One of the most popular novels by the 17th century Japanese realist writer.

IHARA, Saikaku. *Vie d'une amie de la volupté.* Tr. G. Bonmarchand. Paris, Gallimard, [1970 in the press] (Collection Connaissance de l'Orient) (Collection Unesco d'Oeuvres Représentatives – Série Japonaise)
See preceding note.

IKKU, Jippensha. *Shanks' mare: being a translation of the Tokaido volumes of Hizakurige, Japan's great comic novel of travel and ribaldry.* Tr. Thomas Satchell. Rutland, Vt., Tuttle, 1960 P
An amusing early 18th century picaresque novel of the adventures of two rascally travellers.

INOUE, Yasushi. *The Counterfeiter and other stories.* Tr. Leon Picon. Rutland, Vt., Tuttle, 1965 (Unesco Collection of Representative Works – Japanese Series)
Three short stories by a prize-winning author (born 1907), effectively translated.

KAWABATA, Yasunari. *Snow country,* [and] *Thousand cranes.* Tr. Edward G. Seidensticker. New York, Knopf, 1969 (Unesco Collection of Contemporary Works — Asian Series)

> The first of these is a very Japanese novel of a triangle — man, wife, and mistress; the second novel is also famous. Kawabata is widely considered the "most Japanese" of the leading contemporary Japanese novelists.

KAWABATA, Yasunari. *Pays de neige.* Texte français par Bunkichi Fujimore et Armel Guerne. Paris, Albin Michel, 1960 (Collection Unesco d'Auteurs Contemporains — Série Orientale)

> See preceding note.

KONJAKU MONOGATARI. *Ages ago: 37 tales from the Konjaku monogatari.* Tr. S. W. Jones. Cambridge, Mass., Harvard University Press, 1959

> A well-known 11th century Japanese collection of anecdotes and assorted information on the historical and religious past of Japan, China, and India.

KONJAKU MONOGATARI. *Histoires qui sont maintenant du passé.* Tr. B. Frank. Paris, Gallimard, 1968 (Collection Unesco d'Oeuvres Représentatives — Série Japonaise)

> See preceding note.

MINER, Earl (ed. & tr.) *Japanese poetic diaries.* Selected and translated with an introduction by Earl Miner. Berkeley, London, University of California Press, 1969

> The poetic or literary diary is a fictional form, but the contents are sometimes largely based on fact. Four such diaries, written from the 10th to the 19th century, are translated and explained and this little-known literary current is expertly investigated.

MISHIMA, Yukio. *After the banquet.* Translated from the Japanese by Donald Keene. New York, Knopf; Toronto, Random House, 1963; New York, Hearst, 1967 P

> A powerful novel of the conflict between the moralist and the hedonist in present-day Japan, by one of Japan's best writers. Excellent translation.

MISHIMA, Yukio. *Après le banquet.* Traduit du japonais par G. Renondeau. Paris, Gallimard, 1965 P (Collection Du Monde Entier) (Collection Unesco d'Auteurs Contemporains — Série Orientale)

> See preceding note.

MISHIMA, Yukio. *Confessions of a mask.* Tr. Meredith Weatherby. Norfolk, Conn., New Directions, 1958

> A novel in autobiographical form.

MISHIMA, Yukio. *Death in midsummer, and other stories.* Tr. Donald Keene, Ivan Morris, Geoffrey Sargent and Edward Seidensticker. Philadelphia, Lippincott; New York, New Directions, 1966 P
  Short stories in good translation.

MISHIMA, Yukio. *The sound of waves.* Tr. Meredith Weatherby. New York, Knopf, 1956; New York, Berkley, 1965 P
  Love + youth; village + tradition = conflict in modern Japan. A successful novel.

MISHIMA, Yukio. *The Temple of the Golden Pavilion.* Tr. Ivan Morris, New York, Knopf; Toronto, Random House, 1959
  A Zen Buddhist monk's obsession with the ideal of beauty is explored in this interesting novel.

MISHIMA, Yukio. *Le pavillon d'or.* Traduit du japonais par Marc Mécréant. Paris, Gallimard, 1961 (Collection Du Monde Entier) (Collection Unesco d'Auteurs Contemporains – Série Orientale)
  See preceding entry.

MORI, Ōgai. *The wild geese.* Tr. Kingo Ochiai and Sanford Goldstein. Rutland, Vt., Tuttle, 1959 P (and repr.)
  A famous novel (1911-13) set in 1880 which raises the problems of western values in an oriental society.

*MORRIS, Ivan (ed.) *Modern Japanese stories: an anthology.* London, Eyre & Spottiswoode, 1961; Rutland, Vt., Tuttle, 1962 P (and repr.) (Unesco Collection of Representative Works – Japanese Series)
  Twenty-five notable short stories, preceded by a rapid introduction to modern Japanese fiction.

MURASAKI, Shikibu. *The tale of Genji:* a novel in six parts by Lady Murasaki. Tr. Arthur Waley. London, Allen & Unwin, 1935, repr. 1965 C&P; Garden City, N.Y., Doubleday, 1968 P (Unesco Collection of Representative Works – Japanese Series)
  The great 11th century novel of Japanese court society.

MURASAKI, Shikibu. *Le Genji-monogatari.* Introduction et traduction du livre 1, par Charles Haguenauer. Paris, Presses Universitaires de France, 1959
  The first part of the great 11th century six-part classic novel of Japanese court society. ("The world's first novel")

NAGAI, Kafū. *Étrange histoire à l'est de la rivière Sumida.* Tr. A. Féles. Paris, Gallimard, 1970 (Collection Unesco d'Oeuvres Représentatives – Série Japonaise)

The author is one of the major realist writers of the early 20th century, combining Japanese literary influences with those of the West (particularly French).

NAGAI, Kafū. *Kafū the scribbler: a biography* by Edward Seidensticker; [*with*] *the River Sumida; The Peony garden; A strange tale from east of the river; the Decoration,* and other stories, translated by Edward Seidensticker. Stanford, Stanford University Press, 1968 C&P (Unesco Collection of Representative Works — Japanese Series)
See preceding note.

NATSUME, Sōseki. *Grass on the wayside.* Tr. Edwin McClellan. Chicago, London, University of Chicago Press, 1969 (Unesco Collection of Representative Works — Japanese Series)
Skilful translation of a novel by a distinguished modern writer (d. 1916), whose work has been discussed at length by the translator (see McClellan, section 4 above).

NATSUME, Sōseki. *Kokoro.* Tr. Edwin McClellan. London, Peter Owen, 1967; Chicago, Regnery, 1967 P (Unesco Collection of Representative Works — Japanese Series)
A famous novel on man's isolation and despair.

NATSUME, Sōseki. *Le pauvre coeur des hommes.* Tr. Horiguchi Daigaku et Georges Bonneau. Paris, Gallimard, 1957 (Collection Connaissance de l'Orient) (Collection Unesco d'Oeuvres Représentatives — Série Japonaise)
Translation of "Kokoro." See preceding note.

NATSUME, Sōseki. *The three-cornered world.* Tr. Alan Turney. London, Peter Owen, 1965; Chicago, Regnery, 1967 (Unesco Collection of Representative Works — Japanese Series)
The author has written: "An artist is a person who lives in the triangle which remains after the angle which we may call common sense has been removed from this four-cornered world." This book records the reactions of an artist to beauty, nature, and people.

NIWA, Fumio. *The Buddha tree.* Tr. Kenneth Strong. London, Peter Owen, 1966 (Unesco Collection of Contemporary Works — Asian Series)
The materialism of contemporary Japanese Buddhism is the target of this novel about the double life of a Buddhist priest. The prize-winning and prolific author was a Buddhist priest himself for over 20 years.

OOKA, Shōhei. *Fires on the plain.* Tr. Ivan I. Morris. New York, Knopf, 1957
A gripping novel of the Philippine campaign in World War II.

OOKA, Shōhei. *Les feux.* Paris, Seuil, 1959
   See preceding note.

OSARAGI, Jiro. *Homecoming.* Tr. Brewster Horwitz. New York, Knopf, 1955
   A well-known novel about the return of a soldier after World War II.

OSARAGI, Jiro. *Retour au pays.* Traduit du japonais par Kikou Yamata, A.
Mori et S. Regnault-Gattier. Paris, Albin Michel, 1962 (Collection Unesco d'Au-
teurs Contemporains — Série Orientale)
   See preceding note.

SEKI, Keigo (comp.) *Folktales of Japan.* Tr. Robert J. Adams. Chicago, University of Chicago Press; London, Routledge, 1963 (Folk Tales of the World series)
   Sixty-three good representative stories, with folkloristic indexes.

TAKEYAMA, Michio. *Harp of Burma.* Tr. Howard Hibbett. Rutland, Vt., Tuttle; London, Prentice-Hall, 1966; 1969 P (Unesco Collection of Contemporary
Works — Translations Series)
   The reactions of Japanese soldiers to the horrors of World War II and their
   disillusionment following the defeat and collapse of the Japan they used to
   know. Prize-winning but uncheerful.

TANIZAKI, Jun'ichirō. *La confession impudique.* Traduit du japonais par G.
Renondeau. Paris, Gallimard, 1963 P (Collection Du Monde Entier)
   This and the next four works are novels by one of Japan's leading writers
   (b. 1886).

TANIZAKI, Jun'ichirō. *The diary of a mad old man.* Tr. Howard Hibbett.
New York, Knopf; Toronto, Random House; London, Secker, 1965 (Unesco
Collection of Representative Works — Japanese Series)

TANIZAKI, Jun'ichirō. *Journal d'un vieux fou.* Traduit du japonais par
Georges Renondeau. Paris, Gallimard, 1967 P (Collection Du Monde Entier)

TANIZAKI, Jun'ichirō. *Le goû: des orties.* Traduit du japonais par Sylvie Regnault-Gattier et Kyuo Anzaï. Parıs, Gallimard, 1959 P (Collection Du Monde
Entier)

TANIZAKI, Jun'ichirō. *The Makioka sisters.* Tr. Edward Seidensticker. New
York, Knopf, 1957; Toronto. McClelland; London, Secker, 1958; New York,
Grosset, 196– P (Unesco Collection of Representative Works — Japanese Series)
   An important long novel about the decline and fall of an upper middle
   class family.

TANIZAKI, Jun'ichirō. *Quatre soeurs.* Traduit du japonais par Georges Renondeau. Paris, Gallimard, 1964 P (Collection Du Monde Entier)
   See preceding note.

TANIZAKI, Jun'ichirō. *Seven Japanese tales.* Translated from the Japanese by Howard Hibbett. New York, Knopf; Toronto, Random House, 1963; London, Secker, 1964
> Short stories with strong psychological analysis, written over a period of half a century by the famous novelist.

TOKOTOMI, Kenjiro. *Footprints in the snow: a novel of Meiji Japan.* Tr. Kenneth Strong. London, Allen & Unwin; New York, Pegasus, 1970 (Unesco Collection of Representative Works – Japanese Series)
> The work of a successful popular writer of "family" novels (1868-1927).

UEDA, Akinari. *Contes de pluie et de lune.* Tr. René Sieffert. Paris, Gallimard, 1956 (Collection Connaissance d'Orient) (Collection Unesco d'Oeuvres Représentatives – Série Japonaise)
> A collection of tales of the supernatural by a writer of the Tokugawa period.

YOSHIDA, Kenkō. *Essays in idleness: the Tsurezuregusa of Kenkō.* Tr. Donald Keene. New York, London, Columbia University Press, 1967 (Records of Civilization: Sources and Studies) (Unesco Collection of Representative Works – Japanese Series)
> A miscellany of short pithy essays and notes embodying worldly wisdom, as seen by a 14th century Buddhist monk and former court official.

YOSHIDA, Kenkō. *Les heures visives (Tsurezuregusa).* Tr. C. Grosbois et T. Yoshida. Suivies de *Notes de ma cabane de moîne (Hôjôki)* de Kamo no Chômei. Tr. R. P. Candau. Paris, Gallimard, 1968 (Collection Unesco d'Oeuvres Représentatives – Série Japonaise)
> The first of these works is a miscellany of worldly wisdom by a 14th century court official and famous poet who became a Buddhist monk; the second (Hōjōki) are meditations on calamities and the transience of all things by a retired priest, Kamo-no-Chōmei (13th century).

d/Poetry

BLYTH, Reginald Horace. *Haiku.* 4 vols. Rutland, Vt., Tuttle, 1949-52
> Well-known and attractive translations of the 17-syllable popular short verse form called haiku.

BOWNAS, Geoffrey (ed. & tr.) *The Penguin book of Japanese verse.* Translated with an introduction by Geoffrey Bownas and Anthony Thwaite. Harmondsworth, Baltimore, Penguin, 1964
> A moderately successful joint venture by a British scholar of Japanese and an English poet; the poems are from ancient to modern times.

BROWER, Robert H. *Japanese court poetry.* By Robert H. Brower and Earl Miner. Stanford, Stanford University Press, 1961; London, Cresset, 1962
  A very informative standard study of classical poetry even for those without knowledge of Japanese. Good historical introductions and translations. For a good shorter and less specialized treatment see Earl Miner's *An introduction to Japanese court poetry* (below).

FUJIWARA, Teika. *Superior poems of our time.* Tr. Robert H. Brower and Earl Miner. Stanford, Stanford University Press, 1967 (Unesco Collection of Representative Works – Japanese Series)
  A famous classical anthology; the compiler was himself a distinguished poet and philologist (1162-1241).

HAGIWARA, Sakutarō. *Face at the bottom of the world, and other poems.* Tr. G. Wilson. Rutland, Vt., Tuttle, 1969 (Unesco Collection of Representative Works – Japanese Series)

HENDERSON, Harold G. *An introduction to Haiku: an anthology of poems and poets from Bashō to Shiki.* Garden City, N.Y., Doubleday, 1958 C&P (Anchor Books)
  Successful translations.

ISE MONOGATARI. *Tales of Ise: lyrical episodes from tenth-century Japan.* Translated with an introduction and notes by Helen Craig McCullough. Stanford, Stanford University Press, 1968
  Anecdotes consisting of a fictional setting for well-known short poems of court literature; mainly by the 9th century poet Ariwara Narihara. This is a Japanese classic. Excellent introduction.

ISE MONOGATARI. *Contes d'Ise.* Tr. G. Renondeau. Paris, Gallimard, 1969 P (Collection Unesco d'Oeuvres Représentatives – Série Japonaise)
  See preceding note.

ISSA. *The autumn wind.* Tr. & ed. Lewis Mackenzie. London, Murray; New York, Paragon, 1957 (Wisdom of the East series)
  250 fine haiku, well translated, with a good introduction on the great poet's life (1763-1827).

MAN'YŌSHŪ. *The Manyōshū.* The Nippon Gakujutsu Shinkōkai translation of one thousand poems, ... with a new foreword by Donald Keene. New York, London, Columbia University Press, 1965; 1969 P (Records of Civilization: Sources and Studies series) (Unesco Collection of Representative Works – Japanese Series)
  An early classical anthology of poetry on many subjects.

MINER, Earl. *An introduction to Japanese court poetry: with translations by the author and Robert H. Brower.* Stanford, Stanford University Press, 1968
A short but lucid introduction to the forms, conventions, and themes of Japanese poetry written and read in educated circles from the 6th to the 16th centuries; samples in translation; particularly suitable for those who do not know Japanese.

NINOMIYA, Takamichi (comp.) *The poetry of living Japan.* An anthology with an introduction by Takamichi Ninomiya and D. J. Enright. London, Murray, 1957 (Wisdom of the East series)
A balanced selection of "new style" (non-classical) poetry since the 1880s is represented by these "re-creations" (rather than translations).

*WALEY, Arthur (ed. & tr.) *Japanese poetry: the Uta.* London, Lund Humphries; Rutland, Vt., Tuttle, 1946 (and repr.)
Classical poetry beautifully translated.

e/Drama and Cinema†

ANDERSON, Joseph L. *The Japanese film: art and industry.* By Joseph L. Anderson and Donald Richie. New York, Grove; Rutland, Vt., Tuttle, 1960 P
An excellent history of the evolution of Japanese cinema, probably the best developed in Asia.

ARAKI, James T. *The ballad-drama of medieval Japan.* Berkeley, University of California Press; London, Cambridge University Press, 1964
The Kōwaka, which celebrated the exploits of the samurai warriors, was a dramatic form which long rivalled the Nō in popularity. This book gives the history of the form and a study of the librettos.

ARNOLD, Paul. *Le théâtre japonais: Nō, Kabuki, Shimpa.* Paris, L'Arche, 1957
A short review of the development of Japanese drama.

ARNOTT, Peter. *The theatres of Japan.* London, Toronto, Macmillan; New York, St. Martin's, 1969
An expert in the general theatre reviews the various historical forms of theatre in Japan, as well as contemporary developments.

*BOWERS, Faubion. *Japanese theatre.* New York, Hill & Wang, Hermitage House, 1952; 1959 P; London, Owen, 1954
An excellent general introduction, with special emphasis on Kabuki.

CHIKAMATSU, Monzaemon. *Major plays of Chikamatsu.* Tr. Donald Keene. New York, London, Columbia University Press, 1961 (Records of Civilization:

†Including history and criticism of drama.

Sources and Studies series) (Unesco Collection of Representative Works — Japanese Series)

An outstanding translation of 11 plays, with a useful introduction on the puppet theatre. Chikamatsu lived 1653-1725. (The same translator's *Four major plays of Chikamatsu*, Columbia University Press, 1961 P, is a selection from the larger work.)

ERNST, Earle. *The Kabuki theatre*. London, Secker; New York, Oxford University Press, 1956; New York, Grove, 1959 P (Evergreen Books)

A detailed description, mainly of present-day Kabuki.

ERNST, Earle (ed. & tr.) *Three Japanese plays from the traditional theatre*. London, Toronto, New York, Oxford University Press, 1959

Translations of a Nō, a Kabuki, and a puppet play. Each has an excellent introduction to that form of drama.

KAWATAKE, Mokuami. *The love of Izayoi and Seishin*. Tr. Frank T. Motofuji. Rutland, Vt., Tuttle; London, Prentice-Hall, 1966

A domestic play by the last great Kabuki playwright (1816-93).

KEENE, Donald (ed. & tr.) *Twenty plays of the Nō theatre*. Ed. & tr. Donald Keene [and others]. New York, London, Columbia University Press, 1970 (Unesco Collection of Representative Works — Japanese Series)

MISHIMA, Yukio. *Five modern No plays*. Tr. Donald Keene. London, Secker; New York, Knopf, 1957

An interesting attempt by a noted Japanese novelist and short-story writer to modernize the Nō plays.

SAKANISHI, Shio (comp. & tr.) *Japanese folk-plays: the Ink-Smeared Lady and other Kyōgen*. Rutland, Vt., Tuttle, 1960

Excellent translations of humorous plays which constituted the comic relief between Nō plays.

SCOTT, Adolphe Clarence. *The puppet theatre of Japan*. Rutland, Vt., Tuttle, 1963

A readable popular introduction giving a brief history of the art, and the plots of 10 puppet plays.

SCOTT, Adolphe Clarence. *The Kabuki theatre of Japan*. London, Allen & Unwin; New York, Macmillan, 1955; New York, Collier, 1966 P

A good study of an important Japanese popular theatrical tradition.

SEAMI, Motokiyo. *La tradition secrète du Nô, suivie de Une journée de Nô*. Par Zeami. Traduction et commentaires de René Sieffert. Paris, Gallimard,

1960 (Collection Unesco d'Oeuvres Représentatives – Série Japonaise)
This critical work on the aesthetic and technical side of the Nō drama was written by the major figure in the development of these plays. Most of the Nō plays still performed are his work.

UEDA, Makoto (ed. & tr.) *The old pine tree and other Noh plays.* Lincoln, University of Nebraska Press, 1962 P (Bison Books)
A cycle of Nō plays, of which three are by Seami. Good short introduction.

*WALEY, Arthur. *The Nō plays of Japan.* London, Allen & Unwin, 1965 (repr. of 1921 ed.); New York, Grove, 1957 P (repr. of 1921 ed.) (Evergreen Books)
A fine introduction to a notable type of Japanese drama, followed by Waley's famous translations of 20 plays.

6 RELIGION AND IDEAS†

ANESAKI, Masaharu. *History of Japanese religion, with special reference to the social and moral life of the nation.* Rutland, Vt., Tuttle, 1963 (repr. of 1930 ed.); London, Kegan Paul, 1964 (repr. of 1930 ed.)
A classic study.

BUNCE, William K. (ed.) *Religions in Japan: Buddhism, Shinto, Christianity.* Rutland, Vt., Tuttle, 1955
A useful survey, which also includes a section on religions other than those mentioned in the subtitle.

EARHART, Byron. *Japanese religion.* Belmont, Calif., Dickenson, 1969 P
A competent short textbook with lists for further reading.

HORI, Ichirō. *Folk religion in Japan: continuity and change.* Ed. Joseph M. Kitagawa and Alan L. Miller. Chicago, London, University of Chicago Press, 1968 (Haskell Lectures on History of Religions)
An important contribution, dealing with both the past and present.

KITAGAWA, Joseph Mitsuo. *Religion in Japanese history.* New York, London, Columbia University Press, 1966
An absorbing survey covering the past 1700 years.

McFARLAND, Horace Neill. *The rush hour of the gods: a study of new religious movements in Japan.* New York, Macmillan; London, Toronto, Collier-Macmillan, 1967

†For works on Japanese Buddhism, see above subsection B6b. For general works on Buddhism see part III, subsection C4c.

The religious history of Japan is surveyed, characteristics of the "new religions" since World War II are noted, and five of them are individually described in non-technical language.

MOORE, Charles A. (ed.) *The Japanese mind.* Essentials of Japanese philosophy and culture. Honolulu, East-West Center Press (University of Hawaii Press), 1967
Papers of "establishment" thinkers and philosophers given at conferences from 1939 to 1964. Editor justifiably entitles the final chapter "The enigmatic Japanese mind." The papers show the eclecticism of Japanese thought in welding together incompatible elements derived largely from China and India.

OFFNER, Clark B. *Modern Japanese religions, with special emphasis upon their doctrines of healing.* By Clark B. Offner and Henry van Straelen. New York, Twayne, 1963
A review of the "new religions" whose members are said to number 15 per cent of the population, illustrated with photographs.

ONO, Sokyo. *Shinto: the Kami way.* By Sokyo Ono in collaboration with William P. Woodward. Rutland, Vt., Tuttle, 1962
A short lucid description of the native religion of Japan.

ROCHEDIEU, Edmond. *Le shintoïsme et les nouvelles religions du Japon.* Genève, Cercle du Bibliophile, 1968 (Collection Grandes Religions du Monde)
A very general survey.

SIEFFERT, René. *Les religions du Japon.* Paris, Presses Universitaires de France, 1968 (Collection Mythes et Religions)
A good rapid review of main groupings from antiquity to the "new religions."

THOMSEN, Harry. *The new religions of Japan.* Rutland, Vt., Tuttle, 1963
Descriptions of the various and often strange new religions and sects that have developed in recent times.

7 ARTS AND CRAFTS, AND ARCHITECTURE

AKIYAMA, Terukazu. *Japanese painting.* Geneva, Skira; Cleveland, World, 1961 (Treasures of Asia series)
Excellent reproductions of 81 illustrations, together with a good history to the 19th century.

AKIYAMA, Terukazu. *La peinture japonaise.* Genève, Skira, 1961 (Collection Les Tresors de l'Asie)
    See preceding note.

ALEX, William. *Japanese architecture.* New York, Braziller, 1963 C&P (Great Ages of World Architecture series)
    A well-illustrated inexpensive survey.

BOWIE, Henry P. *On the laws of Japanese painting: an introduction to the study of the art of Japan.* New York, Dover, 1951 P (repr. of 1911 ed.)
    On the spirit and technique of traditional Japanese painting.

*BUHOT, Jean. *Histoire des arts du Japon, des origines à 1350.* Paris, Van Oest, 1949
    A first-class work, dealing with all aspects.

FEDDERSEN, Martin. *Japanese decorative art: a handbook for collectors and connoisseurs.* Tr. Katherine Watson. London, Faber, 1962
    Valuable, with excellent bibliography.

HILLIER, J. *Hokusai: paintings, drawings and woodcuts.* London, Phaidon Press, 1955
    A study of the popular 19th century block print designer and book illustrator; contains large clear plates.

KASHIKIE, Isamu. *The ABC of Japanese gardening.* Tr. John Nathan. San Francisco, Japan Publications, 1964 P
    A good short introduction to formal Japanese gardens, well illustrated and lucid.

KULTERMANN, Udo. *New Japanese architecture.* [2nd ed.] London, Thames & Hudson; New York, Praeger, 1967
    The work of leading Japanese architects of the post-World-War-II period, combining Japanese and western concepts and techniques; 199 photographs illustrate the text.

LANE, Richard. *Masters of the Japanese print: their world and their work.* London, Thames & Hudson; Garden City, N.Y., Doubleday, 1962 (World of Art series)
    A good, comparatively inexpensive book, containing 90 coloured and 48 black and white plates. Does not deal with the modern print.

LANE, Richard. *L'estampe japonaise.* Traduit de l'américain par Renée Arbour-Brackman. Paris, Hachette, 1962
    See preceding note.

LEMIÈRE, Alain. *L'art japonais.* 4 vols. Paris, Hazan, 1958
    Four tiny volumes, each containing 15 excellent colour plates and a sketchy
    introduction.

LEMIÈRE, Alain. *Japanese art.* 4 vols. New York, Tudor, 1958
    See preceding note.

MASUDA, Tomoya. *Japon.* Photos par Yukio Futagawa. Fribourg, Office du
Livre, 1969 (Architecture Universelle)
    A rapid review of Japanese architecture, its various styles and techniques,
    historically down to the present. Well illustrated with photographs and
    plans.

*MICHENER, James A. (ed.) *The Hokusai sketch books. Selections from the
Manga.* Rutland, Vt., Tuttle, 1958 (and repr.)
    A delightful book of 187 plates containing hundreds of sketches by Hoku-
    sai Katsushika (1760-1849), one of the liveliest and most popular wood-
    block artists. Good introduction and brief commentaries.

*MICHENER, James A. *The floating world.* New York, Toronto, Random
House, 1954
    The best introduction in English to the Japanese art of wood-block print-
    ing, which flourished from the middle of the 17th to the middle of the 19th
    century.

MIYAGAWA, Torao. *Modern Japanese painting: an art in transition.* Translated
and adapted by Toshizo Imai. Tokyo, Palo Alto, Kodansha; London, Ward Lock,
1967
    A good survey of the period just preceding World War II.

MUNSTERBERG, Hugo. *The arts of Japan: an illustrated history.* Rutland, Vt.,
Tuttle; London, Prentice-Hall, 1957 (and repr.); 1962 P (and repr.)
    A general history for laymen, from the earliest times to the present. Nu-
    merous illustrations, some too small in the reduced format paperback edi-
    tion.

MUNSTERBERG, Hugo. *The ceramic art of Japan: a handbook for collectors.*
Rutland, Vt., Tuttle, 1964
    A useful general treatment, with particularly good coverage of the last 350
    years.

MUNSTERBERG, Hugo. *The folk arts of Japan.* Rutland, Vt., Tuttle, 1958
(and repr.)
    A helpful illustrated introduction to a neglected field; covers pottery, bas-
    ketwork, lacquer, woodwork, metalwork, toys, textiles, painting and sculp-
    ture, peasant houses, and the contemporary folk movement.

Pageant of Japanese art. Edited by staff members of the Tokyo National Museum: Masao Ishizawa, Ichitaro Kondo, Jo Okada, Yutaka Tazawa. 6 vols. Tokyo, Tōtō-Shuppan; Rutland, Vt., Tuttle, deluxe ed., 1953-54; popular ed., 1957-58

> Vol. 1: Painting, 6th-14th centuries; vol. 2: Painting, 14th-19th centuries; vol. 3: Architecture and gardens; vol. 4: Sculpture; vol. 5: Ceramics and metalwork; vol. 6: Textiles and lacquer. An excellent survey. Every volume consists of a long introduction and then a series of plates, each with detailed commentary. The popular edition is unabridged but reduced in size; some illustrations suffer in the reduction.

*PAINE, Robert Treat. *Art and architecture of Japan.* By R. T. Paine and Alexander Soper. 2nd ed. Harmondsworth, Montreal, Baltimore, Penguin, 1966 (Pelican History of Art series)

> An excellent standard work, well illustrated.

QUINN, Lee Early. *The easy magic of Japanese flower arrangement.* Rutland, Vt., Tuttle, 1965

> A simple introduction to a traditional Japanese art, suitable for western beginners.

SMITH, Bradley. *Japan, a history in art.* New York, Simon & Schuster, 1964; London, Weidenfeld, 1965

> An outline of Japanese history, especially social history, brilliantly illustrated by 237 colour plates reproducing outstanding Japanese works of art.

SWANN, Peter C. *The art of Japan from the Jōmon to the Tokugawa period.* London, Toronto, Methuen; New York, Crown, 1966 (Art of the World series)

> A clear, though over-simplified, historical survey from prehistoric times to 1868; 60 coloured plates and an equal number of figures enrich the text.

WARNER, Langdon. *The enduring art of Japan.* Cambridge, Mass., Harvard University Press, 1952; New York, Grove, 1958 P (Evergreen Books)

> A perceptive explanation for the general reader of the artistic philosophy and cultural background which lie behind the Japanese arts, both fine and folk, with many illustrations in support.

YASHIRO, Yukio. *2000 years of Japanese art.* Ed. Peter C. Swann. London, Thames & Hudson; New York, Abrams, 1958

> Reproductions of masterpieces are arranged chronologically; authoritative introductory essays discuss the development of the Japanese arts, and of the various forms and styles illustrated.

YOSHIDA, Tetsuro. *The Japanese house and garden.* Translated from the German by Marcus G. Sims. Rev. [2nd] ed. New York, Praeger, 1969

> Mainly modern, with historical introduction. Copious illustrations.

8 MODERN JAPAN

DENING, Esler. *Japan.* London, Benn; New York, Praeger, 1961 (Nations of
the Modern World series)
   Aspects of modern Japan, preceded by a historical review.

HALLORAN, Richard. *Japan: images and realities.* New York, Knopf; Toronto,
Random House, 1969
   A good analysis of modern Japan, with the thesis that westernization is
   only external.

IKE, Nobutaka. *Japanese politics: an introductory survey.* London, Eyre &
Spottiswoode; New York, Knopf, 1957
   Emphasis on the recent period and on the social forces which affect politics.

*KEENE, Donald. *Living Japan.* London, Heinemann; Garden City, N.Y.,
Doubleday, 1959
   A good view of modern Japan in words and numerous pictures. Attractive
   to beginners.

MAKI, John M. *Government and politics in Japan: the road to democracy.* New
York, Praeger, 1962 P
   Mainly concerned with the post-World-War-II period.

MARAINI, Fosco. *Meeting with Japan.* Translated from the Italian by Eric
Mosbacher. London, Hutchinson, 1959 (and repr.); New York, Viking, 1960
   An enjoyable description of a journey in Japan, with numerous informative
   digressions on many subjects. Gives a vivid picture of contemporary Japan,
   its past history, and its culture. Excellent illustrations.

MARAINI, Fosco. *Japon.* Traduit de l'italien par Angélique Lévi. Grenoble,
Paris, Arthaud, 1964 (Collection Les Beaux Pays)
   See preceding note.

*REISCHAUER, Edwin O. *The United States and Japan.* 3rd ed. New York,
Viking, 1962 P; Cambridge, Mass., Harvard University Press; London, Oxford
University Press, 1965
   Good analysis of the Japanese character, and Japan's place in the modern
   world, particularly since World War II.

SCALAPINO, Robert A. *Parties and politics in contemporary Japan.* By Rob-
ert A. Scalapino and Junnosuke Masumi. Berkeley, University of California
Press, 1962; 1964 P
   A useful succinct analysis of recent Japanese politics.

WARD, Robert E. *Japan's political system.* Englewood Cliffs, N.J., Prentice-Hall, 1967 P
    A first-rate work on modern politics and their historical background.

YÉFIME. *Japon.* Paris, Seuil, 1959 (Collection Petite Planète)
    A vivid impressionistic picture of the Japan of today, combining striking photographs and lightly written description in a small book.

YÉFIME. *Japan.* Tr. Raymond Johnes. London, Vista; New York, Viking, 1962 (Vista Books)
    See preceding note.

D KOREA

CHAE, Kyun-oh. *Handbook of Korea.* By Chae Kyung Oh. 2nd ed. New York, Pageant, 1959
  A factual description of modern Korea, with introduction on Korean history and society.

CHUNG, Kyung Cho. *New Korea: new land of the morning calm.* New York, Macmillan, 1962
  A useful general work.

*HYUN, Peter (ed. & tr.) *Voices of the dawn.* London, Murray; New York, Paragon, 1960 (Wisdom of the East series) (Unesco Collection of Representative Works — Korean Series)
  A broad selection of poems, well translated, with a useful introduction on Korean literary forms.

IM BANG. *Korean folk tales: imps, ghosts, and fairies.* Translated from the Korean of Im Bang and Yi Ryuk by James Gale. Rutland, Vt., Tuttle, 1962
  The original compilers lived in the 16th and 17th centuries; the translation was first published in 1913.

KIM, Chae-wŏn. *The arts of Korea: ceramics, sculpture, gold, bronze and lacquer.* By Chewon Kim and Won-Yong Kim. London, Thames & Hudson, 1966. American edition entitled: *Treasures of Korean art: 2000 years of ceramics, sculpture and jeweled arts.* New York, Abrams, 1966
  A general review omitting graphic art and architecture.

KIM, Chae-wŏn. *Corée: 2000 ans de création artistique.* Par Chewon Kim et Won-Yong Kim. Version français par Madeleine Paul-David Fribourg, Office du Livre, 1966 (Collection Aspects de l'Art)
  See preceding note.

KIM, So-un. *The story bag: a collection of Korean folktales.* Tr. Setsu Higashi. Rutland, Vt., Tuttle, 1955
  A pleasant selection.

LEE, Chong-sik. *The politics of Korean nationalism.* Berkeley, University of California Press; London, Cambridge University Press, 1963
  A detailed and documented study.

*LEE, Peter Hacksoo (comp. & tr.) *Anthology of Korean poetry: from the earliest era to the present.* New York, Day, 1964 (Unesco Collection of Representative Works — Korean Series)

A useful introduction, covering the past 2000 years. Includes adaptations of western poetry and experimentation in the 20th century.

*LEE, Peter Hacksoo. *Korean literature: topics and themes.* Tucson, University of Arizona Press, 1965 (Association for Asian Studies: Monographs and Papers)
A good short account with some translations. Also an outline of Korean history and culture.

LI, Ogg. *Histoire de la Corée.* Paris, Presses Universitaires de France, 1969 P (Collection "Que sais-je?")
A crowded short outline.

*McCUNE, Evelyn. *The arts of Korea: an illustrated history.* Rutland, Vt., Tuttle, 1962
A comprehensive, excellently illustrated survey of Korean arts, with details of the cultural background in which they flourished.

McCUNE, Shannon. *Korea's heritage: a regional and social geography.* Rutland, Vt., Tuttle, 1956 (and repr.)
Geography in a very broad sense: contains much cultural material.

McCUNE, Shannon. *Korea: land of broken calm.* New York, Toronto, London, Van Nostrand, 1966 (Asia Library series)
A general account for laymen, by an expert who was brought up in Korea.

OH, John Kie-chiang. *Korea: democracy on trial.* Ithaca, Cornell University Press, 1968
The ins and outs of Korean politics from 1945 to 1967.

OSGOOD, Cornelius. *The Koreans and their culture.* New York, Ronald, 1951
A general work by an anthropologist, describing village life, customs of upper classes, political history, and cultural history (the latter based on out-of-date material).

REEVE, W. D. *The republic of Korea: a political and economic study.* London, Toronto, New York, Oxford University Press (for Royal Institute of International Affairs), 1963
The post-World-War-II period up to 1962, preceded by a historical outline.

Index of names*

Abaï/see Avezov, Mukhtar. *Abaï*
- see Avezov, Mukhtar. *La jeunesse d'Abaï*
Abasıyanık, Sait Faik/see Faik, Sait
Abbott, Freeland. *Islam and Pakistan/124*
Abbouchi, W. F. *Political systems of the Middle East in the 20th century/113*
Abd-el-Jalil, Jean-M. *Aspects intérieurs de l'Islam/89*
- *Brève histoire de la littérature arabe/59*
'Abd al-Malik, Anwar/see Abdel-Malek, Anouar
Abdel-Malek, Anouar. *Idéologie et renaissance nationale: l'Égypte moderne/39*
- (ed. & tr.)/see *Anthologie de la littérature arabe contemporaine*
'Abduh, Muhammad. *The theology of Unity/101*
Abe, Kōbō. *The face of another/255*
- *Friends/255*
- *The ruined map/255*
- *The woman in the dunes/255*
Abel, Armand (ed.) *Le monde arabe et musulman/33*
Abramsky, Samuel. *Ancient towns in Israel/52*
Acker, William (tr.)/see T'ao, Ch'ien. *T'ao the hermit*
Adams, Charles J. (ed.) *A reader's guide to the great religions/11*
Adams, Robert J. (tr.)/see Seki, Keigo (comp.) *Folktales of Japan*
Ādi Granth. *Selections from the sacred writings of the Sikhs/168*
Adie, W. A. C./see Goodrich, Luther Carrington. *A short history of the Chinese people*
Adigal, Ilangô/see Ilangōvatikal
Afnan, Soheil Muhsin. *Avicenna: his life and works/96*
Ageron, Charles Robert. *Histoire de l'Algérie contemporaine/42*
Agnon, Samuel Joseph. *The bridal canopy/84*
- *A guest for the night/84*
- *In the heart of the seas/85*
- *Two tales: Betrothed, and Edo and Enam/85*

- see Band, Arnold J. *Nostalgia and nightmare: a study in the fiction of S. Y. Agnon*
Ahmad, Aziz. *An intellectual history of Islam in India/101*
- *Islamic modernism in India and Pakistan/101*
- *Studies in Islamic culture in the Indian environment/89, 54*
Ahmad, Khurshid (tr. & ed.)/see Maudūdī, Abul A'lā. *The Islamic law and constitution*
- (tr.)/see Maudūdī, Abul A'lā. *Towards understanding Islam*
Aini, Sadriddin. *Boukhara/73*
Akhundov, Fath 'Alī. *Comédies/79*
Akinari, Ueda/see Ueda, Akinari
Akiyama, Terukazu. *Japanese painting/267*
- *La peinture japonaise/268*
Aksan, Akil (ed. & tr.) *Anthologie de la nouvelle poésie turque/79*
Akurgal, Ekrem. *Treasures of Turkey/105*
- *Les trésors de Turquie/105*
Akutagawa, Ryūnosuke. *Exotic Japanese stories/255*
- *Rashomon/256*
Alazard, Jean. *Initiation à l'Algérie/120*
Alem, Jean-Pierre. *Juifs et arabes/33*
- *Le Liban/116*
- *Le Proche-Orient arabe/115*
Alex, William. *Japanese architecture/268*
Ali, Ahmed (ed. & tr.) *The bulbul and the rose/82*
Ali, Syed Ameer. *The spirit of Islam/101*
Ali Shah, Omar (tr.)/see Khayyam, Omar. *The Rubaiyyat of Omar Khayaam*
- (tr.)/see Sa'dī. *Le jardin de roses – Gulistan*
'Alī Shīr Navā'ī/see Navā'ī
Allchin, Bridget. *The birth of Indian civilization/141*
Allchin, F. R. (tr.)/see Tulasīdāsa. *The petition to Rām*
Allen, John (ed.)/see *Cambridge shorter history of India*
Allen, Richard. *Malaysia – prospect and retrospect/192*
Allen, William Edward David. *Problems of Turkish power in the sixteenth century/47*

---

*Of authors, main editors, compilers, and translators, as well as the subjects of biographies.

Index of titles